WHY MOVEMENTS SUCCEED OR FAIL

PRINCETON STUDIES IN AMERICAN POLITICS: HISTORICAL, INTERNATIONAL, AND COMPARATIVE PERSPECTIVES

SERIES EDITORS

IRA KATZNELSON, MARTIN SHEFTER, THEDA SKOCPOL

WHY MOVEMENTS SUCCEED OR FAIL

OPPORTUNITY, CULTURE, AND THE STRUGGLE FOR WOMAN SUFFRAGE

Lee Ann Banaszak

PRINCETON UNIVERSITY PRESS

PRINCETON, NEW JERSEY

LIBRARY OF CONGRESS CATALOGING-IN-PUBLICATION DATA

BANASZAK, LEE ANN, 1960–

WHY MOVEMENTS SUCCEED OR FAIL : OPPORTUNITY, CULTURE,
AND THE STRUGGLE FOR WOMAN SUFFRAGE / LEE ANN BANASZAK.

P.   CM.—(PRINCETON STUDIES IN AMERICAN POLITICS)

INCLUDES BIBLIOGRAPHICAL REFERENCES AND INDEX.

ISBN 0-691-02640-8 (CL : ALK. PAPER).—ISBN 0-691-02639-4 (PB : ALK. PAPER)

1. WOMEN—SUFFRAGE—UNITED STATES—HISTORY.   2. WOMEN—
SUFFRAGE—SWITZERLAND—HISTORY.   I. TITLE   II. SERIES.

JK1896.B38   1996

324.6′23′09494—DC20   96-2190   CIP

THIS BOOK HAS BEEN COMPOSED IN SABON

PRINCETON UNIVERSITY PRESS BOOKS ARE PRINTED ON ACID-FREE PAPER,
AND MEET THE GUIDELINES FOR PERMANENCE AND DURABILITY OF THE
COMMITTEE ON PRODUCTION GUIDELINES FOR BOOK LONGEVITY OF THE
COUNCIL ON LIBRARY RESOURCES

PRINTED IN THE UNITED STATES OF AMERICA
BY PRINCETON ACADEMIC PRESS

1   3   5   7   9   10   8   6   4   2

1   3   5   7   9   10   8   6   4   2
(PBK.)

IN MEMORY OF

Barbara Salert

CONTENTS

TABLES

FIGURES

PREFACE AND ACKNOWLEDGMENTS

A S A COLLEGE SENIOR I spent a semester in Basel, Switzerland, during the battle for an equal rights amendment. I was shocked when Swiss mentioned that women still could not vote in several cantons. Like most women coming of age in the late 1970s, I took my political rights for granted and assumed that all "democratic" countries had enfranchised women generations ago. I knew nothing about the American woman suffrage movement, but as I learned more (episodically at first, systematically later), I was struck by the fact that many histories of the U.S. suffrage movement noted the early adoption of women's voting rights in Wyoming. Yet none attempted to explore state differences in a systematic fashion. Social movement theories seemed a good place to start to unravel the mysteries of the timing of suffrage, but as I enthusiastically examined one theory after another, each left some aspects unanswered or raised more questions. I was also astonished by the way that many theories ignored the decisions, statements, and values of movement activists in trying to derive a theoretical framework to understand movement success and failure. This seemed to bypass other developments in political science. Chief among these were increased understandings of how beliefs and values affect individual behavior, rational choice explorations in decision-making behavior, and examinations of the mechanics by which macro-level contexts influence the individual. This work contributes both to our understanding of woman suffrage movements and to ways that we can examine movement success and failure more generally.

While many consider academic scholarship to be a solitary pursuit, I have not found this to be so. Like the activists I write about, I have been influenced by a rich and supportive context of family, friends, and colleagues. To all of them, I owe a tremendous debt of gratitude.

Because this project has evolved and grown over a period of years, many institutions provided material support that enabled me to develop this work. The initial research utilized in my dissertation was supported by a Swiss Government Grant and a Washington University Dissertation Fellowship. Iowa State University and the American Political Science Small Grant Award provided additional financial support that allowed me to return to Switzerland to collect additional data and interviews. In addition, Iowa State University, Pennsylvania State University, and the Alexander von Humboldt Bundeskanzler Program furnished release time from teaching, which allowed me to code data, develop theoretical arguments, and mold the research into its final form.

I am especially indebted to my colleagues, friends, and mentors who have provided advice and comments on the numerous versions of this work: Michael Bernhard, Peter Dombrowski, Lynn Kamenitsa, John Kautsky, Hanspeter Kriesi, Wolf Linder, Richard Mansbach, Eileen Mc-Donagh, Carol Mershon, Joel Moses, Dieter Rucht, Barbara Salert, Steffen Schmidt, and John Sprague. Many of the ideas in this book were developed as a result of their suggestions, which forced me to rethink and refine my initial thoughts. Elizabeth Clemens, who reviewed the manuscript, also gave me several important insights into the American suffrage movement. Most of all, Theda Skocpol provided numerous substantive and organizational comments that helped clarify the argument and make the manuscript more readable. If this book falls short in any way, it is not for lack of sage advice.

I am also grateful for the capable aid rendered by my research assistants. Mira Canion, Trudi Matthews, and Tanja Sopcak all provided assistance with translation and the transcription of my interviews with Swiss suffrage activists. Trudi Matthews also helped with the coding and cleaning of the legislative history data in the United States. Jean Mayer provided some translation assistance in the final preparation of the manuscript. Librarians at the Library of Congress, the Landesbibliotek in Bern, and the Gosteli Stiftung deserve much thanks for their assistance in locating appropriate materials.

This research would not have been possible without the assistance of numerous people in both Switzerland and the United States. At the University of Bern, Beatrix Mesmer gave me an academic home when I conducted the initial interviews in 1987. While a number of Swiss women activists aided my search for archives and suffrage activists, two deserve special mention. Marthe Gosteli, whose advocacy for the importance of women's history has saved many of the records of the suffrage movement from destruction, brought important materials to my attention and introduced me to many of the suffrage activists I later interviewed. During my 1987 stay, Lydia Benz-Burger gave me practical advice and introduced me to several key activists at the Schweizerischer Verband für Frauenstimmrecht meeting in Appenzell.

Above all, this work owes much to the warm environment that surrounded me. In addition to providing constant encouragement and love, my parents, Len and Joyce Banaszak, fostered the intellectual curiosity that drives much of this work. I also thank them for *not* regularly asking how the book was going. To Eric Plutzer, I owe the deepest debt of gratitude. He has read virtually all of the drafts of this work, helping me alter my most turgid prose. More importantly, he has played many roles in my life—colleague, friend, lover and soulmate. In each of these, he has influenced my being and hence this book in innumerable ways.

Finally, I have found inspiration in the lives and activities of the suffrage activists about whom I write. More than anything else, the interviews with the Swiss suffrage activists brought home to me what a large and sometimes discouraging battle this was. In comparison, this research has seemed an insignificant task. I never had the opportunity to meet the American woman suffrage activists or those Swiss activists who died before I began this project. Many of the Swiss suffrage activists I interviewed have passed away in the intervening years. Yet, the stories of these activists have, in the course of this research, also become a part of me. I hope that, in some small way, I can assure that their stories continue to inspire.

WHY MOVEMENTS SUCCEED OR FAIL

1

COMPARING THE U.S. AND SWISS
WOMAN SUFFRAGE MOVEMENTS

SWITZERLAND AND THE UNITED STATES have both been characterized as "cradles of democracy." Although one is a tiny Old World country with a sovereign history stretching back to the thirteenth century and the other is a huge New World nation founded only a couple of centuries ago, both became democracies for men quite early in comparison to other Western countries. Universal suffrage for men was enshrined in the Swiss Constitution of 1848, although in some areas it existed even earlier. American men (except black slaves) gained virtually universal suffrage rights by the 1830s and 1840s. In global terms, both tiny Switzerland and the huge, growing United States were early democratizers for men.

In contrast, democratic rights for women came in sharply contrasting tempos to these two countries. At the national level, the United States enfranchised all women through the adoption of the Nineteenth Amendment to the Constitution in 1920, even as many European nations were in the process of allowing female suffrage (see Table 1.1). Switzerland, however, delayed its constitutional amendment adopting woman suffrage until 1971 and, even then, individual cantons within Switzerland had the option of limiting some types of elections to men. As early as 1929, the famous U.S. suffrage activist Carrie Chapman Catt remarked on the unusual delay in Swiss woman suffrage: "Switzerland, being a Republic and a democratic one, is quite behind the times, since in Europe where most women vote, it has not yet enfranchised its women. We know your situation there, but find it difficult to understand why the men and the women of Switzerland do not follow the example of all the rest of the world."[1] Little did Catt realize that Swiss women would have to wait several more decades for the vote.

The national contrasts between the United States and Switzerland are only heightened by the variations within their respective federal governmental structures. The Swiss constitutional amendment of 1971 did not fully settle the issue of female enfranchisement because it permitted cantons to determine their own voting rules for local elections and for one house of the Swiss Parliament. Two cantons took advantage of this op-

TABLE 1.1

Year Women Are Enfranchised in Selected Countries,
U.S. States, and Swiss Cantons

Year	Country	U.S. State	Swiss Canton
1869		Wyoming Territory	
1893	New Zealand	Colorado	
1906	Finland		
1910		Washington, California	
1913	Norway	Illinois[a]	
1915	Denmark		
1917	Netherlands	New York	
1918	Germany		
1919	Sweden		
1920	**United States**		
1944	France		
1945	Italy		
1952	Greece		
1959			Vaud, Neuchâtel
1969			Basel-stadt
1971	**Switzerland**		
1989			Appenzell A.R.
1990			Appenzell I.R.

Source: Woodtli 1983: 248–50
[a] Right to vote for presidential electors only

tion to remain bastions of male-only suffrage for nearly two decades after 1971. Appenzell Ausserrhoden finally adopted full woman suffrage in 1989. Two years later, on November 27, 1990, the women of Appenzell Innerrhoden, a small agricultural canton of about 13,000 people, attained the right to vote—finally completing the long-delayed process of female enfranchisement in Switzerland.

If federalism delayed the complete enfranchisement of Swiss women, it speeded the transition to female voting in the United States. In 1869, a remarkable 121 years before the culmination of Swiss woman suffrage, the U.S. territory of Wyoming became the first polity to allow all women to vote in all elections. Utah followed suit the following year (only to have its woman suffrage repealed by the U.S. Congress because the Mormon Church had actively supported it). In 1893, the same year that New Zealand became the first nation to adopt woman suffrage, women in the state of Colorado also won the right to vote. Although only a few U.S. states and territories granted female suffrage in these early years, the fact is that state-level variations enabled some American women to become the world's pioneer voters of their gender, while cantonal options served to further delay woman suffrage in an already-very-tardy Switzerland.

This book seeks to explain why the United States and Switzerland differed so sharply in this crucial aspect of democratization. I explore the reasons for the sixty-year gap in national adoptions of woman suffrage and for the differences in timing permitted by federalism *within* each country. The two sources of variation—international and intranational—lead to an additional question: Can we find factors that elucidate both the national differences and the differences within the United States and Switzerland?

There are many potential explanations for the differences between and within Switzerland and the United States in the enactment of voting rights for women. Some might suppose that the answer lies in broad national features such as patterns of socioeconomic modernization, educational access, or cultural variety. As I discuss in Chapter 2, such "macroscopic" features cannot explain entirely the puzzles that motivate this book. While there are several reasons why these factors are insufficient, let me offer one simple one here. Woman suffrage was not a simple byproduct of overall economic and cultural conditions. Rather, it was an object of prolonged struggle. Groups of Swiss and American women founded organizations that constituted decades-long political movements. These movements mobilized resources, found allies and enemies, discovered opportunities or faced obstacles, and took or failed to take advantage of their opportunities. Out of such struggles women were enfranchised— sooner or later—at different moments in the national and subnational histories of the United States and Switzerland.

A Brief History of the U.S. Woman Suffrage Movement

The traditional date for the founding of the American woman suffrage movement—the 1848 convention for women's rights in Seneca Falls, New York—is at once too late and too early. On the one hand, women's activism had already found its expression in benevolent associations, the temperance movement, moral reform organizations, missionary societies, anti-slavery groups, and working women clubs (Scott 1984, 1991) as well as in the writings of several American women on the condition of women and women's rights. On the other hand, although suffrage was mentioned in the Seneca Falls Declaration of Sentiments, it was less important than other issues during this initial phase of the women's rights movement. In fact, many activists attending the convention opposed including a voting rights resolution in the Declaration of Sentiments (Stanton et al.

1881a), preferring to focus on other forms of discrimination such as the lack of property rights for married women, limited access to education, and poor wages and conditions for working women. Only after 1865 did the women's movement begin to concentrate on enfranchisement.

In contrast to later phases of the movement, no women's rights organization existed between 1848 and 1865. Rather, women's activities centered around annual conventions where women met to communicate with activists from other states and to promulgate women's rights propaganda. Between conventions, individuals or a small group of activists with close personal ties might occasionally give speeches, testify before a legislature, or run a petition drive, but these were always the activities of informal networks rather than organizations.

Despite the lack of formal organization, several advances in women's rights occurred prior to 1865. The rights of married women to control their own property and wages were adopted by most states by 1855 (Stanton et al. 1881a: 256; Flexner 1975: 64). Although women's enfranchisement was not the focus of attention during these early years, most states considered woman suffrage bills, usually as a result of petitions filed by women's rights activists. However, few of these pieces of legislation were voted on and none received much support from legislators or convention delegates. The onset of the Civil War ended this phase of the women's rights movement since most women's rights activists switched their focus to war work or anti-slavery politics. Women's rights disappeared from legislative agendas and did not reappear until the war's end.

1865–1890: Divisions in the Woman Suffrage Movement and the Rise of the Suffrage Issue

Immediately after the war, women's rights activists continued their pre-war tradition of cooperation with abolitionists by joining in the creation of the American Equal Rights Association (AERA). While the organization's purpose was to further the interests of blacks and women, fundamental disagreements over whether women's rights or rights for blacks should take precedence split the AERA within four years. In particular, the willingness of abolitionists to incorporate the word "male" in the Fourteenth Amendment, which extended basic civil rights to blacks and served as the basis for Reconstruction, and exclude women from the Fifteenth Amendment, which extended voting rights to all races, disappointed many women's rights activists. However, these events focused women activists' attention on the question of voting rights.

In 1869, two national organizations for suffrage were founded: the National Woman Suffrage Association (NWSA) and the American

Woman Suffrage Association (AWSA). The two fundamental issues that divided the organizations were: (1) the relationship between women's voting rights and the right of blacks, and (2) the approval of existing social and political institutions.

Elizabeth Cady Stanton and Susan B. Anthony, leaders of the NWSA, reacted to their disappointment over the Fourteenth and Fifteenth Amendments by withdrawing support from abolitionist causes, arguing that women's voting rights should be top priority. In their fight for female suffrage, they alienated many abolitionists by accepting funding for their women's rights journal, *The Revolution*, from a well-known racist, George Francis Train (Sinclair 1965). The specific impetus for the creation of the NWSA was the AERA's refusal to endorse a federal woman suffrage amendment. Indeed, during its first few years, the NWSA pushed for a federal amendment. However, by the 1880s, NWSA concentrated mainly on state legislation.

The AWSA, led by Lucy Stone and Henry Ward Beecher, maintained its connection to the abolitionist movement. Although many AWSA members also expressed their disappointment at the lack of support for woman suffrage by abolitionists, they argued that the anti-slavery movement should have first priority (Sinclair 1965: 189). When Anthony and Stanton began to associate with opponents of black voting rights and formed the NWSA to fight for a national woman suffrage amendment, Stone and her associates refused to join, creating instead a separate organization that continued to support the abolitionist cause and advocated achieving women's voting rights on the state level first.

The NWSA and the AWSA also differed in their acceptance of existing social institutions. The American Woman Suffrage Association supported the traditional institutions of marriage, the family, and the church. The AWSA's journal, the *Woman's Journal,* financed by middle- and upper-class men and women, was very conservative in style and often downplayed the suffrage issue (Deckard 1983: 261). The NWSA was more revolutionary, making strident demands for suffrage, attacking existing institutions, and refusing to admit men into the organization (Banks 1981; Deckard 1983). Its journal, *The Revolution*, published writings of "free love" advocates and often attacked the church as a source of sexism. Elizabeth Cady Stanton's belief that sexism is inherent in religious institutions led her to reject the Bible, which she saw as the major source of discrimination against women (Banks 1981; Deckard 1983).

The creation of the NWSA and the AWSA marked the beginning of a new phase in the women's rights movement—the rise of formal organizations working for the enfranchisement of women. With the spread of the

NWSA and AWSA, state and local chapters began to spring up. Most of these sections were in the East and the Middle West. Southern states were the very last to organize; formal suffrage associations did not appear there until the 1890s and 1900s. However, building membership was not a priority for these groups and relatively few individuals were attracted to these fledgling organizations. Generally, new members joined of their own accord, having come in contact with the organizations through social ties or public lectures. Moreover, Elizabeth Cady Stanton's association with Victoria Woodhull, an advocate of "free love," discouraged many women from joining the movement and gave it a tarnished reputation that only began to fade in the 1880s.

During the years when the suffrage movement suffered from scandal, the Women's Christian Temperance Union (WCTU) often carried the suffrage banner. The WCTU's membership far outnumbered that of suffrage organizations and Frances Willard, president from 1879 to 1897, fostered support for women's voting rights by arguing that the ballot was necessary for the temperance cause (Earhart 1944). In fact, until Willard's death in 1898, "the WCTU put more money and organizers into the suffrage campaigns than the official suffrage associations" (Deckard 1983: 264).

Despite the splits and scandals that plagued the suffrage cause from 1869 to 1890, the movement achieved its first successes—female suffrage in Wyoming and Utah—during this period. While female voting rights first appeared in the West, state legislatures in the East and the Middle West were also considering legislation enfranchising women. On average, in every year between 1870 and 1890, 4.4 states considered legislation giving women the vote. The large majority of these bills stalled in legislative committees or failed to pass at least one house of the state legislature. However, eight state woman suffrage amendments were rejected by voters in referenda.[2]

Working within the WCTU and the two suffrage organizations, activists campaigned in state legislatures and among the electorate for the right to vote. In addition, during the 1870s NWSA activists tried a number of confrontational tactics such as attempting to vote, running women candidates, and protesting the lack of suffrage at public events. The NWSA also supported attempts to enfranchise women through judicial challenges to the Constitution during the early 1870s. However, these activities were short-lived and none resulted in any additional voting rights for women. Otherwise, suffrage activists continued to use the same methods they had utilized in the earlier women's rights movements: petitioning legislatures and testifying before committees to convince lawmakers to consider woman suffrage bills, and giving public speeches and conducting referendum campaigns to rouse public support for the enfranchisement of women.

1890–1910: The Unification of Suffrage Organizations and the Intergenerational Years

As the memories of the battle over the Fourteenth and Fifteenth Amendments faded and the two suffrage organizations grew more and more similar, the rationale for the division within the suffrage movement disappeared. In 1886, the NWSA and AWSA began negotiations to unify (Anthony and Harper 1902). By 1890, the merger was complete and an amalgamated suffrage organization, the National American Woman Suffrage Association (NAWSA) was created.

Unification did not immediately bring greater success. In fact, suffrage activists labeled the period between 1896 and 1910 "the doldrums" (Flexner 1975: 256). On the national level, neither the House of Representatives nor the Senate reported a woman suffrage amendment from committee between 1896 and 1913 (Catt and Shuler 1926; Flexner 1975). Nor were there any state victories during this period. While Colorado enfranchised women in 1893 and Utah and Idaho followed suit in 1896, it took fourteen years until another state gave women the right to vote.

Organizational changes were partially responsible for this period of low achievement (Deckard 1983; Flexner 1975; Kraditor 1981; Sinclair 1965). After 1904, the NAWSA national organization abandoned the strategy of pressuring Congress and focused instead on state amendments. For example, the NAWSA changed its policy of holding its annual convention in Washington, D.C., in order to allow the suffrage organization to carry the suffrage message to the states. In addition, the lack of a national headquarters and of board meetings (decisions were generally made by mail) diminished the decision-making power of the organization.

Yet, women's voting rights was not a dead issue between 1896 and 1910. Six state referenda on woman suffrage amendments were held and, although state legislatures did not pass suffrage legislation, they continued to consider and debate it. Every year between 1896 and 1909, an average of eight states deliberated suffrage bills, almost twice as many as in the previous period. In addition, the NAWSA doubled in size between 1896 and 1910. Thus, while successes were few, the issue of women's voting rights was by no means absent during "the doldrums."

However, the movement itself was in a state of flux during this period. By the 1890s, many of those women who had actively fought for women's rights before the Civil War, such as Lucy Stone and Elizabeth Cady Stanton, were dying. While Susan B. Anthony continued to serve as president of the organization until 1900, she was already in her seventies. By 1897, she was no longer embarking on the rigorous speaking tours which had been her trademark (Harper 1969 [1898], vols. 2 and 3). Indeed, in her last years as president, she focused on documenting the history of the movement, beginning her biography and the fourth volume of the *History of Woman Suffrage* in 1897 (Harper 1969 [1898], vol. 2). Although she continued to attend NAWSA conferences and work for suffrage until her death in 1906, age was slowing her down.

As the first generation of suffrage activists disappeared, the second generation moved into positions of leadership in the national and local suffrage movements. However, this transition was not complete until 1910. Anna Howard Shaw's presidency of the NAWSA personified this intergenerational period.[3] Shaw was younger than the first-generation activists but older than Carrie Chapman Catt, Alice Paul, and others of the second generation. Despite the age difference between her and the first-generation activists, Shaw shared their beliefs and strategies, including their emphasis on (and talents in) propaganda and public speaking rather than organization.

In some state-level organizations during this period the tactics that would dominate the national level during the last decade of the suffrage movement were already being developed. Carrie Chapman Catt, working in Iowa and later in New York, began organizing suffrage sections around electoral districts. Some local sections, like the Texas Equal Rights Association began supporting pro-suffrage candidates and opposing those who believed women should not vote. Finally, the first suffrage parades occurred in Iowa and New York during the first decade of the twentieth century (Cott 1987; Noun 1969).

In addition, the coalitions between women's organizations and populist and progressive organizations, which were important for the passage of women's voting rights legislation, developed during this period. New allies—the Grange, the populist People's party and the Progressive party—supported women's enfranchisement and worked with suffrage activists, putting pressure on the major political parties to address the issue. Successes in Colorado and Idaho were linked to surges in support for the populist movement (Deckard 1983: 267). In addition, suffrage activists supported their proposed reforms, such as the initiative and referendum, in the hope of aiding their own cause (Kraditor 1981: 56). Both the new generation of suffrage leaders and the coalitions that developed between 1890 and 1910 would become increasingly consequential in the final phase of the struggle for the vote.

1910–1920: The Woman's Party, the Winning Plan, and Victory

Although Anna Howard Shaw remained president until 1915, the character of the National American Woman Suffrage Association was largely changed by 1910. Carrie Chapman Catt formed the Woman Suffrage party in New York and chaired a national petition drive for the NAWSA. Other second generation activists, such as Harriet Stanton Blanch and Alice Paul, were returning from England where they had experienced the battles of the English suffragettes. In 1913, Alice Paul took control of the NAWSA's Congressional Committee, which was responsible for lobbying for a national amendment. With these new leaders came the tactics that fundamentally altered the battle for the vote.

Alice Paul and Lucy Burns attracted attention to the idea of a national amendment with their flamboyant tactics. As heads of the NAWSA Congressional Committee, they staged a parade in Washington, D.C., during Woodrow Wilson's 1913 inauguration which brought woman suffrage to the headlines. By 1914, they formed an independent organization (the Congressional Union or the Woman's party[4]), modeled after the British suffrage movement. They campaigned against the Democrats in elections, arguing that, as the party in power, it was responsible for delays in women's enfranchisement. They utilized militant tactics, including picketing the White House, burning speeches of Woodrow Wilson, and hunger strikes, to confront the government and publicize the suffrage cause.

Although many of the new generation of NAWSA leaders were horrified by these tactics, they also altered their tactics. When Carrie Chapman Catt accepted the NAWSA presidency in 1915, she brought an emphasis on professional organizers and lobbyists, as well as an electoral strategy for winning the vote. Her 1916 "Winning Plan" for a federal amendment assigned states a role commensurate with their circumstances. The NAWSA split its resources between state campaigns that had a chance of winning and lobbying efforts in Washington. In the final years of the struggle, the NAWSA even entered partisan politics by fighting the reelection of a few anti-suffrage senators.

Both the militant activities of the Woman's party and the careful organizing and lobbying of the NAWSA led to many new successes. First, the number of women engaged in suffrage organizations rose dramatically. Membership in the NAWSA doubled between 1910 and 1912 and again between 1912 and 1915. This expansion signaled an increased interest in the issue of women's voting rights and provided new armies to be marched into the suffrage battle. State legislatures became increasingly willing to consider woman suffrage legislation. Between 1910 and 1920 an average of 15 states considered suffrage legislation each year, and there were more state referenda on women's voting rights than in the previous forty years combined.

Breakthroughs occurred first in the Midwest, then in the East and finally in the South. Beginning in 1910, Arizona, California, Kansas, Michigan, Montana, Nevada, New York, Oklahoma, Oregon, South Dakota, Washington, and the territory of Alaska all passed constitutional amendments enfranchising women. In states where the rules for amending the constitution were more arduous, the suffrage activists sought voting rights for specific elections which could be granted by legislative act (such as the vote for presidential electors) (Catt 1917). In fact, the first advance in women's voting rights east of the Mississippi occurred in 1913, when Illinois enacted this form of presidential suffrage legislation. By the time the Nineteenth Amendment was adopted in 1920, all the Midwest states had some form of women's voting rights, two southern states had adopted suffrage in primary elections, and a few Eastern states, most notably New York, had enacted women's voting rights legislation.

As women entered the electorate in more and more states, pressure mounted on Congress to pass the Nineteenth Amendment. In 1918, the amendment passed the House of Representatives but failed in the Senate by just two votes. The NAWSA opposed and defeated two anti-suffrage senators in the next election. As a result, in 1919 the amendment passed and was sent on to the states for ratification. It took 15 months and 19 hard-fought state campaigns to ratify the amendment (Deckard 1983).

By the time of ratification in August 1920, 12 European countries had already enfranchised women. Swiss women would wait five more decades after that before they could go to the polls.

A Brief History of the Swiss Woman Suffrage Movement

Switzerland's woman suffrage movement does not break down neatly into phases like the U.S. movement. Throughout its history, the Swiss woman suffrage movement remained a collection of small local bands with weak national ties whose activities differed greatly from canton to canton. Nonetheless, even as the different local organizations pursued separate courses of actions, national events and trends allow us to make some generalizations about the movement.

1868–1909: The Development of a National Woman Suffrage Organization

The first phase of the Swiss movement is characterized by the development of the first women's rights organizations and the first demands for equal rights for women. As in the United States, various women's organizations were formed in the first half of the nineteenth century (Mesmer 1988). Yet, the first women's organization to promote women's rights, the Association internationale des femmes (AIF), was not founded until 1868. In that same year, three anonymous groups of women petitioned for equal rights in divorce, inheritance, and education during the revision of Zürich's constitution (Mesmer 1988; Woodtli 1983). Despite these events, equal rights was not the explicit focus of most women's organizations. Rather, the first women's organizations were created to support the interests of working women (largely within the growing socialist movement), or to conduct charity and moral reform work.

Indeed, the Swiss socialist movement, which was strongest in the French-speaking western cantons of Switzerland, spawned a number of women's organizations in addition to the AIF. Within the socialist movement, women workers also organized and by 1890 were strong enough to form a national organization, der Schweizerische Arbeiterinnenverband (Eidgenössische Kommission für Frauenfragen 1984). The principal focus of these organizations was to provide better living and working conditions for working women by demanding higher wages, reduced working hours, and the adoption of state health and unemployment insurance. After the turn of the century, the fledgling Social Democratic party (SP) also began to take an interest in organizing women and endorsed equal rights for women (Mesmer 1988).

Despite socialists' support for women's rights, early Swiss women's rights efforts had closer ties to women's social reform organizations. A major impetus for the development of the social reform associations came from Josephine Butler's moral reform movement in Britain. This movement, which focused on the laws regulating prostitution, was quite separate from suffrage organizations. For Butler, the prostitution problem expressed the quintessence of women's oppression, making other questions of women's rights less important (Lovenduski 1986: 26).

Butler cultivated many contacts on the Continent and greatly influenced women's movements in Germany, France, and Switzerland (Evans 1976; Hause and Kenney 1984; Mesmer 1988). Almost all of the early Swiss women's rights activists were connected to Josephine Butler. She was a member of the AIF, which developed local committees in other countries (Mesmer 1988). During a Swiss lecture tour, Butler attracted many early women reformers to her cause (including Helene von Mülinen, founder of the Bund Schweizerischer Frauen, see Mesmer 1988; Woodtli 1983). Many of these first-generation activists retained their interest in moral reform even as they turned to the issue of women's rights.

The first organization devoted exclusively to women's rights, Zürich's Union für Frauenbestrebungen, was founded in 1893 (Ruckstuhl 1986; Woodtli 1983). Other local suffrage organizations were not formed until after the turn of the century and it was only in 1909 that the national woman suffrage organization—the Schweizerischer Verband für Frauenstimmrecht (SVF)—was founded. In that year, seven local suffrage organizations decided to create the national organization (SVF 1934).

Even as local suffrage organizations emerged, public discussion of women's voting rights was rare in Switzerland. In a few cantons, women petitioned for the right to serve on some local commissions (Mesmer 1988). However, the only success during this 50-year period occurred in Vaud, where women won the right to vote for church boards in 1908 (Ruckstuhl 1986). Women's organizations did not promote women's enfranchisement among a wider audience (as did their American contemporaries), preferring instead to stress other issues. The Union des femmes, one of the earliest women's associations in Genève, is typical of women's organizations during this period. Its main activities were providing social services for working women and fostering moral reform, but it also held occasional open discussions of women's rights (Woodtli 1983: 68).

1910–1929: The Rise of the Suffrage Issue

It was only in the late 1910s that voting rights for women reached the public agenda and the fledgling woman suffrage movement took root in Switzerland. As the rest of Europe and the United States enfranchised women, demands for voting rights for women increased within Switzerland. Outside of the burgeoning women's rights organizations, the socialist movement and the Social Democratic party (SP) played important roles in the expansion of the suffrage issue. In 1912, the SP platform stated that the party should "use every opportunity to agitate for woman suffrage" (Ruckstuhl 1986: 18; translated by author). When a general strike was called in February of 1918, the strike committee also included women's voting rights on its list of demands. Later in 1918, a Social Democratic representative in the Nationalrat, Herman Greulich, introduced the first motion for woman suffrage in the Swiss Parliament.[5] This motion, asking the government (Bundesrat) to consider enfranchising women, passed the Nationalrat but neither the Bundesrat nor the other branch of Parliament (the Ständerat) took any further action for almost forty years. Between 1910 and 1929, woman suffrage legislation was also discussed for the first time in 11 of the 25 cantons; in 7 cantons referenda were held.

Two sorts of suffrage legislation were considered at this point, each with differing bases of support, regional emphases, and success rates. The SP and, to a lessor extent, the Swiss Communist party (the Partei der Arbeit or PdA) were very active in introducing unqualified voting rights for women (full suffrage). Of the seven motions for full woman suffrage introduced in cantonal parliaments during this period where the political party of the responsible legislator could be identified,[6] all but one stemmed from SP or PdA members. Moreover, with only one exception, only those cantonal parliaments where the SP and PdA were heavily represented passed bills for full women's voting rights.[7]

On the other hand, partial suffrage bills, which permitted women to vote only for a limited set of offices (usually church councils or school boards), were acceptable to a wider array of parties. Center and right parties, opposed to women participating in politics, saw the value of allowing women to serve on church, school, and charity boards. As a result, between 1910 and 1920, four cantons (Neuchâtel, Bern, Basel-stadt, and Graubünden) extended this highly limited franchise to women.

The expansion in consideration of the suffrage issue was matched by increased mobilization into suffrage organizations. While only seven suffrage organizations existed in 1909, by 1929 that number had more than doubled and these groups also increased their participation in the suffrage debate. The national SVF sent appeals to the national government and sponsored a 1928 national petition drive that gathered about 250,000 signatures in six months (Ruckstuhl 1986; Woodtli 1983). Cantonal sections often reacted to motions for woman suffrage by making their own entreaties to cantonal governments. The most aggressive cantonal section was in Genève where suffrage activists successfully launched an initiative (later defeated at the polls) after suffrage motions failed in the cantonal parliament.

Despite the increase in the activities and size of the Swiss suffrage organization, it remained weaker and less aggressive than its American counterpart. Many local Swiss women's rights organizations were dependent on a few women leaders for survival. If these champions left an organization, the group often disbanded. Moreover, many suffrage organizations were unwilling to unequivocally support female suffrage. For example, when Social Democrats introduced a motion calling for the full enfranchisement of women in St. Gallen, the local suffrage organization argued that the motion provided too much suffrage (Ruckstuhl 1986). Thus, Swiss activists were just beginning to focus on votes for women. Nonetheless, in comparison to the years that followed, the period from 1909 to 1929 was one of intense activity.

1930–1944: The Quiet in the Storm

Beginning in 1930, Switzerland underwent a prolonged period of crisis starting with the economic depression, which lasted until 1936 (Fahrni 1983) and was followed by World War II. When the war began in 1939, Switzerland remained neutral but feared invasion. Thus, even though Switzerland did not suffer the destruction of other European countries during World War II, it experienced extreme changes as most male citizens remained mobilized in the army between 1939 and 1945.

During these crises, the woman suffrage issue virtually disappeared from the public agenda. On the national level, no mention was made of women's voting rights in the Swiss Parliament until 1944. Even Swiss women suffrage activists focused on other activities during this period, taking over the jobs in industry and agriculture held by soldiers and providing extensive aid for the families of soldiers and the refugees pouring into the country. The SVF made only one appeal to the Swiss Parliament for women's enfranchisement during this period and that constituted the bulk of the SVF's suffrage work during the crises. Instead, the national suffrage organization focused on problems caused by the depression and war such as discriminatory rules against women's employment and the price and scarcity of food.

Most cantonal organizations also reduced suffrage activities during the crises. Zürich's suffrage section, for example, continued to hold regular meetings but altered the focus of their lecture series. Instead of women's rights, lecture topics centered more on women's work and the war (*Die Staatsbürgerin*, November 1968). Only a few cantonal suffrage organizations continued to actively pursue the enfranchisement of women. In Genève, activists successfully launched a second initiative petition drive for full woman suffrage in 1938 that was rejected by voters in 1940. In addition, the Bern suffrage section founded a special Aktionskomitee in 1940 that organized a petition drive to ask the cantonal government for the vote in local elections. However, most local organizations, overwhelmed by national and international events, ignored the suffrage issue during this period.

Nor were local politicians pushing for women's enfranchisement. During this 15-year period only nine motions for woman suffrage were introduced in cantonal parliaments and only four of these were for unlimited voting rights. Except for the Genève suffrage initiative, only one canton held a referendum on women's voting rights, and then only for partial suffrage.

1945–1967: The Postwar Drive for Suffrage

As the war ended and as France and Italy enfranchised women, interest in the question of women's rights increased in Switzerland and woman suffrage organizations became increasingly active.

The Swiss Parliament's 1944 motion for national woman suffrage was followed by another in 1949 asking the Bundesrat to consider the extension of political rights for women. In 1951, the government reported that it was too early to attempt a national referendum on woman suffrage since all previous attempts on the cantonal level had failed. Although conditions in the cantons did not change, in 1957 it announced it would submit a national constitutional amendment enfranchising women to the voters in 1959. The change of heart was largely political: a government-sponsored constitutional amendment requiring women to serve in civil defense had been jeopardized by the indignant reactions of women's rights groups who rejected additional responsibilities for women who lacked basic political rights.[8] While the resulting woman suffrage referendum was rejected by an overwhelming majority of the voters, majorities endorsed suffrage in three cantons, leading to the first enactments of full voting rights for women on the cantonal level.

Indeed, the end of World War II heralded more interest in woman suffrage on the cantonal level than ever before. In all, legislation providing full enfranchisement of women was introduced 47 times between 1945 and 1967, resulting in 15 cantonal referenda. In addition, 12 cantons held referenda on partial voting rights for women. Several cantonal referenda were successful. In 1957, voters in the canton of Basel-stadt elected to allow individual towns to decide whether women could vote in local elections, allowing two of the canton's three towns to enfranchise women. In 1959, Vaud and Neuchâtel became the first two cantons to adopt full woman suffrage. In 1960, the canton of Genève followed suit, and in 1966 voters in Basel-stadt enfranchised women in all elections.

The mobilization and activities of woman suffrage organizations underwent fundamental changes during the postwar period. Membership in the SVF, which had declined during the war years, rose steadily in the late 1950s and early 1960s. Between 1951 and 1966, for example, the organization grew by 48 percent. Moreover, other outlets developed for women who supported the enfranchisement of women but found the SVF too radical. During this period, the Staatsbürgerlicher Verband katholischer Schweizerinnen (STAKA), was founded (Ruckstuhl 1986). Officially, STAKA emphasized civic education for women so that they could fulfill their traditional roles as mothers, philanthropists, and supporters of the church, although many activists claimed the real purpose was to increase support for women's entrance into politics. Other women's organizations that previously had not supported women's voting rights also became active in the suffrage struggle. They coordinated their activities in the Arbeitsgemeinschaft für die politischen Rechte der Frau. While most groups in the Arbeitsgemeinschaft played a minor role in the battle for suffrage, their willingness to send appeals to the Swiss government and to help organize the 1959 referendum campaign meant the base of support for women's voting rights had widened considerably.

During this period, there was also a slight change in the tactics suffrage activists utilized. Previously, activists focused almost exclusively on two types of tactics: public education on the suffrage issue and petitions or appeals to governments. Indeed, suffrage activists were often careful to avoid any hint of controversy. During the 1959 national referendum, suffrage activists argued that women conducting publicity work should take special care to avoid offending anyone. While public education and petitioning continued to be the primary tactics, activists in a few cantons began employing protest, such as trying to register to vote and torchlight demonstrations. These acts occurred infrequently, but they heralded a new phase in the movement.

1968–1971: The Rise of the New Women's Movement and the National Woman Suffrage Amendment

The four years encompassing 1968 to 1971 deserve special attention because the development of the new women's liberation movement, and the rise of protest more generally, had an impact on the suffrage movement. The women's liberation movement, or Frauenbefreiungsbewegung (FBB), was influenced by the radical student activity in the late 1960s (Woodtli 1983). Women's second-class treatment by male leaders within the student movement and their refusal to consider women's status within the movement an issue was a specific impetus for the creation of the FBB (see the group's founding statement in Woodtli 1983: 207–8).

Generally, FBB members were unwilling to join forces with the older, more conservative suffrage activists. In fact, women's liberation activists belittled the activities of the SVF and accused the organization of being complacent about their disenfranchisement. When the Zürich woman suffrage organization gathered to celebrate their seventy-fifth anniversary, the FBB women protested the celebration: "We were having the evening celebration when the '68 women [the FBB] . . . disturbed the celebration. They said over the megaphone, '75 years working for suffrage is no reason to celebrate'" (interview with suffrage activist, January 15, 1988).[9] Thereafter, suffrage activists consciously tried to attract FBB women into their organizations. While they never succeeded, some local sections cooperated on occasional projects.

The most important of these was the March on Bern. In 1968, the Swiss government indicated it would sign the European Human Rights Convention with a specific proviso excluding the sections granting political rights to women. Together with the FBB, suffrage activists from Zürich and Basel-stadt organized a demonstration in front of Bern's Bundeshaus.[10] While the national women's organizations did not sanction the March on Bern, even some of the more conservative suffrage activists attended. While a demonstration against the government would have previously appalled these women, the advent of the new social movements enhanced their convictions that such protest was acceptable and even necessary.

Both the March on Bern and the strong disapproval by all of the national women's organizations of the provisos to the Human Rights Convention spurred the Swiss government to announce a second national referendum on woman suffrage. The circumstances of this referendum were quite different from the first. All of the major women's organizations and the major political parties supported its passage. Moreover, two-thirds of all cantons had already granted women substantial voting rights—either full cantonal suffrage or optional city suffrage.[11] On February 7, 1971, 66 percent of the (male) voters approved the inclusion of a woman suffrage amendment in the Swiss constitution. On the same day, voters in four cantons approved cantonal voting rights for women. However, not all the results were positive; voters in eight cantons rejected the national suffrage amendment.

1972–1990: Completing the Enfranchisement of Women

This continued opposition was important because the Swiss woman suffrage amendment was explicitly limited to the right to vote in national referenda and elections for the lower house of Parliament. Cantons were still permitted to make their own laws regarding voting eligibility in cantonal and local elections. The independence of cantons resulted in inequities for some women. In some areas, women elected to the Swiss Parliament were prohibited from participating in their canton's elections. Thus, the suffrage movement was forced to continue its battle in several cantons and communities.

Most of the localities where women were still disenfranchised immediately moved to adopt full voting rights for women. Between February 1971 and December 1972, eight cantons adopted full woman suffrage legislation. After 1972, only four cantons remained where women were disenfranchised. In Solothurn and Graubünden, some local communities continued to restrict women's voting rights until 1983. The two Appenzells denied women voting rights until 1989 (Ausserrhoden) and 1990 (Innerrhoden).

Most cantons rushed to change their voting laws after the national referendum in 1971, and women's rights organizations subsequently moved on to other issues. Indeed, the woman suffrage organization renamed itself the Swiss Association for Women's Rights (Schweizerischer Verband für Frauenrechte). In 1975, a number of the former suffrage activists organized an initiative campaign for an Equal Rights Amendment, which passed in a 1981 referendum. Women in the two Appenzells were left to struggle for cantonal voting rights largely on their own.

Conclusion

As even this brief overview suggests, there are a number of factors that might account for the differences in the timing of women's enfranchisement in the United States and Switzerland. The American suffrage movement created stronger national structures and grew faster than its Swiss counterpart. The two movements reacted to events by choosing different tactics. The Swiss suffrage movement found allies in the Socialist party and movements and other women's organizations while the American movement benefitted from ties to the abolitionists, WCTU, Populists, and Progressives. Each movement also operated within and was affected by very different historical and political contexts. Women's voting rights were temporarily ignored during the Civil War in the United States and during the depression and World War II in Switzerland. All of these factors, and others, may have affected the timing of women's voting rights in each country.

The autonomy that federalism imparted to states and cantons created profound variation in the timing of woman suffrage on the local level. It allowed some U.S. states to be trailblazers in the enfranchisement of women, but it had the opposite effect in Switzerland where federalism permitted a few cantons to deny women the vote long after it had become a *fait accompli* nearly everywhere else in the world. To understand the success and failure of suffrage movements in the United States and Switzerland, we must also explain the differences within each country. In the chapters that follow, I unravel the complex histories of both the local and national movements and determine which factors explain the different patterns and timing of success in both the United States and Switzerland.

2

INFORMATION, PREFERENCES, BELIEFS, AND
VALUES IN THE POLITICAL PROCESS

IN ORDER to understand the success and failure of the American and Swiss woman suffrage movements, this book raises three questions, each drawing on a different comparison. First, in contrasting the two nations, I examine why American women acquired voting rights so much sooner than their Swiss sisters. Second, I compare local suffrage movements within each country by asking: Why did women in some U.S. states and some Swiss cantons achieve suffrage sooner than women living elsewhere in the same nation? Third, I examine individual movements over time in order to inquire why some early efforts failed, only to succeed much later. For possible answers to these questions, I look initially at broad societal conditions that others have linked to democratization or extensions of the franchise and show that these cannot make sense of the tempos of success and failure. I then elaborate a more promising approach, which focuses on the woman suffrage movements themselves and their actions within the various national, cantonal and state-level contexts.

Modernization, Women's Education, and Culture in the Swiss and American Woman Suffrage Movements

While this study examines several theoretical perspectives on *movement* success or failure, necessitating a focus on political groups, other approaches have sought explanations for the expansion of the franchise in terms of broad aspects of social structure. We can quickly see why such conditions as socioeconomic modernization, women's education, and cultural variations do not sufficiently explain the extension of woman suffrage in the United States and Switzerland.

Modernization

Numerous scholars (among them, Cutright 1963; Cutright and Wiley 1969; Lipset 1959; Neubauer 1967; and Smith 1969) have argued that economic development, particularly industrialization and urbanization, contributes to the expansion of democracy by increasing the economic wealth of many groups and by spreading new ideas and ideologies among the mass public. Moreover, by dislocating existing social groups and creating new ones, modernization creates more demands for political participation. Modernization theories have not been used specifically to explain the spread of women's voting rights. Nonetheless, it is logical that women's demands may have increased along with the changes wrought by modernization since women as a group also experience changes in work, income, and opportunities with economic development.

Despite its apparent applicability to the case of woman suffrage, the concept of modernization is of limited usefulness in understanding the timing of woman suffrage in Switzerland and the United States. For one thing, the pace of industrialization in the two nations was very similar. Both industrialized earlier and faster than most other European countries. Indeed, Switzerland was the first country on the European continent to experience the industrial revolution, with the growth of its textile industry in the late eighteenth century (Fahrni 1983; Schaffer 1972). By 1850, Switzerland was the second most industrialized country in Europe after Great Britain (Fahrni 1983: 56). Industrial development in the United States also began with the development of the textile industry, especially after the 1830s in factories, as steam engines and mechanization helped to increase production (Cott 1977; Faulkner 1960). In both countries, manufacturing became an important source of employment. By 1920, over 33 percent of the American working population were employed in manufacturing, mechanical, and mining industries (U.S. Bureau of the Census 1920). In comparison, 44 percent of the Swiss population were employed in manufacturing and mining in 1920 (Eidgenössiches Statistisches Amt 1951). Thus, industrialization cannot have been the driving force in the enfranchisement of women since Switzerland's industrial development equaled or even surpassed that of the United States.

If the pace of industrialization cannot account for the extension of the franchise to women, is it possible that the lack of urbanization is related to the lateness of Swiss suffrage? Although Switzerland and the U.S. followed similar paths of industrialization, they diverged in the degree to which the expansion of industry coincided with the concentration of the population in large cities. Switzerland's industry, particularly the textile factories, was not concentrated in urban areas but spread throughout the countryside in order to capitalize on the free energy provided by Swiss waterways (Fahrni 1983). Despite the increase in industrialization, only 29 percent of the population lived in cities with a population of 10,000 or more in 1920.[1] In contrast, in 1913, 39 percent of the American population was already living in urban areas of comparable size (Banks 1971: 95).

Yet, within the United States and in an international perspective, urbanization cannot explain women's voting rights. Those U.S. states that first granted woman suffrage—Wyoming, Utah, Idaho, and Colorado—were not great urban centers and the most urbanized states—Massachusetts, New Jersey, and Connecticut—did not enfranchise women until the ratification of the Nineteenth Amendment.[2] From an international comparison, even Swiss suffrage activists noted that less urbanized countries like Cambodia and Ghana had voting rights for women long before Switzerland.

On the other hand, urbanized cantons in Switzerland were, on average, more likely to enact woman suffrage legislation earlier than rural cantons. Those cantons that enacted suffrage by 1960—Neuchâtel, Genève, and Vaud—had 59 percent of their population in cities over 10,000, while in cantons with no women's voting rights, only 27 percent of the population lived in cities over 10,000.[3] However, these three cantons shared a number of characteristics (for example, similar linguistic backgrounds and strong left parties) which may explain this relationship.

Moreover, although urban areas were thought to facilitate the spread of ideas and the creation of new demands, two characteristics made urbanization less important in the case of Swiss woman suffrage. First, the density of towns and Switzerland's small size meant that those living outside of cities were still relatively close. Even in the Alps, a trip to a city of over 10,000 was never more than 50 miles away. Indeed, the two Appenzell cantons lie within a 20-mile radius of one of Switzerland's larger cities, St. Gallen, and many of their smaller towns serve as its suburbs. Second, because much of the Swiss suffrage movement occurred later than the American, communications technology further reduced the separation between urbanized and rural areas. While U.S. suffrage activists had access to newspapers, railways, and the telegraph, Swiss suffrage activists had radio, telephones, and automobiles, which eased the problems of communication and increased the diffusion of ideas between urban and rural areas.

Thus, overall it is difficult to argue that modernization was a significant factor in the extension of the franchise to women. Switzerland industrialized relatively early compared to most European countries but was the last to adopt woman suffrage. The growth of urban areas is not related to the timing of woman suffrage internationally or in the United States. Further, geography and the lateness of the woman suffrage movement reduced the significance of the urban/rural division in Switzerland.

Women's Education

In the United States, scholars have argued that extensive changes in women's education beginning in the 1800s led to changes in women's political condition (for example, Cott 1977; Deckard 1983; Skocpol

1992). Can differences in the levels of women's education therefore explain the variation in the timing of women's enfranchisement?

On the one hand, both nations were innovators in the area of women's education, in part because of a need for female teachers. The first teacher training school for women was opened by the canton Bern in 1838 (Mesmer 1988). In the United States, institutions of higher education for women, like Mount Holyoke, proliferated in the 1830s and began to focus on the academic subjects necessary to prepare women for careers in teaching (Newcomer 1959; Skocpol 1992). Interestingly, both countries claim the honor of being the first in the world to graduate women from existing postsecondary institutions,[4] although women had attended lectures for years without receiving diplomas. Moreover, the United States and Switzerland were both early supporters of compulsory education. After revisions in 1874, the Swiss Constitution included obligatory primary school for both sexes (Mesmer 1988: 133).[5] About the same time, the United States instituted a policy of compulsory education in the primary levels (Skocpol 1992).

Despite these similarities, women's education in the United States and Switzerland ultimately took on very different characteristics. While educational opportunities in both countries expanded during the nineteenth century, the changes in Swiss education were much more limited. Although a higher percentage of the Swiss population was attending postprimary institutions in 1900, by 1920 a greater proportion of U.S. citizens were being educated at this level (Banks 1971). Moreover, while women quickly became about half of the students in colleges and universities in the United States, the percentage of women in Swiss universities remained less than 25 percent until the 1970s (Heidenheimer 1994). In part, the low enrollment of women reflects the fact that education for traditional women's occupations—social work, nursing, and teaching—was provided at other types of schools (for example, Hochschule). Finally, women were not pushed into the field of public education as rapidly in Switzerland as in the United States. In 1900, 73 percent of all American teachers were women, while in 1910 only 52 percent of Swiss teachers were female (U.S. Bureau of the Census 1900; Statistische Bureau der Schweiz 1910).[6]

Can the differences in women's education (and subsequent employment) account for the differences in timing of woman suffrage? Again, the evidence is mixed. In advanced industrialized countries, women's access to universities and women's voting rights were not related.[7] In Europe, France and Switzerland were among the first countries to allow women to acquire university degrees but among the last to grant them voting rights; Germany enfranchised women in 1918, but did not allow women to receive diplomas until 1900.

Nonetheless, *within* Switzerland and the United States there is a connection between higher education and success. States that adopted women's voting rights by 1920 gave a higher percentage of their baccalaureate degrees to women than states where women could not vote.[8] In Switzerland, cantons that had enacted women's voting rights legislation by 1970 gave 30 percent of all diplomas to women, while the other cantons bestowed only 19.5 percent of their diplomas on women. Similarly, I looked at the percentage of women in Ober and Untere Mittelschulen (that is, secondary schools of all types). In the three cantons enfranchising women by 1960, 48 percent of students at this level were women; cantons without suffrage had only 23 percent women in these grades.[9] Before I discuss the implications of these relationships, let us examine the link between culture and suffrage in Switzerland.

Cultural Diversity

Switzerland is often touted for its ability to combine a mix of cultures within a stable democratic system.[10] Three different linguistic groups exist side by side; 65 percent of the Swiss speak German dialects, approximately 20 percent are French-speaking, and about 10 percent Italian. While most cantons are dominated by a single linguistic group, several, such as Freiburg/Fribourg and Wallis/Yalais, are divided by language.

The governmental institutions that facilitate this system are discussed in other chapters. However, to many Swiss the linguistic differences also denote a diversity of cultures. For example, Linder (1994) points out that French-speaking Swiss are more internationalist (that is, interested in joining the UN and the European Economic Area) and less supportive of government policies (but see Inglehart 1990: 28–29). Many of the woman suffrage activists I interviewed argued that French-speaking Swiss have a cultural connection to the traditions of the French Revolution that makes them more supportive of woman suffrage, while German-speakers are stubborn, less spontaneous, and less willing to change. These characteristics in turn have been used to explain why French-speaking cantons—Neuchâtel, Genève, and Vaud—were the first to enfranchise women within Switzerland.

Interestingly, the Swiss stereotypes of how French-speaking culture affected women's enfranchisement do not correspond with the realities in France. There, the ideology of the French Revolution did not lead to woman suffrage. Indeed, Hause and Kenney (1984: 14–17) note that even strong supporters of the French Republic fought women's voting rights, arguing that women were not yet ready for the vote. Moreover, the French women's rights movement, despite the ideology of the French Revolution, was one of the weaker in Europe (Lovenduski 1986).[11]

If the Swiss stereotypes of French-speakers clash with the realities of French politics, French-speaking cantons were, nonetheless, the first to enfranchise women. By 1971, all of the cantons where French was spoken by more than 30 percent of the population had enacted women's voting rights legislation. If the ascribed cultural characteristics that supposedly influenced the timing of suffrage cannot be attributed to French culture, we must explore more carefully the mechanisms by which linguistic differences affected women's enfranchisement.

Decomposing Urbanization, Women's Education, and Cultural Diversity

The above discussion indicates that none of the three variables—modernization, women's education, and cultural factors—withstand international comparisons. While all three appear related to women's enfranchisement within Switzerland, many of these factors overlapped. French-speaking cantons shared a multitude of characteristics, including being more urbanized and having high percentages of women in higher education. As a result, it is difficult to isolate which of these factors was of major importance in determining the timing of woman suffrage.

I have chosen to approach these puzzles by focusing on the major *mechanisms* by which urbanization, women's education, and culture might affect the spread of woman suffrage. These three factors alter the demands made by women for suffrage, the resources they then utilize in the battle for woman suffrage, the distribution of power within society, and the spread of new beliefs and values throughout society. These mechanisms translate into political change by affecting small groups, large political organizations, and political parties. Without looking at groups, the connection between modernization, women's education, and culture—and the timing of suffrage—remains vague (McAdam 1983). Nor is the relationship straightforward. At each step, groups are also influenced by the political context and interactions with other political actors. Thus, looking at the women's movement requires that we widen our focus to look at other political actors and key aspects of the political context. As a result, we must turn to the literature on social movements and in particular to the three recent perspectives—resource mobilization theories, theories of political opportunity structures, and treatments of collective beliefs and values—that try to explain the outcomes of social movements.

In what ways does each perspective help us to answer our questions about the Swiss and American woman suffrage movements? Just as broad societal factors are insufficient to explain woman suffrage, so is a restricted focus only on resources and political opportunities available to the movements. Resources and opportunities matter, but they can take us only part way in understanding the timing of suffrage in the two countries. A focus on conditions, resources, or opportunities alone minimizes or ignores the role that information, values, and beliefs play in the tactical decision making of woman suffrage activists. Drawing on key insights from recent approaches that emphasize the role of "frames," "discourses," and "culture" in movement success or failure, I contend that beliefs and values may aid a movement, as they did in the case of the U.S. suffrage movement, by predisposing it to take advantage of opportunities. On the other hand, these same factors may explain why a movement foregoes existing opportunities, as in Switzerland.

Resource Mobilization and Movement Success

The first scholars to explicitly explore the causes of social movement success and failure were resource mobilization theorists (Jenkins 1983; Jenkins and Perrow 1977; Oberschall 1973; McCarthy and Zald 1977; and Zald and McCarthy 1979).[12] Reacting to "classical theorists," who explained the existence of social movements by referring to aggression rooted in individual grievances (Gurr 1970) or structural stresses and strains (Smelser 1963), they viewed participants and movements as rational actors who weigh the relative costs and benefits of their actions. This approach explains individual participation and movement growth by focusing on organizational resources, organizational structure, movement recruitment strategies, and the role of leaders (McCarthy and Zald 1977; Zald and McCarthy 1979, 1987).[13] According to this view, the development of social movements depends mainly on the availability of "resources" such as money, facilities, a communication network, and a group of committed volunteers (both skilled and unskilled) willing to commit time to the movement.

Although some movements may control their own resources, they frequently acquire resources from two other sources. One important source is "political entrepreneurs." These are individual activists, interest groups, or other social movements who finance the costs of the movement because they hope to receive some personal benefit, such as a leadership position or the achievement of a highly valued goal (Jenkins and Perrow 1977; Oberschall 1973; Popkin 1988). Another source is groups that inadvertently provide resources to the movement (Freeman 1975; Jenkins and Perrow 1977). For example, Freeman (1975: 58–59) argues that other protest movements in the 1960s provided the communications network necessary for the development of the younger branch of the women's movement in the United States.

If resource mobilization theories are correct, we would expect to find that the Swiss suffrage movement, and the local suffrage movements in both countries where suffrage was enacted relatively late, lacked resources. Examining the role of movement resources in the timing of woman suffrage, however, requires first a definitive list of which resources are important. Here we run into one of the weaknesses of resource mobilization theory. Despite the centrality of the concept of resources, the definition of resources remains vague, incorporating virtually anything which might affect a movement.[14] For example, Oberschall (1973) defines resources in terms of tangible assets, such as money and material goods, and intangible assets, such as networks with other groups and the skills of movement activists (see also Jenkins 1983). Unfortunately, these definitions are problematic. "It would be exceedingly difficult, given the all-inclusive definitions . . . to find a social movement that was not preceded by *some* increase in *some* type of 'resource' " (McAdam 1982: 33; emphasis in original). Moreover, many "resources," such as allies and networks, also play a role in theories of political opportunity structure. To avoid a limitless measure of resources and to distinguish the two theories, I discuss two tangible assets available to the U.S. and Swiss suffrage movements—volunteers and finances—in Chapters 3 and 4. The role of networks with other organizations (see Rosenthal et al. 1985) is discussed under the concept of political opportunity structure.

The Theory of Political Opportunity Structures

An explanation for suffrage success that relies exclusively on resource mobilization is at best incomplete. For one thing, resource mobilization's emphasis on outside resources may exaggerate their influence. Mass-based movements, although economically poor, have their own resources and do not necessarily require outside help (McAdam 1982; Morris 1993; Piven and Cloward 1979). More fundamentally, even unconditional aid to the movement by other political actors may act to reduce a movement's success. In Chapter 5, for example, I illustrate the positive effects of U.S. suffrage movement's alliances with the temperance movement and some progressive organizations. I also show how these gains were, in part, offset by the growth of an anti-suffrage alliance that reacted to these groups' support of women's enfranchisement. Thus, the influence of political entrepreneurs and other collective political actors on a social movement can be both positive and negative.

Second, social movements are not just affected by the "resources" available to them from other groups but also by the constraints and opportunities produced by alliances, state structures, and political processes

(McAdam 1982; Tilly 1978; and Tarrow 1989a, 1989b, 1994). The historical context creates "specific configurations of resources, institutional arrangements, and historical precedents" (Kitschelt 1986: 58) that may constrain or help a movement. In some U.S. states, for example, the right to initiate constitutional amendments provided an opportunity for woman suffrage activists. On the other hand, electoral stability and the nature of Swiss government coalitions virtually assured continued rule of the major parties, limiting the suffrage movement's ability to influence their platforms. Thus, political opportunity structure theories incorporate a new influence—the political context—in addition to many aspects of resource mobilization.

The constraints and opportunities of the political process have two effects on the calculus of rational movements. On the one hand, formal and informal political structures may alter the costs of taking a particular collective action. For example, the costs associated with the Woman's party picketing of the White House were increased when, after the United States declared war in 1917, women were arrested in these picket lines (Irwin 1921). On the other hand, the political opportunity structure may also alter the benefits that result from collective action. For example, the return on collecting signatures on petitions increases where they can be used to initiate a referendum vote. Here, the amount of resources available to the movement is not of primary importance; rather, it is a question of what a movement can achieve from those resources.[15] At the extreme, it is possible for the state to so restrict the range of possible outcomes that the movement cannot realize any of its objectives no matter what strategy it utilizes or how many resources it expends (see, for example, Tilly 1978: 139–40).

To apply this approach to the U.S. and Swiss woman suffrage movements, we must delineate the important aspects of political opportunity structure. However, this is not as easy as it might seem. The specific characteristics of the political opportunity structure are systemwide phenomena that are shared by all movements in the same society, but each movement is differentially affected by these factors (Tarrow 1994). The characteristics and resources of a movement may determine which aspects of the political opportunity structure most affect its development and success.[16] Moreover, "movements create opportunities for themselves" (Tarrow 1994: 82). Consider the role of U.S. woman suffrage movements in the alliance that fought to acquire initiative rights. By helping to acquire this right in a number of states, suffrage movements increased their opportunities for pressing their claim for the vote (see Chapter 7). The result is a continuously changing political context affecting and affected by an evolving social movement (see also, McAdam 1982; Tarrow 1989b; Tilly 1978; and Kriesi 1991).

While political opportunity structure theorists have outlined different theoretical dimensions of opportunities (compare Eisinger 1973; Tarrow 1989a, 1994; Kitschelt 1986; Kriesi 1995), they generally agree on the factors most important to movement development and success.[17] First, many note the importance of some formal rules and institutions of the state (Eisinger 1973; Kitschelt 1986; Kriesi 1995). In particular, formal institutions may provide challengers with many points of access. These include the independence of legislative and executive branches, federalism, and direct democratic institutions. Interestingly, both the United States and, especially, Switzerland, according to this view, provide greater access than many other countries (Kriesi 1995; Kitschelt 1986). Indeed, Switzerland, with its direct democratic institutions on the national level, surpasses the United States in its openness to outside challengers. Therefore, formal institutions cannot help to explain why the American movement was the first to succeed.

A second important aspect of the political opportunity structure is the constellation of other political actors. Political actors are defined as political parties, interest groups, social movements, and other contenders for power within the population (see Tilly 1978: 52). The extent to which power is divided (or concentrated) among various actors, and the divisions and alliances among them, may affect a movement's success. Opposition political parties in both countries are particularly important since they were most likely to adopt the woman suffrage issue as a means of attacking those in power (Kriesi 1995; Tarrow 1994). Again, Switzerland and the United States, and the states and cantons within them, share a number of common characteristics. Parties in both countries are weaker on the national level than at the local level. Although the United States is normally considered a two-party system and Switzerland a multiparty system, during the fight for women suffrage, the United States experienced a number of significant third party challenges. The greater number of parties in Switzerland might lead us to believe that Swiss suffrage movements had greater opportunities to find allies among political parties. However, electoral and governmental stability in Switzerland reduced the competition among parties which, in turn, limited the availability of allies to the Swiss suffrage movement.

Interest associations and other social movements also provide multiple points of access into the system and numerous potential allies for the woman suffrage movements (Kriesi 1995; Tarrow 1989a, 1994). The U.S. and Swiss woman suffrage movements existed within very similar constellations of interest groups; both countries enjoyed an extensive system of voluntary associations that played an important role in politics. However, the U.S. suffrage movement benefitted from the existence of the abolitionist and temperance movements, while the Swiss movement lacked similar movement allies (see Chapter 5). Although important, I argue that this difference alone cannot explain why Switzerland delayed suffrage so long.

Switzerland and the United States differed along a third dimension of the political opportunity structure as well: the informal procedures of decision making and strategies of those in power. The United States is normally described as competitive and pluralist, while Switzerland's decision-making is based on consensus (Steiner 1974; Steiner and Dorff 1980). Kriesi (1995) argues that consensus building in Switzerland facilitates access to the system because the tradition tries to incorporate challengers. In Chapter 6, I argue that this generalization does not apply to the woman suffrage movement, which was excluded from the consensus system. Nevertheless, the negative consequences of the consensus system cannot completely account for the slowness of suffrage because it cannot explain why Swiss suffrage organizations did not take advantage of other opportunities. To understand the successes and failures of the U.S. and Swiss movements, we must examine their perceptions and strategic decisions.

Strategic Decisions, Perceptions, and Collective Beliefs and Values

Political opportunity structure theory inadequately explains the success and failure of the U.S. and Swiss woman suffrage movements largely because it makes a number of simplifying assumptions that are untenable in these cases. While most researchers in this tradition (Klandermans 1984; Kriesi 1988; McAdam 1982; Tilly 1978; and Tarrow 1989b) recognize that the true cognitive inputs are actors' *perceptions* of the "objective conditions," these authors do not fully explore the implications of this fact.[18] Indeed, they have focused on the political environment and outcomes while brushing over movements' strategic and tactical choices. In so doing, they tend to make the simplifying assumption that social movements know the current state of the political opportunity structure and base their choice of tactics on that knowledge. They also assume that the goals of the group are straightforward and are not themselves influenced by the political context.

While movements and activists within the movement make strategic decisions based on their perceptions about the resources available to them and the structure of political opportunities, their perceptions will not always mirror reality. The lenses through which suffrage movements viewed their society and political system colored their perceptions and even filtered out certain pieces of information. As a result, the Swiss suffrage movement did not perceive all the strategic options open to it, although it made rational decisions based on its perceptions. If social movements rely so heavily on perceptions to make strategic decisions, we need to understand how they acquire their perceptions. To do so, we must move beyond the political opportunity structure and examine theories about how collective values and beliefs play a role in the processing of information and how perceptions, especially those affecting action, are developed.

Recently, scholars have begun to focus on the effect of collective beliefs and values on the perceptions of social movements in discussions of "frames" (Snow, Rochford, Worden, and Benford 1986; Snow and Benford 1988, 1992; Tarrow 1994), "discourses" (Jenson 1987; Moaddel 1992; Gamson 1992), or "cultures" (Swidler 1986; Tarrow 1994).[19] In using the term "collective beliefs and values," I rely heavily on Snow, Rochford, Worden and Benford, who define values as "modes of conduct or states of existence" that are attributed with a positive or negative value and beliefs as "presumed relationships" between things and/or characteristics (1986: 469). Values and beliefs are collective to the extent that they are shared by a group of individuals. In my discussion of the Swiss and American woman suffrage movements, I focus on the elements of politics that are valued, the beliefs about the way that politics can and should be conducted, and the "boundaries of political discussion" (Jenson 1987: 65). These particular values and beliefs influenced the strategies of the two movements and their success.

The timing of women's enfranchisement in the United States and Switzerland was greatly affected by the role collective beliefs and values played in the strategic choices of the woman suffrage movements. The U.S. suffrage movement, for a variety of reasons, developed beliefs and values that reinforced the idea of challenging the state. The collective values and beliefs that governed Swiss tactics derived not from within the movement itself nor from interaction with other social movements or political actors. Rather, they were spread by advocates of the existing political system who assigned positive worth to existing state institutions and processes. In order to understand the tactical choices of the two movements, we need a theoretical framework for understanding collective beliefs and values. Three specific aspects of such a framework are important: (1) how collective beliefs and values affect a movement's strategic decisions; (2) which types of collective beliefs and values might be relevant to the two movements; and (3) how the political context helps to determine which collective beliefs and values the two movements adopted.

How Collective Beliefs and Values
Affect Strategic Decisions

Strategic decisions of social movements are affected by collective beliefs and values in two ways. First, beliefs and values determine which actions movements will evaluate as having utility and which will be considered counterproductive or useless. Under resource mobilization and political opportunity structure theories, the only collective value we need to know in order to understand the Swiss and American woman suffrage movements' choice of strategies and tactics is that their goal was the enfranchisement of women. However, if we are to understand how collective beliefs and values shape strategic choices, we must examine more than just movement goals. Movements may value a specific tactic for reasons other than its effectiveness in achieving their goal (Swidler 1986). For example, Tocqueville ([1845] 1969) noted that American culture treasured the use of voluntarist organizations to pursue specific aims, and therefore Americans faced with political goals were likely to create such associations.

Often the effect of collective values on strategic choices may be even more indirect than the Tocqueville example implies. The American anti–woman suffrage movement's campaigns, for example, languished during World War I because women opposed to suffrage dropped all political activity in favor of war relief efforts (Marshall 1985). The decision to switch activities, Marshall argues, resulted from anti-suffrage activists' idealized view of women as the moral, peaceful, and caring sex. Although the temporary switch in emphasis may eventually have contributed to anti-suffrage activists losing the fight against women's voting rights, they switched goals because they valued this role for women very highly. Similarly, I maintain that the Swiss woman suffrage movement was greatly affected by its idealization of the federal structure of Switzerland. Swiss suffrage activists internalized federalism as a norm, making them unwilling to aid movements outside their own canton. Understanding the course of action taken by a movement thus requires exploring a broader range of collective beliefs and values beyond mere goals.

Second, collective beliefs and values serve as a lens filtering information about the political universe and especially about potential political strategies (Snow et al. 1986). Self-selection of information, especially to correspond with an individual's political preferences, has been documented in studies of U.S. elections (Lazarsfeld, Berelson, and Gaudet 1968; Huckfeldt and Sprague 1987). The most relevant beliefs and values in the case of the two suffrage movements concern how the political system operates. In the United States, Alice Paul's Woman's Party (WP), influenced by British suffragettes, believed that ruling political parties were responsible for policies. Following this belief, WP activists decided that electoral campaigns against Democratic politicians would hasten the passage of a federal woman suffrage amendment. In making this decision, they did not give credence to information suggesting that individual politicians and local parties often made decisions about women's voting rights legislation independent of their national party's policy. On the other hand, Swiss activists believed that the general public, and not political elites, were ultimately responsible for policies. Swiss suffrage activists therefore did not perceive that electing or lobbying sympathetic politicians was a necessary strategy, although these strategies were used successfully by other political actors (see Chapter 6). In both cases, movements' values and beliefs selected or biased their perceptions about potential strategies.

Information may also be biased or edited before it even reaches a social movement. Other political actors or the mass media will select specific aspects to communicate and will reinterpret these in light of their own beliefs and values (Klandermans 1992). Even the most "unbiased" media sources must select from a myriad of possible events the limited number of stories they will feature on a particular day, thereby filtering out other information and determining how events will be portrayed (Tarrow 1994: 127–28). Thus, whether information is perceived directly or transmitted by others, it is incomplete and biased.[20]

The Pluralism of Collective Beliefs and Values

At any specific time and place, we can expect to find multiple, and sometimes even contradictory, sets of beliefs and values coexisting (Klandermans 1992). Indeed, a single political actor may possess and be influenced by beliefs and values acquired from different sources simultaneously, all of which may act on their perceptions. Since social movement decisions exist in a world of multiple values and beliefs, we must have some method of determining which sets of values will be most significant in social movement decisions. This, in turn, requires understanding how movements adopt collective values and beliefs and how actors resolve conflicting values and beliefs.

To simplify, I classify collective beliefs and values into three categories according to the level at which they are shared: (1) *group* values and beliefs are developed and shared by a group of similar individuals, such as actors within a social movement; (2) *coalition* values and beliefs are common to two or more interacting groups; and (3) *status quo* beliefs and values reflect the current "configuration of power" (Kriesi 1995: 5), are promoted by the state institutions and polity members, and are widely

TABLE 2.1

Levels of Beliefs and Values and Their Instruments of Transmission

Level	Type of Collective Beliefs and Values	Key Sources of Transmission
Macro-Level (Social Structure)	Status quo	Most mass media Social interaction
Meso-Level (Interaction of Groups)	Coalition	Social interaction between groups Media shared by groups
Micro-Level (Individual Experience)	Group	Social interaction among group members Group-specific media

distributed in the society.[21] As illustrated in Table 2.1, these three levels mirror similar divisions between macro-, meso-, and micro-levels used by other social movement theorists (Gerhards and Rucht 1992; Neidhardt and Rucht 1992).[22]

The most widespread collective beliefs and values are those inculcated at the macro-level. These status quo values and beliefs include those that have developed out of the historical context as well as those explicitly supported by the government and polity members. One value common to most status quo philosophies is the positive worth placed on the use of existing channels when participating in politics and the condemnation given to attempts to challenge status quo institutions (see Piven and Cloward 1979 and Tarrow 1992 on "system-supporting political culture").

Groups of like-minded individuals, joined together through networks of interaction and sharing common experiences or characteristics, may also develop their own set of values and beliefs. Through these networks of interaction, common values and beliefs are created and reinforced (Klandermans 1992). For example, the "tight-knit politically based community" of Freedom Summer participants acquired a set of beliefs and values that they continued to hold even decades after the event ended (McAdam 1988: 235). Close ties or a strong community within the movement thus become an important facilitator of the dissemination of group beliefs and values within a social movement.

Between the levels of the status quo and the group lies another—a shared outlook developed through the ties a movement has to other groups. While groups may develop similar philosophies independently of one another, the label "coalition" refers only to a set of values and beliefs that evolves through the interaction of more than one group.[23] For example, while each new social movement in western Europe during the 1970s and 1980s had its own distinct perspective, it also shared a broader set of values and beliefs with the other new social movements.[24] Group interaction is key to defining coalition values and beliefs. The sharing of these beliefs and attitudes is fostered by the development of joint interests, the necessity of successful political cooperation, or routine communication among political actors.

The distinction among different levels of collective beliefs and values helps explain the strategic decisions of the American and Swiss woman suffrage movements. While their tactical choices were affected by available resources and the political opportunity structures in both countries, collective beliefs and values played an even larger role in those decisions. Suffrage activists in the United States had close ties to each other and to a number of other political organizations. These links produced group and coalition philosophies that challenged status quo dogma. Consequently, the American suffrage movement was able to perceive a wide range of political opportunities and chose successful tactics. On the other hand, the Swiss suffrage movement never developed strong group values and beliefs, nor were they networked with other political actors who might have encouraged coalition perspectives that differed from those of the status quo. Instead, the tactical decisions of Swiss suffrage activists were strongly influenced by status quo beliefs and values. As a result, the Swiss suffrage movement rarely chose tactics that challenged the government, although these were used successfully by other political actors and, occasionally, by local suffrage movements.

Since different levels of collective values and beliefs can conflict, we need to understand how one set might replace or take precedence over another. Of particular interest is how the status quo philosophy might be supplanted by that of a group or coalition. Since status quo values tend to support existing institutions, the development of alternative values and beliefs is imperative to social movements challenging the system. To understand how group and coalition perspectives can displace those of the status quo, we must examine how different types of beliefs and values are transmitted and how that affects their ability to contradict existing dogma.

The Transmission of Collective Beliefs and Values

Collective values and beliefs are, in fact, conveyed in much the same way as information, although it takes longer for a group to internalize a new value than to receive a new piece of information. Thus, values and beliefs partially determine what is transmitted through the media or through personal interaction, but they are also part of the message that accompanies information. Whether they are embraced depends on both the messenger, that is the method of transmission, and the degree to which the new beliefs and values correspond with existing philosophies (McAdam and Rucht 1993). I distinguish between two broad categories of transmission, which are defined by the relationship of the actor to the source of the information: personal interaction and mass media.[25] Personal interaction is defined as one actor dealing with another, even when one represents a larger institution such as the military, police, or a religion. Mass media involve communication through indirect observation; examples include party newspapers, religious pamphlets, and Army recruitment advertisements.

Social interaction and impersonal transmission do not play equal roles in the formation of values and beliefs. Although technological advances have greatly increased the amount of information available through the mass media, personal interaction is still more important in the creation of perceptions and even in the communication of information (Grofman and Norrander 1990). This is particularly true where personal interaction bridges groups or results from strong ties, which are emotionally intense, mutual, and the result of frequent contact (Granovetter 1973: 1361). Even where mass media may be the initial source of an idea or belief, it is frequently reinterpreted and reinforced by social interaction (Klandermans 1992; Popkin 1993). Indeed, the survival of many religious, ethnic, and opposition groups in communist-bloc countries, despite state attempts to "resocialize" these populations through absolute control of mass media, indicates the power of strong interpersonal ties. Scholars of social movements have also emphasized the role of social interaction and personal ties in the development of movement values and beliefs (Klandermans 1992; Gamson 1992; Friedman and McAdam 1992; Oberschall 1973; McAdam 1982).

While each level of values and beliefs may be transmitted by both social interaction and mass media, social interaction generally becomes more important as one moves from the macro- to the micro-level (see Table 2.1). The bonds that hold all individuals and all groups together in society are weaker than those that bind smaller, more cohesive groups. Even though group and coalition values and beliefs will not always be produced by strong ties, stronger ties will tend to become more prevalent as one moves toward smaller groups. On the other hand, groups and coalitions, especially those connected to social movements, will generally lack extended access to the media. The larger mass media—major television networks, radio stations, and the principal newspapers—are usually unavailable to challengers of existing institutions. Even when they provide information about social movements, the message is often distorted (Tarrow 1994: 128). While movements can create alternative media sources, these rarely rival mass media in size and scope. Thus, movements and movement coalitions rely less frequently on media for the transmission of their values and beliefs than do elements of the status quo.

The role of social interaction in the development of group and coalition values or beliefs becomes particularly important in the case of the Swiss woman suffrage movement. While the U.S. woman suffrage movement developed strong personal ties among activists, the Swiss movement did not. Divisions within the Swiss suffrage movement impeded the spread of group values and beliefs. Linguistic, political, and religious differences between activists as well as organizational characteristics that hindered the flow of information and ideas reduced the ability of the Swiss suffrage movement to build a group identity, develop mutual interests, and cement emotional bonds. These differences also reduced the frequency of contacts between activists, which would have encouraged the development of group values or beliefs. Most Swiss activists were members of political parties and religious organizations and their ties to those groups affected their values and beliefs more than their connections within the suffrage movement itself. As a result, the values and beliefs that developed out of the suffrage movement were not as influential as those of the status quo or activists' other social networks.

How do group or coalition values and beliefs become more significant than those of the status quo or other existing sets of beliefs and values? New values or beliefs may either supplement or contradict established values and beliefs.[26] A set of beliefs and values may supplement another where the other is silent on particular aspects or contains several contradictory values or beliefs. Status quo philosophies are often open to this sort of augmentation because they are so broad that they may not provide clear interpretations of specific points or may include potentially contradictory elements (Snow and Benford 1992; Snow et al. 1986). Group or coalition values and beliefs may provide convictions where the status quo is silent. Here, because group and coalition beliefs and values are not supplanting those of the status quo, the likelihood of their adoption is less dependent on the strength of interpersonal bonds. The development of additional values or beliefs, as long as they speak to issues that other sets of beliefs and values do not address, is a relatively easy process (Snow et al. 1986).

Contradicting existing dogma is much more difficult. Only the powerful influence of social interaction through strong ties may negate deeply ingrained values and beliefs.[27] The individuals or movements that develop lasting contradictory values and beliefs must have a strong group identity and be integrated into networks of interaction through strong social ties (McAdam 1982; Snow et al. 1986). The American woman suffrage movement was such a movement. Suffrage activists not only created a close-knit community within the movement itself but they had strong social ties to other movements—abolitionist, temperance, populist, and progressive—that also challenged the status quo. Extensive social interaction with these movements created coalition values and beliefs that encouraged the use of specific tactics. In addition, the development of a strong suffrage identity, encouraged by the activities of the national organizations and by the social cohesiveness of the women themselves, helped to create and maintain the group's own philosophy.

How the Political Opportunity Structure Changes
Collective Values and Beliefs

The political opportunity structure and collective values and beliefs are not independent determinants of social movement success. Political opportunity structures affect not only the resources and opportunities of a movement but also the development of collective beliefs and values. While these two effects of political opportunities usually work together, as was the case in the U.S. woman suffrage movement, they can, as in Switzerland, also counteract each other.

Because social interaction is so important, widespread changes in social interactions between political actors create changes in coalition values and beliefs. If one group begins to collaborate with another, the new interaction may fundamentally alter its members perceptions and values. The degree of change will depend on three things: the number and strength of ties between the two groups, the degree to which the groups already share other values and beliefs, and the degree to which strong bonds exist within each group.[28] When there are few shared values and the ties between the two groups are weak, interaction is not likely to result in much exchange or modification of values or beliefs. Moreover, even where groups already share strong ties and similar ideologies, newly introduced values or beliefs are not likely to diffuse through a group where the ties binding individuals to the group are weak.

The strength of social interaction and the correspondence of different philosophies are, in turn, heavily influenced by the alliances and conflicts between movement activists and other political actors. Freeman (1987) provides the example of the alliance between the feminist movement and the Democratic party in the United States. Because the Republicans forced Republican feminists out of the party (despite a long tradition of bipartisanship within the women's movement), a closer alliance between the feminist movement and the Democratic party developed. With this new alliance the feminist movement accepted certain norms such as the willingness "to curb one's commitment to one's own agenda" (Freeman 1987: 241). Thus, by constraining certain networks and expanding others, the political opportunity structure may alter the values, beliefs, and tactics of a social movement and its activists.

Political opportunity structures also influence status quo beliefs or values. Well-established formal or informal political structures often become a norm by which politics is expected to work, as in the case of Swiss federalism (Elazar 1987; Steinberg 1976). Therefore, political opportunity structures are more than mere "reality" about which political actors must be informed; they also generate a set of values that supports the maintenance of these structures. Status quo dogma is, in large part, the aggregate of current and past political opportunity structures, social configurations, and economic systems.[29]

The collective values and beliefs created by aspects of the political opportunity structure affected the success and failure of the Swiss and American woman suffrage movements. Coalition values and beliefs developed from alliances within the political system in the United States aided American suffrage activists in their struggle for the vote. On the other hand, Swiss federalism and political divisions among elites played a role in inhibiting the evolution of close ties within the Swiss suffrage movement, limiting the development and spread of useful tactics.

My emphasis on the strategic choices made by movements and their specific actions and tactics is an unusual one. While other theorists (for example, Kitschelt 1986) have examined the types of tactics used by social movements, they have usually not focused explicitly on why and how the decision to utilize a certain tactic was made. Thus, some discussion of the sources of evidence is in order.

Using Historical Evidence in the Evaluation of Beliefs, Values, Tactics, and Strategies

Analyzing complex political decisions is difficult, but especially so when dealing with historical movements. In arguing that success or failure is determined largely by perceptions, I could not rely solely on the activities of the suffrage movements; tactics that activists considered but did not pursue are equally important. Therefore, I analyzed two types of materials that reflect the perceptions of suffrage activists. First, retrospective, autobiographical accounts provide the activists' own versions of the movement's history. In Switzerland, published accounts were rare. However, the timing of suffrage afforded the possibility of speaking with Swiss suffrage activists. Thus, between 1987 and 1990, I interviewed 62 activists representing all 25 cantons.[30] These interviews are described in greater detail in Appendix A. The autobiographical accounts—both the written records of U.S. suffrage activists and the discussions I had with Swiss activists—include many interpretations of the resource and opportunity problems the movement faced.

Second, I relied heavily on the written debates and discussions that were recorded in the course of the two movements. By emphasizing certain problems and ignoring others, these records indicate which political opportunities suffrage activists perceived and which they missed. Using this evidence, I identified those aspects of the political opportunity structure the suffrage activists themselves stressed (or in the Swiss case, did not recognize) and the extent of their knowledge about the political process.

By focusing on two federal countries where local suffrage movements could act independently, I also have been able to compare the movements within each country. While there are numerous factors that might plausibly account for the differences in timing of woman suffrage on the national level, many of those explanations can be rejected once we compare states within the United States or cantons in Switzerland. In addition, comparisons of various cantonal suffrage movements indicate that a few managed to utilize successful strategies that were ignored by activists living in other Swiss cantons.

These methods and the sum total of the evidence they produce indicate that perceptions were a critical factor in each movement's choice of tactics and later success. The exploitation of initiative rights in Switzerland provides a good example. A few local suffrage movements used initiative petitions to bring suffrage amendments before voters. Where initiative rights were used, women were enfranchised earlier. Nonetheless, documents from board meetings of the national suffrage association show that this tactic was rarely discussed. Retrospective interviews with suffrage activists also reveal few references to the initiative and even, in some cases, inaccurate information about women's right to utilize this tactic. All of this suggests perceptions and information played an important role for Swiss suffrage activists. The most tentative conclusions in the analyses that follow are, perhaps, those concerning the spread of status quo or coalition beliefs and values. These are difficult to trace since the transfer of perceptions from other groups and political institutions must be inferred. Unlike donations of material resources, the adoption of a new belief is not recorded in balance sheets or heralded in the press, but appears only in its affects on the decisions of and debates within the movement. Nonetheless, I think the weight of evidence is persuasive: perceptions, values, and beliefs played an important role in both movements and represent a significant element in social movement success.

Social Movement Perspectives of the U.S. and
Swiss Woman Suffrage Movements

In the chapters that follow, I examine the role of resources, political opportunities, and collective values and beliefs in explaining the success and
failure of the Swiss and American woman suffrage movements. In Chapters 3 and 4, I explore the initial mobilization of women and resources
into the two suffrage movements and the effect of those resources on
women's enfranchisement. Chapter 3 focuses on the founding and
growth of suffrage organizations in Switzerland and the United States. It
suggests that the U.S. woman suffrage movement greatly increased membership through their mobilizing tactics. While Swiss women were initially well mobilized in pursuit of the right to vote, the societal emphasis
on federalism inhibited organizational activities to mobilize women in
Switzerland, resulting in a decline in membership. Chapter 4 focuses on
the effect of resources on the success of suffrage movements. I discuss
differences in the monetary resources of the two movements and analyze
the effect of membership on success. Neither money nor membership
completely explains why the American movement succeeded more
quickly than the Swiss movement.

From there I turn to the role of political opportunities in the battle for
woman suffrage. I begin by exploring how alliances affected the achievement of women's voting rights. Chapter 5 chronicles the development of
the pro- and anti-suffrage coalitions in Switzerland and the United States.
The pro- and anti-suffrage alliances were interdependent; coalitions
evolved as a reaction to the activities of opponents. Perceptions, and ultimately success, were influenced by this web of movement and counter-
movement coalitions. In the United States, political parties and interest
groups coalesced around the pro- and anti-position, often reacting to the
perceived menace to their interests presented by their opponents. In Switzerland, the structure of Swiss politics and the character of the movement itself reduced potential opponents' perceptions of threat resulting
in blurred lines of combat between pro- and anti-suffrage forces. Nonetheless, coalitional support, however weak, still affected women's
enfranchisement.

In Chapter 6, I examine the opportunities the Swiss and U.S. movement had to affect legislation in both countries. Lobbying tactics are associated with the passage of women's voting rights legislation in both countries, although American activists were much more likely to use these
techniques. To some extent, the lack of competition between political
elites constrained the Swiss woman suffrage movement's tactics in comparison to their U.S. counterparts. However, the structure of political op-

portunities cannot fully account for the differences between the Swiss and the U.S. suffrage movement. Swiss suffrage activists absorbed many of the values of status quo politics, thereby failing to perceive when political opportunities were in their favor. Without information and values emphasizing the usefulness of lobbying, which is hidden in the consensus decision-making process, Swiss suffrage movements missed political opportunities.

In Chapter 7, I explore the tactics of the two movements outside normal legislative channels. In contrast to their Swiss counterparts, the U.S. suffrage movements chose tactics designed to confront the public more often; within both countries, however, local movements differed significantly. The choice of tactics was not merely constrained by the structure of political opportunities but was also determined by available information and perceptions of the political process. The success of suffrage movements in both countries was, in turn, related to the use of more confrontational tactics. Together Chapters 6 and 7 examine the reciprocal relationship between the structure of political opportunities and perceptions of movement actors as well as how these factors affected the enfranchisement of Swiss and American women.

I elaborate on the different sources of perceptions, information, and values for the two suffrage movements in Chapter 8. In Switzerland, interactions with other political groups—women's charitable and moral reform associations, socialist groups and Catholic organizations—did not provide information about lobbying, initiative, or confrontational tactics. Instead, the social networks of Swiss suffrage activists reinforced status quo values and encouraged divisions in the suffrage movement. On the other hand, American suffrage activists had strong ties to other movements, which provided both information and values that encouraged those tactics and strategies that helped suffrage activists take advantage of the existing political opportunities.

Finally, in Chapter 9, I reexamine the usefulness of previous models of social movements, concluding that political and sociocultural contexts must be reinstilled in the study of social movements. Context is not merely a set of rules, conditions, or alliances that restrict or expand what movements can achieve. It also includes beliefs and values, developed within and through the political opportunity structure, that influence the perceptions of movement actors and, hence, their tactics, strategies, and ultimate success.

3

BUILDING SUFFRAGE ORGANIZATIONS

IN 1868, the Zürich cantonal government, which was revising its constitution, received a petition, signed by "numerous women out of the people," asking that women's voting rights be included (Mesmer 1988: 84–85, translated by author; see also, Woodtli 1983). Without the power of mobilized supporters and the legitimacy of a formal organization, these women received no serious consideration. This was typical of women's petitions made before the creation of women's rights associations. It suggests that organization is important both as a resource for marshaling movement support and for the efficient use of all resources. Thus, while Swiss and American suffrage supporters' ultimate goal was the adoption of woman suffrage, they also needed to mobilize and organize movement support. This chapter considers several aspects of building suffrage organizations: size, mobilization, and tactics.

Comparing the Size of Swiss and American Suffrage Organizations

Can the timing of women's voting rights in Switzerland and the United States be explained by the creation and expansion of Swiss and American suffrage associations? Certainly resource mobilization theorists would argue that organization and supporters are a significant resource for social movements and therefore important precursors to success. Given the relative slowness with which Swiss women were enfranchised, resource mobilization theory would lead us to expect that Swiss suffrage movements had fewer members than their U.S. counterparts. Surprisingly, this is not the case.

While it is impossible to find membership data on all of the suffrage organizations in Switzerland and the United States in all years, I located membership data for the largest suffrage organizations in both countries—in the United States for the National American Woman Suffrage Association (NAWSA) and in Switzerland for the Schweizerischer Verband für Frauenstimmrecht (SVF).[1] At first glance, the Swiss suffrage association seems smaller than its American counterpart. In absolute numbers, the SVF was always outstripped by the NAWSA (see Table 3.1). However, comparing absolute membership in the two countries is highly

TABLE 3.1
Absolute and Per Capita Membership in Swiss and
American Woman Suffrage Organizations[a]

	United States			Switzerland	
Year	Membership	Per 1,000 pop.	Year	Membership	Per 1,000 pop.
1893	7,241	0.109	1934	5,546	1.340
1894	8,032	0.119	1937	4,664	1.112
1895	7,826	0.114	1951	4,133	0.863
1896	8,885	0.127	1952	4,690	0.965
1897	9,860	0.138	1954	5,564	1.113
1898	9,936	0.137	1955	5,718	1.127
1899	8,548	0.115	1958	5,657	1.070
1900	8,944	0.119	1959	6,056	1.130
1901	9,833	0.128	1964	6,454	1.153
1902	9,939	0.126	1965	6,305	1.110
1903	12,045	0.150	1966	6,130	1.033
1904	12,453	0.152	1969	6,973	1.127
1905	15,461	0.185	1975	5,538	0.912
1906	15,865	0.186	1976	5,203	0.857
1907	16,305	0.188			
1908	16,668	0.189			
1909	16,705	0.186			
1910	16,637	0.182			
1911	19,013	0.204			
1912	32,052	0.340			
1913	45,658	0.477			
1914	65,946	0.679			
1915	53,320	0.542			
1916	59,765	0.599			
1917	59,072	0.584			
1919	65,322	0.629			
1920	85,135	0.809			

[a] In the United States, the table indicates membership in the National American Woman Suffrage Association; in Switzerland, membership is in Schweizerischer Verband für das Frauenstimmrecht. In noncensus years, the population is determined by a linear interpolation between census years.

misleading. After all, in 1920 the population of the United States was over 105 million. In comparison, the Swiss population barely exceeded 6.5 million in 1980. Given the tremendous differences in population, mobilization into suffrage organizations is more appropriately measured by membership per capita.

Taking population into account, the SVF was much larger than the American suffrage organization. Even when the NAWSA made great gains in membership after 1910, it never equaled the per capita size of the

SVF. Indeed, it was only in the last years of the American suffrage movement that NAWSA per capita membership even approached levels achieved by the Swiss suffrage organization. When participation in the NAWSA peaked in 1920, one year after the final suffrage campaign that mobilized many women into the suffrage organizations, the number of dues payers per capita was only two-thirds of the top Swiss membership rate in 1934. Thus, variation in membership cannot account for the differences in the timing of women's enfranchisement on the national level. A comparison of the memberships of the two national suffrage organizations suggests that it was the American not the Swiss suffrage movement that lacked members.

However, the data in Table 3.1 also indicate that the two organizations had very different life cycles. The NAWSA experienced almost continuous growth—both in absolute and per capita membership—from 1893 until it disbanded in 1920. In fact, during the last ten years of the suffrage campaign, the suffrage association expanded at a phenomenal rate. Between 1911 and 1913, the NAWSA more than doubled in both absolute and per capita size. It came close to doubling again between 1913 and 1920. These increases greatly exceeded the growth of the U.S. population during this time.

In comparison, membership in the Swiss suffrage organization was extremely stable. In absolute size, the membership of the SVF in 1934 was almost exactly the same (5,546 members) as in 1975 (5,538 members). While the membership declined in the late 1930s and early 1950s and increased in the 1960s, it remained within 25 percent of its original level for more than six decades. Because the Swiss population also increased over time (although more slowly than in the United States), the growth in suffrage membership in the 1960s did not enlarge the per capita membership of the SVF. In fact, the highest per capita membership is found in 1934, the earliest year for which we have membership figures. After that year, the relative size of the suffrage organization remains relatively stable or declines slightly.

Thus, the trajectories of membership in the Swiss and American suffrage movements differ substantially. The National American Woman Suffrage Association started out small, grew steadily from 1893 to 1909, and then expanded rapidly until ratification of the Nineteenth Amendment. The Schweizerischer Verband für Frauenstimmrecht began as a much larger organization but never enlarged its membership during its six decades of existence. Even at the peak of absolute membership in 1969, the SVF counted only 1,400 more members than in 1934.

If the NAWSA was always smaller than the Swiss suffrage association, it appears to have had a healthier organizational life. While the Swiss organization peaked early and then stagnated for decades, the NAWSA continued to grow. To understand why the Swiss and American suffrage organizations had such fundamentally different patterns of membership growth, it is necessary to examine their recruitment activities.

Mobilization Tactics of the National American Woman Suffrage Association

Leading women's rights activists in the United States developed a tradition of mobilizing supporters and organizing outside of their own states as early as the 1850s. Before 1870, women's rights activists created informal networks of suffrage supporters through yearly meetings at women's rights conventions, but they did not erect enduring formal suffrage organizations (Harper 1969).[2] Instead, they focused on raising public consciousness by using conventions to attract a wider audience to women's rights lectures. Convention calls published in newspapers attracted interested women who in turn joined the organizers in an ever-expanding network of activists. For example, the 1848 Seneca Falls convention attracted a number of women who then organized a larger convention in Rochester two weeks later (Stanton et al. 1881a). The publicity of the first conventions inspired women in other areas, such as the Midwestern states of Ohio and Indiana, to issue calls for local conventions as well (Stanton et al. 1881a). Between conventions, suffrage activists kept in contact through correspondence and informal networking.

Public speaking tours allowed recruitment work to continue between conventions. While the first speeches occurred at conventions, women's rights activists soon discovered that other audiences would pay to hear women's rights lectures. Previously, women's associations had relied on volunteers who often placed family or other activities before organization work. Now, suffrage activists had another method of organizing: the full-time paid activist. Like the earlier abolitionists, suffrage activists financed their full-time organizing and campaigning in two ways. Initially, the money paid to the full-time activists was raised on the road, by selling literature and charging speaking fees. Thus, Anthony wrote from Kansas in 1867 that between speaking fees and the sale of suffrage literature, she was able to finance her entire trip (Stanton et al. 1881b: 242). After national organizations developed in the 1870s, a portion of their budgets was used to pay for organizational work in the states.

A critical step for U.S. woman suffrage organizations was recognizing that organizational activities need not be confined to one's own town or state. Women's voluntary associations had traditionally been local groups. However, the early experiences of suffrage activists in other movements also led to the belief that national "interference" in the affairs of other states was an appropriate method of organizing. Many woman suffrage activists assumed that sending organizers or speakers into unorganized states would further the cause. While some suffrage activists (particularly in western and southern states) expressed resentment toward the intrusion of paid organizers, national suffrage leaders were never discouraged from organizing in these states.

When the new generation of suffrage activists replaced the movement's founders, the organizing and recruiting strategies of the suffrage movement also changed. Early organizing activities revolved around the speaking tour or agitation for legislation. An activist would enter a state and speak in several places, urging people to sign petitions for women's rights legislation and encouraging the women to form local associations. While organization building was important, so was raising the issue before the general public or pushing a specific legislative agenda. Organizing was viewed as only one part of mobilization and was not seen as having greater worth than other activities. As a result, the emphasis on organization varied from activist to activist; there was no expectation that the activist's hightest priority was to develop a sustainable organization (cf. Stapler 1917 and Stanton et al. 1881a).

The new generation of suffrage activists, notably Carrie Chapman Catt, felt one of the problems with the earlier generation was that "the chief work of suffragists for the past forty years has been education and agitation, and not organization" (cited in Fowler 1986: 106). Under Catt's leadership, the NAWSA focused mobilization plans explicitly on the development and maintenance of suffrage associations. Although public speeches by well-known activists still provided most of the opportunities to create local suffrage clubs, organizing became the focus of activity and raising public consciousness declined in relative importance (Kraditor 1981: 8). Indeed, when the NAWSA was not financing state referendum campaigns, it underwrote organizing campaigns. State suffrage associations even raised money expressly for this purpose; their donations paid the salaries of full-time organizers who were then sent into states lacking suffrage groups (Park 1940). In some years, more than 50 percent of the NAWSA's budget was spent on organizing and most of this money paid the expenses and salaries of organizers (NAWSA 1896).

While earlier activists had developed speaking into a full-time profession, the second generation developed a cadre of professional organizers. Within the NAWSA, the Organization Committee was created to conceive of and execute strategies for organizing suffrage auxiliaries. Its first head, Carrie Chapman Catt, instituted Suffrage Schools, which taught organizational techniques "often down to the last practical detail" (Fowler 1986: 111). These trained professionals were then dispatched to states with little or no suffrage organization. Second-generation suffrage activists also believed that the form an organization took affected suffrage movement success (Fowler 1986; Taylor 1987). In order to influence both state and national legislatures, the national organization attempted to organize local auxiliaries around electoral districts.

Despite these subtle differences between generations, mobilizing supporters and organizing was of paramount importance starting in the 1870s. The emphasis on organization increased after 1890 as more resources were devoted to this goal and specific forms were emphasized. In spite of occasional resistance from local women, national suffrage activists established local suffrage groups in many states. Equally important, state suffrage sections also adopted the same strategy, targeting unorganized localities within their own state. Paid speakers and, later, full-time professional organizers were able to organize in areas that would have been unreachable by part-time volunteer activists.

Mobilization Tactics of the Swiss Woman Suffrage Association

Compared to American activists, Swiss women made few attempts to organize suffrage clubs on the national or cantonal level. Instead, their primary goal was consciousness raising. Although they sponsored lectures on woman suffrage, they emphasized the development of support for suffrage ideas among the public. In the interviews I conducted, some suffrage activists implied that raising consciousness among the public was an organizational tactic. However, it was virtually the only strategy for most suffrage organizations. Furthermore, compared to the American movement, the Swiss suffrage movement was handicapped in its organizational and consciousness-raising strategies by its reliance on part-time volunteers. As a result, organizing attempts were sporadic and there were few advances or changes in recruitment strategies over the 70-year period of the suffrage movement.

Unlike their American counterparts, the first Swiss suffrage activists did not travel widely spreading the suffrage message. Although the first local suffrage group (Zürich's Union für Frauenbestrebungen) began in 1893, there is no record of Zürich activists attempting to organize suffrage associations in other cantons before 1903. Suffrage activists who gave lecture tours were such a rarity that the president of the Zürich organization between 1903 and 1911, Klara Honegger, was later praised as a great propagandist in part because of her willingness to speak in the rural parts of Zürich (*Die Staatsbürgerin*, November 1968: 7; Mesmer 1988). Even the development of a national suffrage organization was delayed until seven local suffrage organizations appeared independently of one another, indicating that the focus of these first groups did not extend much beyond their own area (Mesmer 1988).

Once established, the national SVF had little in the way of an organizational strategy. SVF minutes and records contain only one mention of building suffrage organizations: A 1948 Aktionsprogramm provided "suggestions for active Propaganda Methods." [3] Even then, this plan emphasized schooling women in the operations of government, disseminating information during referenda (with no mention of woman suffrage referenda), and encouraging women to utilize the political rights they already had. The suggestion that organizations actively recruit new members was hidden in a section entitled "Propaganda in Wider Circles" (SVF 1948; translated by author). These recommendations totaling three short sentences suggested that existing clubs use meetings and small-group discussions at private houses to recruit new members, and that those expressing an interest in joining should be visited by suffrage activists at home. Even these suggestions reflect an assumption that organizational work entails building the membership of *existing* local organizations and not creating new clubs in unorganized areas.

Second-generation suffrage activists, like their predecessors, tried to spread suffrage ideas by lecturing in unorganized areas. When I asked about helping suffrage organizations in other cantons, several suffrage activists mentioned their lecturing activities. Although this tactic was useful for organizing in the United States, three factors reduced its effectiveness in the Swiss case.

First, when suffrage activists lectured, they often refused to agitate for the creation of local suffrage groups. While all of the leaders interviewed said that lectures served as places of recruitment, the primary purpose was education. Many who lectured argued that membership should not be stressed since it might reduce their ability to spread suffrage ideas. One activist recalled: "Not all the women who participated in these lectures and visits were members. . . . We made sure to invite all women . . . but we did not try very hard to make them become members because we wanted them to come and learn something and not feel if they came they would have to become members" (interview of May 16, 1988). Other activists argued that even mentioning women's voting rights repelled potential listeners. Therefore, to convert individuals (and particularly women) to the cause, it was better to avoid mentioning the enfranchisement of women at all. As a result, most lectures and courses given by suffrage activists were *not* on the issue of women's voting rights but on current policy debates or themes such as the structure of local government. Suffrage activists generally felt that lecturing on such topics in rural areas or nonorganized towns was the best way to raise suffrage consciousness without repulsing their audience with radical ideas.

Second, Swiss suffrage activists, many of whom were employed full-time in other professions, were always part-time volunteers. Although activists sacrificed much of their valuable free time to suffrage work, they were simply unable to lecture as often as American suffrage activists. Nor were they able to travel the distances necessary to reach remote, unorganized areas like the eastern mountain regions. Although the distances were much shorter than in the United States, a trip of several hours made an evening lecture after a full day of work very difficult. Also, while the paid full-time activists in the American movement were constantly developing lecturing and organizing skills (in the suffrage and other movements), the sporadic and part-time nature of their lecturing did not provide Swiss suffrage activists with such opportunities.

Third, suffrage leaders believed that women within each canton were responsible for building their own associations. One woman in an unorganized canton requested organizational help from visiting lecturers but recalled, "They said that we had to work from the bottom up and try to motivate the women" (interview of May 6, 1988). In interviews, many suffrage activists defended this position by arguing that local citizens would react negatively to an "outsider" trying to influence cantonal affairs. To suffrage leaders, creating a new suffrage section was as dangerous as trying to influence the vote in a local suffrage referendum. Any action for woman suffrage by an "outsider" would be counterproductive.

Although feelings of local autonomy may have discouraged national leaders from developing local affiliates, one might expect local associations in one canton to help organize in those cantons where they had special connections to others because of geography, history, or culture (for example, Appenzell Innerrhoden and Appenzell Ausserrhoden). Yet, suffrage activists in these cantons rarely encouraged their unorganized neighbors to create organizations. Such interference was thought to be dangerous. "If our organization went into the canton and organized it, it would have caused a national scandal. It would be said that that was mixing in the internal affairs of the canton" (interview of May 19, 1988). On the rare occasions when local activists did encourage others to organize, they provided no organizing expertise or resources (as the American suffrage activists did). Instead, they assisted with moral and verbal encouragement. For example, when suffrage supporters in Basel-land decided to rebuild their own association, after spending seven years as part of the Basel-stadt section, its president urged them to do so but there is no indication that she supplied other forms of assistance.

Even within cantons, most existing local sections did not help create affiliates in other towns or villages. When activists from the larger, urban suffrage associations, such as Bern and Zürich, sent lecturers into unorganized areas, prospective new members were encouraged to join existing associations or, if the distance was too great, to pay dues to the national SVF. The local focus of SVF sections is also illustrated in the statements of local suffrage activists about cooperation among sections in the same canton. The canton Bern is typical of the larger cantons containing more than one local section; there was no sustained contact between the suffrage organizations in the cities of Bern, Biel, and Thun except for coordination during referendum and initiative campaigns.

In contrast to the United States, there was no level of organization between local sections and the national organization in the SVF. Local clubs and the national SVF did not expect sections in the same canton to create cantonal organizations. While local U.S. suffrage organizations in the same state were generally required to form or join state associations, the decision to organize on the cantonal level was left up to the local sections. Indeed, several cantons with multiple local sections (such as Bern and Solothurn) never developed canton-level organizations at all. In three cantons—Vaud in 1907, Zürich in 1920, and Ticino in 1953—local activists formed such cantonwide suffrage organizations on their own initiative. However, the Zürich cantonal organization was created not as an umbrella association of local auxiliaries but as an association of supporters in rural areas. It accepted single members into its ranks but made no attempt to organize these individuals into local clubs except for a short period in the 1930s (*Die Staatsbürgerin*, November 1968).

The Vaud and Ticino cantonal organizations appear closer to the American model of state-level suffrage associations. Although they placed far less emphasis on organization building than American suffrage groups, the Vaud and Ticino cantonal associations were exceptional organizers in the Swiss context. They were the only local affiliates to even mention organizational work and the creation of new sections in their reports to the national SVF (SVF 1959).

Thus, the national Swiss suffrage organization and local sections rarely had explicit strategies for actively recruiting members or for creating suffrage groups in unorganized areas. Rather, they focused on raising public consciousness through lectures and citizenship courses, assuming that the creation of associations and recruitment of new members would be a side effect of this activity. Could the Swiss suffrage organizations have increased their membership using the organizational techniques of the U.S. movement? Several examples suggest that these strategies could have succeeded in Switzerland.

First, in a few exceptional cases, activists in other women's rights associations used organizational techniques to create sizable, sustained local sections, from both outside and inside the canton. Thus, the national Staatsbürgerlicher Verband katholischer Schweizerinnen (STAKA) generated an auxiliary in one eastern mountain canton by asking individual members in that canton to form a section and aiding them in that process (interview of May 16, 1988). In addition, some leaders of cantonal political parties (particularly the Free Democratic party[4] and the Christian Democratic People's party) encouraged the formation of women's associations within their party in order to mobilize women in the fight for suffrage.

Second, other social movements and interest groups in Switzerland successfully used such organizing strategies. In the most exhaustive study of Swiss political movements to date, Kriesi notes that anti-nuclear power groups did not limit themselves to creating organizations within their own canton: "The movement is, to be sure, focused on the location where nuclear power plants are planned and the groups we studied are localized in a presumed region. The movement, however, reached out from these local foci and recruited on the national level from these areas" (1985: 387; translated by author). In fact, Frenkel (1978) argues that one reason why Swiss interest groups dominate national politics is that they are tightly organized on the national level. Thus, organizing techniques appear to have been successful both within women's associations and for at least some other Swiss organizations and social movements.

A Comparison of Local Organizational Tactics in the United States and Switzerland.

Additional evidence on the usefulness of recruitment and organizing strategies can be gleaned from an examination of the tactics of local suffrage associations in each nation. Indeed, without closely examining the relationship between recruitment strategies and organizational growth in the United States, we cannot even be sure that suffrage association strategies had an impact on the number of dues-paying members. Although suffrage movement organizing strategies coincided with membership expansion on the national level in the United States, it may have resulted from other causes. By concentrating on the organizing strategies of state-level organizations, we can examine how specific activities were related to changes in membership within particular states. In Switzerland, local suffrage associations can provide additional confirmation of the usefulness of recruiting and mobilizing strategies for the Swiss woman suffrage movement.

The United States

Unfortunately, an investigation of NAWSA local sections recruitment and organizing is not equally viable in all states.[5] It is impossible to examine the influence of organizing tactics on membership in eastern or western states because of the limited time period for which membership data are available (1893–1920). Organizational work in the East began in the 1840s and 1850s, and so most suffrage organizations were well established by the 1890s. On the other hand, many western states, after enfranchising women, were no longer the target of organizational or recruitment activities.

To examine the effect of strategy on membership, I utilize the histories of three different states: Texas, Florida, and Iowa. Each of these states have well-documented histories that include descriptions of their organizational activities. Of the states discussed here, Texas and Florida are typical of southern states, which first acquired suffrage organizations in the 1890s. However, until institutional efforts were made to create and sustain these organizations, they existed only where dynamic leaders committed to mobilization strategies held them together. Consequently, most southern states were unable to create sustained suffrage associations until after the turn of the twentieth century. Iowa, on the other hand, was one of the earliest states to have a strong suffrage movement; in this way, it resembles many eastern states. Nonetheless, it continued to be a target of suffrage activists' organizational strategies, documented in two very specific histories (Noun 1969 and Gallaher 1918). As a result, it is a convenient example of organizational work outside of the South.

TEXAS

In 1893, Rebecca Henry Hayes assembled a group of interested parties in Dallas to form a Texas Equal Rights Association, the first avowed suffrage organization of the state. During the next two years, Hayes traveled more than 9,000 miles speaking and organizing groups in other parts of Texas (Taylor 1987). Even though Hayes was able to organize smaller suffrage groups in seven Texas cities, Figure 3.1 shows that the membership in suffrage organizations between 1894 and 1896 remained small. Indeed, most of these groups had only a handful of members. When Hayes resigned from the suffrage association after losing a battle for its presidency in 1895, the Texas Equal Rights Association soon withered away. Taylor attributes the decline to the "loss of Mrs. Hayes's leadership" (1987: 23).

The Texas suffrage movement remained dormant until 1903, when three sisters created a suffrage association in Houston. They invited Carrie Chapman Catt to speak, and they also organized a suffrage club in nearby Galveston. A year later, they created a third suffrage club and held a state convention where Anna Howard Shaw was the guest speaker. However, when the original organizers moved from Texas in 1905, the three associations quickly dissolved (Taylor 1987).

It was only in 1908 that a permanent suffrage association was created

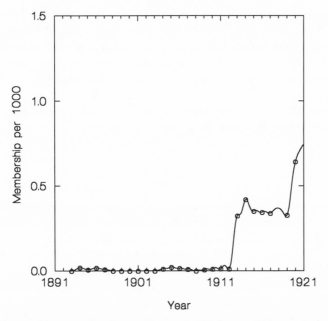

Figure 3.1 Membership in Texas NAWSA per 1,000 population
(1893–1920)

in Texas. The impetus came from the NAWSA; Anna Howard Shaw was sent to lecture after Texas had been without any suffrage activity for several years (Taylor 1987). A few months after her visit, a woman suffrage club formed in Austin and remained the only suffrage organization until 1912. After a second section was formed in San Antonio, Shaw visited again to stimulate further interest in suffrage clubs. Existing local auxiliaries also created a state association in 1912, which then made concerted efforts to organize other Texas communities (Taylor 1987). In 1914, Texas suffragists gathered $1,600 for organizational work, and in 1916 they devoted considerable effort to organizing within the state (Taylor 1987: 28–30). As Figure 3.1 shows, the national and local suffrage groups' combined focus on organization after 1912 resulted in a sustainable suffrage association. The previous efforts, while successful in creating clubs and recruiting members in the short term, were highly dependent on their respective leaders. When they left, mobilizing efforts stopped and suffrage associations suffered.

The Texas case also illustrates the scope of local dislike of outside interference in the United States. A recurring theme in interviews with Swiss suffrage activists was local resentment against outsider interference. These attitudes existed in many American states as well, particularly in the South and West. In Texas, Rebecca Henry Hayes, the founder of the Texas suffrage association, withdrew from the suffrage cause in 1895 over the issue of whether Susan B. Anthony should be invited to Texas. Hayes, along with some other Texas activists, maintained "that suffrage work should be conducted by Texas women, not by outsiders" (Taylor 1987: 21–23). After a year-long battle over the issue, during which other association officers even attempted to depose her, Hayes lost a bid for reelection as the association president after which she stopped engaging in suffrage activities. The acrimony of this debate indicates that beliefs in local autonomy also motivated some suffrage activists in the United States.

Florida

Florida's first suffrage organization also developed because of the leadership of a single activist. After attending a suffrage convention in Iowa, Ella C. Chamberlain of Tampa converted to the suffrage cause and "resolved to begin crusading in her home state, especially in the realm of . . . organizational work" (Taylor 1957a: 42). In 1893, she created a suffrage club in Tampa and then encouraged the group to organize other affiliates. During the next two years, the suffrage organization grew rapidly (see fig. 3.2). However, the Florida suffrage association suffered when Chamberlain left Florida in 1897. Without its leader, "the Florida organization became less active. It stopped sending reports to the national association and apparently disbanded" (Taylor 1957a: 44). Between 1897 and 1912, there are no indications that remaining local supporters or the national suffrage association attempted to organize in Florida. Like the early Texas club, only the charisma of a single leader had held the organization together.

Only after a new suffrage association developed in Jacksonville did national suffrage activists again focus attention on Florida. After 1912, speakers came to Florida on a regular basis. Anna Howard Shaw spoke in Florida four times between 1915 and 1919, and Kate Gordon, the Louisiana suffrage activist famous for organizing the Southern States Woman Suffrage Conference, periodically toured the state starting in 1914. In addition, suffrage activists from Jacksonville and, later, other existing clubs organized suffrage affiliates in Florida towns that lacked a suffrage group (Taylor 1957a). As in Texas, the organizing activities of local groups and national suffragists resulted in permanent, burgeoning suffrage organizations after 1912.

Iowa

One problem with examining the effect of recruitment tactics in the older suffrage organizations is that many such activities precede 1893, the first year when membership data are available. However, the early phases of

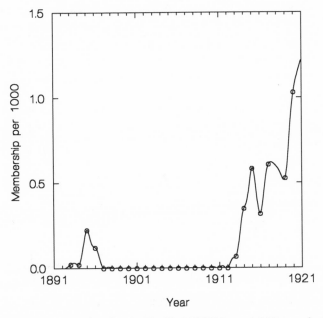

Figure 3.2 Membership in Florida NAWSA per 1,000 population
(1893–1920)

the movement are important in understanding how organizational and recruitment strategies evolved over time. Early Iowa suffrage activists were clearly concerned about organization and recruitment, although they believed this was best accomplished by acquiring good public speakers. Hence, lecture tours by famous women's rights activists such as Anna Dickinson, Elizabeth Cady Stanton, Lucy Stone, and Susan B. Anthony were arranged between 1868 and 1871 (Noun 1969). Some of these lecturers, particularly Martha Brinkerhoff (of Missouri), made special efforts to organize societies for woman suffrage. Local suffrage activists were also cognizant of the importance of these lectures for local organization and recruitment. Thus, Annie Savery of Des Moines postponed the founding convention of the Iowa Woman Suffrage Association for several months with the explanation, "Unless we could get good speakers such as Lucy Stone or Mrs. Stanton, I fear the results would not be satisfactory" (cited in Noun 1969: 137).

The interest in organizing that was so prevalent during the 1870s disappeared from Iowa during the 1880s. In the wake of the free love debate and the Beecher-Tilton scandal, which implicated prominent suffrage activists in a love triangle and the subsequent highly publicized civil suit, many suffrage societies became divided and disbanded. The remaining suffrage associations focused less on building strong organizational net-

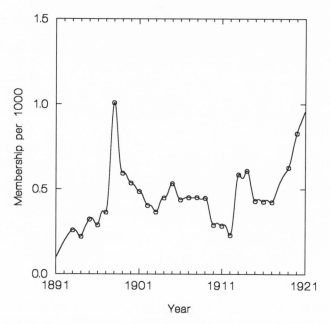

Figure 3.3   Membership in Iowa NAWSA per 1,000 population
(1893–1920)

works. Instead, "their object was chiefly to get the women interested in government and to develop in them a sense of civic responsibility" (Gallaher 1918: 191).

Recruitment and organizational tactics were revived in 1888 when "the Iowa Woman Suffrage Association adopted the plan of choosing a president for every congressional district and a superintendent for every county" (Gallaher 1918: 191). A year later, Carrie Chapman Catt started organizing for suffrage in Iowa, visiting a number of towns for the state society (Noun 1969). Thereafter, the Iowa suffrage organization worked steadily on organization, emphasizing the creation of groups around electoral districts. In 1893 alone, officers reported 33 new clubs to the state convention (Gallaher 1918: 201). Figure 3.3 shows that by 1893 the per capita NAWSA membership in Iowa was roughly double the national average of .11 per 1,000 population.

This continued emphasis on organization and recruitment produced relatively stable membership in the Iowa suffrage association through 1917 with one exception. In 1897, when the annual convention of the National Woman Suffrage Association met in Des Moines, national leaders urged Iowa groups to start an organizational campaign to influence the state legislature (Anthony and Harper 1902; Noun 1969). As head of the NAWSA's Organization Committee that year, Carrie Chapman Catt launched a full-scale attempt at recruitment in Iowa with conventions and national speakers in every county of the state (Noun 1969: 241). The result was a huge, though mostly temporary, rise in association membership in 1897 (see fig. 3.3).

These three case studies indicate the importance of state-level mobilizing efforts for the growth of membership in the NAWSA. Both institutional and individual efforts to increase membership in suffrage associations had positive results. However, when such tactics were the result of the efforts of individual leaders, the associations were often temporary. If these leaders left the suffrage society, it usually disbanded rather quickly. It was only when recruitment strategies were institutionalized within local clubs or the national association that permanent, local affiliates flourished. Moreover, the NAWSA also faced resistance, even among local suffrage activists, when they tried to organize in some states (like Texas). In spite of this opposition to interference by the national organization, the NAWSA did send organizers into these areas, usually with considerable success.

Switzerland

In contrast to the United States, organizing new sections or trying to raise membership levels were rarely explicit tactics of Swiss suffrage organizations. Hence, it is difficult to talk about changes in organizational strategies except in a few cases. However, local suffrage groups did put more effort into mobilization techniques during referenda campaigns. Then, suffrage associations spoke more explicitly about women's voting rights and increased their propaganda and lecturing efforts. These referenda campaigns and the few other cases of emphasized organization had a positive effect on membership levels. To illustrate the connection between these activities and organization membership on the local level, I examine the histories of suffrage organizations in two Swiss cantons: Aargau and Zürich.[6] Like the American examples given above, these represent different types of suffrage societies. Aargau suffrage associations were dependent on dynamic leadership for survival. Zürich, on the other hand, was a larger canton that occasionally engaged in active propaganda work, although it never explicitly chose organizational tactics. Unfortunately, because Swiss membership data are not available in every year, it is hard to attribute jumps or declines in membership to specific events as I was able to do in the United States. Nevertheless, increases in membership in the following two examples correspond to publicity work, particularly during referenda.

AARGAU

The history of the suffrage movement in Aargau can be divided into two periods separated by an era of relative dormancy: (1) 1918–1942, when the suffrage association was dependent on dynamic leaders for organization and mobilization; and (2) 1959–1969, when referenda campaigns and an increased focus on woman suffrage drew new members into the organization. Until 1942, local women's rights clubs in Aargau were dominated by two activists who initiated and organized the woman suffrage movement there. Elisabeth Flühmann founded the first women's rights association, Verein für Frauenbildung und Frauenfragen, in 1918–1919. As president she emphasized the importance of organization, creating new suffrage clubs in three towns (Aarau, Baden, and Freiamt) and later the cantonal women's center (Joho n.d.).

After the death of Flühmann, Dr. Helen Dünner became the president of the new Aarau suffrage section in 1938. She transformed the earlier Verein für Frauenbildung und Frauenfragen into a section of the SVF. However, Dünner's interest lay less in organization than in lobbying, and so the other local sections of Baden and Freiamt, which were inspired by Flühmann's leadership, soon disbanded, leaving only the local Aarau section. Under Dünner's administration, this organization remained active, advocating the right to vote in school boards, juvenile boards, and church boards.

The importance of these two leaders for the local suffrage section became obvious after Dünner moved away from Aargau in 1942. Under the next president, membership fell (see fig. 3.4) and the suffrage association ceased almost all suffrage activities. During the late 1940s and early 1950s, the group's activities consisted of campaigns to have streets and Pro-Juventute stamps named after important women and writing letters to Swiss writers asking them to deal with women's issues (Joho, n.d.).

Only after 1959 and another change in leadership did the organization begin to revive, increasing its membership and its focus on the issue of women's enfranchisement. Beginning in 1960, public lectures on woman suffrage were held every year. The club also sponsored citizenship courses for women in 1965 and 1969. At the same time, the cantonal government began to consider women's voting rights legislation. In 1961, two years after the first national referendum on women's voting rights, the first motion for enfranchising women in cantonal affairs was introduced in the Aargau cantonal parliament. A second motion followed in 1966, with the Governing Council of Aargau finally submitting a voting rights bill to the cantonal parliament in 1969.

In many ways, the history of the Aargau suffrage association resembles its counterparts in Texas and Florida. In all three cases, single leaders dominated the early suffrage movement, concentrated on building the

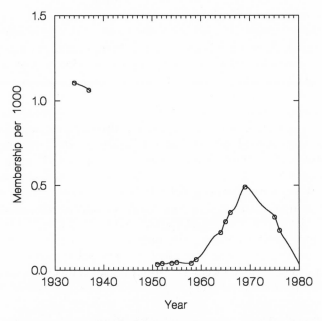

Figure 3.4   Membership in Aargau SVF per 1,000 population
(1930–1980)

organization, and emphasized the issue of women's voting rights. When these dynamic leaders left the movement, the associations were unable to survive. The major difference between the Swiss case and the two American cases was the impact these leaders had on membership. In Florida and Texas, the clubs these leaders built were dwarfed by those that developed once explicit organizing tactics were institutionalized. In contrast, Aargau's suffrage association was largest under the influence of these leaders, as the canton was never the target of explicit national or local mobilizing tactics. In the 1960s and 1970s, an increased focus on women's enfranchisement drew new members into the suffrage organization. Between referenda campaigns, the suffrage issue was kept alive through group-sponsored lectures and citizenship courses and by the publicity surrounding motions and votes in the cantonal parliaments. However, these events did not create the type of membership gains associated with the explicit organizational activities of early suffrage leaders.

ZÜRICH

The Zürich suffrage association was considerably different from its Aargau counterpart. The suffrage section in the city of Zürich was the oldest in Switzerland and was relatively successful in maintaining its membership. Several lecture series in the Zürich countryside and a cantonal level organization attracted rural women into the movement (*Die Staatsbürgerin*, November 1968). In addition, the organization itself controlled more resources than most local groups, including its own newsletter, *Die Staatsbürgerin*,[7] which was used to communicate among with local Zürich sections and, on occasion, the wider public.

Nonetheless, organizing and recruiting were not major focuses of the association with the exception of one membership campaign in 1928 when activists invited petition signers to attend their meetings (*Die Staatsbürgerin*, November 1968: 23–24). As in Aargau, suffrage association activities were not even always related to the enfranchisement of women. When women's voting rights legislation was not on the horizon, suffrage activists addressed a wide range of issues—some related to women's rights but many not. Typical lecture topics included literary themes and political controversies unrelated to women's rights. Even when women's rights were the major concern, suffrage was rarely the explicit theme of public meetings. Moreover, some functions sponsored by the suffrage association were purely social events such as boat rides on Lake Zürich.

However, during the five suffrage referenda between 1920 and 1970, the organization's publicity work and speeches focused almost exclusively on the topic of women's voting rights. Former association presidents reminiscing about their terms in a commemorative edition of *Die Staatsbürgerin* (November 1968) mentioned more propaganda work related to women's enfranchisement during referendum campaigns than in other years. Activists also appear to have lectured more frequently in other parts of the canton during referendum campaigns. In the 1920 referendum campaign, activists gave suffrage lectures in over 70 different communities. One president of the organization mentioned "countless . . . events" during the 1966 referendum campaign (*Die Staatsbürgerin*, November 1968: 15, 49; translated by author). Because of approaching suffrage referenda, activists were also invited by political parties and other women's organizations to lecture on or debate women's voting rights, allowing them to speak to a wider audience than could be reached during normal times. Thus, the peak of the suffrage association's activity occurred during referenda campaigns: They focused only on women's voting rights, had access to new audiences, and organized more events.

Comparing the increases in suffrage association activity to the sporadically available cantonal membership data, however, is difficult. Only four of the five suffrage referenda—in 1947, 1954, 1966, and 1969—occurred after 1934 when the membership figures for the entire canton are first available. In addition, membership data during the 1940s are missing (see fig. 3.5), so we cannot directly observe a relationship between cantonal suffrage organization membership and the 1947 referendum campaign.

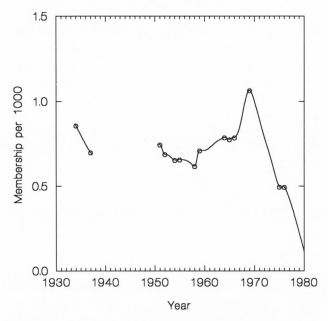

Figure 3.5 Membership in Zürich SVF per 1,000 population
(1930–1980)

Nonetheless, membership changes in Figure 3.5 are largely consistent with the idea that suffrage referenda brought new members into the organization. The suffrage organization grows in 1966 and 1969. Moreover, the group increased its membership between 1937 and 1951 (the years closest to the 1947 suffrage referendum when data was available). The gain is consistent with the supposition that new members were attracted to the association during the 1947 suffrage referendum, especially since most cantons lost membership during the 1930s and 1940s. Zürich was one of only four cantons to register an increase in per capita membership during those years.

Additional information about suffrage organization membership during these referenda is available for the Zürich-city section from the organization's publication, *Die Staatsbürgerin* and the Schweizerisches Sozialarchiv Zürich. These data are presented in Figure 3.6, with arrows indicating the dates of the four referenda. Given that referendum propaganda usually began when the parliament considered the legislation, approximately one or two years before the actual referendum, these data show a clear rise in membership around 1947 as well as in 1966 and 1969, the year of the last cantonal referendum. Thus, in three cases, referenda are preceded by an expansion in the number of dues-paying members, supporting the idea that the mobilization activities of suffrage organizations during referenda campaigns increased membership.

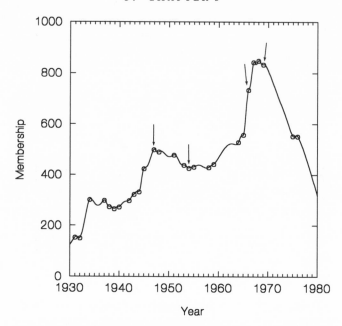

Figure 3.6   Membership in Zürich City Suffrage Organization
(1930–1980)

However, during the 1954 referendum campaign, membership in the suffrage organization fails to register any increase; in fact, between 1952 and 1954, the per capita membership declined in both the city and the canton. On the surface, this would appear to contradict my argument that membership increased with suffrage organization activity. In fact, it does not. The 1954 suffrage referendum was unique precisely because the suffrage organization chose *not* to do any publicity work during the campaign. Because the referendum was a product of an initiative by the Communist party, the conservative-leaning suffrage association decided "after a lengthy deep discussion [to] keep quiet, which meant that we published merely one resolution" (*Die Staatsbürgerin*, November 1968: 36; translated by author). Without the lectures, propaganda, and campaigning of the suffrage association, recruitment suffered. Thus, it was the activities of the suffrage organization, and not simply the occurrence of referenda that caused new women to join the movement.

These case studies of local suffrage organizations in the United States and Switzerland indicate that organizational strategies affected the size of the organization. In both countries, charismatic local leaders who focused on recruitment and organization increased the number and size of local suffrage affiliates, although only as long as they were active. In the United

States, professional NAWSA organizers and speakers helped to increase and stabilize the local suffrage associations. Local suffrage societies also initiated recruiting and organizing drives to increase their size. In Switzerland, national and local suffrage organizations often had no comprehensive organizational strategy. Their only explicit strategies were to increase public consciousness of and support for woman suffrage, mainly through lecturing and citizenship courses for women. However, since they lacked professional activists and were unwilling to push the suffrage issue, they rarely attracted members or created new clubs with these strategies. Nonetheless, evidence from Zürich and Aargau indicates that increased publicity work and lectures could increase membership when activists emphasized women's enfranchisement, which was mainly during referenda campaigns. The increase in propaganda that occurred during the later years of the Swiss suffrage movement is largely a result of the increased number of woman suffrage referenda. Unfortunately, such campaigns were rare in most cantons.

As a result of the lack of organizational activity on both the national and local levels, many local suffrage clubs in Switzerland had a precarious existence as did early suffrage organizations in the southern United States. Many local associations were small and heavily dependent on the leadership of a single activist who kept the whole organization running. For example, the local sections in Wallis/Valais, Horgen (canton Zürich) and Bulle (canton Fribourg/Freiburg) all have been described as relying on the inspiration and leadership of one or two individuals.[8] Unfortunately, dependence on a single leader spelled death for the organization once the individual left. Thus, the Horgen section deteriorated after Lina Lienhart and F. Liggensdorfer moved from the area; and the suffrage organization in Bulle lasted only while Mme. Reichlin, its first president, lived there. On the other hand, most American suffrage associations were well established by 1910.

Why Were the Swiss and American Organizational Tactics Different?

The discussion above suggests that American suffrage organizations chose highly successful organizing techniques while Swiss suffrage organizations, although initially quite strong, eschewed such tactics, even though they would probably have been successful. Since examples of successful organizing do exist in Switzerland, both among other social movements and within a few local suffrage organizations (like Aargau in the 1920s), we must ask why these techniques were not widely utilized. Each theoretical perspective discussed in Chapter 2 provides a different explanation for the variation in tactics. Resource mobilization theories focus on the availability of resources to a movement, arguing that these affect its activities and success. Political opportunity structure theories try to account for these same characteristics by examining the political system in which the movement operates. A focus on perceptions explains the activities of a movement by exploring the specific values and beliefs that influence decisions. How do each of these models apply to the differences in recruiting techniques in the United States and Switzerland?

The American woman suffrage movement enjoyed a clear advantage in organizational resources in the form of full-time organizers and speakers. Moreover, even before the U.S. suffrage movement paid their own full-time lecturers, they were helped by organizers employed by other movements—particularly abolitionist groups—who were sympathetic to the cause of women's rights. The American Anti-Slavery Society, headed by William Lloyd Garrison, hired 70 paid agents to organize new auxiliaries and mobilize individuals into the abolitionist cause (Fogel 1989; Rice 1975). Several early suffrage activists, such as Sarah and Angelina Grimke, Lucy Stone, and Susan B. Anthony, were employed as paid organizers and speakers in the abolitionist movement. As paid lecturers for the abolitionist movement, these women were able to utilize their time and skills in the cause of women's rights as well. The Grimke sisters mixed the themes of equal rights for women and blacks together, while Lucy Stone lectured for abolitionism on weekends and women's rights during the week (Ryan 1992). The Swiss suffrage movement lacked such external sources. While there were strong connections between women's rights organizations and other women's voluntary associations, particularly in the early years (see Mesmer 1988), these did not provide the resources that American suffrage activists received from the abolitionist movement. Although Swiss women's voluntary associations of the nineteenth century included many committed women, they had few full-time activists. Thus, national differences in organizational strength vary with the availability of resources, both internal and external.

On the local level, however, resource mobilization theory cannot explain the variation in organizational strategies and membership levels among Swiss cantons. Suffrage associations with comparatively more resources, like the Zürich section, did not utilize more organizing and recruiting strategies than groups with fewer resources. Moreover, within the various Swiss cantons, local affiliates do not appear to alter their tactics because of changes in resource availability. If anything, political considerations appear to be more important. Hence, we must look further to explain why movements chose such tactics.

Swiss suffrage activists themselves believed that they were constrained from engaging in U.S.-style recruitment by the political opportunity structure. Despite occasional successes on the local level, suffrage activists maintained in interviews that federalist attitudes were too strong to permit women to organize outside their own locale. The unique characteristics of Swiss federalism forced them, in their eyes, to follow noninterventionist strategies. However, as we have seen, Swiss federalism did not keep some Swiss women's rights organizations like STAKA or other social movements from successfully "interfering" in cantons by helping to create organizations. Moreover, there were opportunities for existing groups to initiate recruiting strategies in their own areas as indicated by the rise in membership during referenda.

Indeed, similar beliefs and attitudes toward federalism, and the role that federalism plays in the political culture of the country, existed in both countries.[9] While the cultural attachment of Americans to their local governments has not been examined by scholars in detail, the level of cultural federalism in the United States is generally regarded as being higher than most countries (Elazar 1987). Certainly, Swiss citizens are well known for their strong attachment to their canton or community (Elazar 1987; Steinberg 1976); but, especially in the latter half of the nineteenth century, citizens in the southern and western United States also felt greater affinity for local governments, distrusted the federal government, and loathed federal interference into state affairs. As we have seen, those attitudes were sometimes utilized to argue against outside organizers in the U.S. woman suffrage movement. However, in the end, these beliefs did not obstruct the use of organizing and recruiting tactics in the U.S. woman suffrage movement. Thus, Swiss suffrage activists were mistaken; the structure of political opportunities *did* permit such mobilization strategies by outsiders.

Why did U.S. activists understand their opportunities while their Swiss counterparts clung to a view that underestimated theirs? In answering this, it is helpful to examine the development of these beliefs. In the beginning of the American movement, abolitionists not only provided American suffrage activists with resources to organize but also with a model of successful organizing and a belief in the usefulness of organizational techniques even in the face of opposing values (such as a belief in local autonomy). As the abolitionist movement gained ground in the 1860s, women's rights activists discovered that paid agents could rapidly mobilize the public and create new organizations. The abolitionists provided an excellent example. Even though they faced hostile mobs in many places, abolitionists could enter a state and successfully mobilize individuals to form organizations. The abolitionists also had a habit of pledging part of the organization's budget toward paying full-time organizers.

Thus, through their experiences in the abolitionist movements, several of the early influential suffrage activists learned firsthand how the explicit emphasis on building organizations aided the abolitionist movement.

This is not to say that women lacked experiences with voluntary organizations prior to the abolitionist movement. Even before the close association between the women's rights and abolition movements in the late 1840s, voluntary women's clubs were instrumental in raising funds for various causes and coordinating petition drives for legislation (Cott 1977; Kraditor 1969; Scott 1991). The practice of inviting speakers to lecture on political, social, or literary topics was also common. Thus, women were not strangers to associational life, and they had experience in raising the resources necessary to keep an organization running. However, women's voluntary associations lacked, particularly in the first phase of the women's rights movement, a model of using paid organizers and lecturers to organize other areas of the country. The experiences of women in voluntary associations prior to the abolitionist movement were generally limited to organizing within a single city or town. Thus, the organizing strategies the American suffrage movement later developed could not have come from existing women's organizations alone. Moreover, the abolitionist movement was not the only model upon which early suffrage activists depended. They also had ties with the early temperance movement, which also sponsored organizers and lecturers. Indeed, Susan B. Anthony began her activism in the temperance movement (Harper 1969, vol. 1).

Second-generation suffrage activists did not participate in the abolitionist movement, but they learned new and slightly different models of organizing in other movements. Particularly important was the Women's Christian Temperance Union (WCTU), which in the 1880s was a large, influential organization and included many suffrage activists in its ranks. For example, the emphasis on electoral organization was largely inspired by the WCTU (although other organizations played a role as well). "From the very beginning, local unions [of the WCTU] were organized by congressional district. Women learned the techniques of lobbying and pioneered in voter education" (Scott 1991: 103). Indeed Fowler (1986) attributes many of Carrie Chapman Catt's organizational ideas to Frances Willard, second president of the WCTU. Other organizational models were provided by the Grange (Marti 1991), Chautauqua (Bordin 1981: 34), and networks of progressive reformers (Fowler 1986). In all of these cases, the networks between the woman suffrage movement and the other movements provided activists with ideas about potential organizing tactics. Thus, beliefs and values shared at the coalition level appear important in helping American suffrage activists take full advantage of their political opportunities and resources.

In the Swiss case, suffrage movements lacked strong ties to movements or other political actors that might have contradicted their belief in the necessity of local autonomy. In the early years, the women's rights movement was well connected with other women's organizations. As in the United States, these were largely local organizations that performed charitable work, advanced the cause of women's education, and advocated moral reform. Many capable women were educated into organizational life in these groups; however, the skills they developed centered on organizing and running local organizations. When other women's associations did create national organizations, it was largely out of necessity. Responsibility and financing for many of their concerns began to move from local governments to the hands of the federal government (although local governments continued play a major role in education and charitable work). As a result, women's associations developed national institutions—largely umbrella organizations of local affiliates—to deal with the changing structure of political opportunities (Mesmer 1988). However, because these national associations developed largely for the purpose of acquiring more resources for existing local groups, they never sought to organize new chapters. Hence, they could not serve as a model of national organizing for Swiss suffrage activists.

Some early women's rights activists like Marie Goegg-Pouchoulin also had ties to the early socialist movement, within which both full-time activism and outside agitation were common. Why, then did the early women's rights movement not pick up on those strategies? First, Swiss socialist women followed decisions of the International Women's Conferences in 1907 and 1910 not to work with middle-class suffrage associations (Mesmer 1988: 257). Consequently, just as the SVF and its auxiliaries were taking root, many of the women who might have spread these models of organizing were leaving the suffrage movement.

Second, middle-class suffrage activists were overly careful to divorce their activities from those of the socialist movement. As Mesmer points out, socialist party support for woman suffrage created the suspicion that even school and church suffrage "would prepare the way for socialism" (1988: 254; translated by author). The more conservative parties questioned the motives of the socialist activists, arguing that socialists promoted women's enfranchisement only because they thought they could benefit from it (Woodtli 1983: 147). Woman suffrage activists, therefore, were continually separating themselves from the socialists. For example, when woman suffrage was named as one of the demands of the 1918 general strike, the leadership of the SVF condemned the activities of the socialist strikers (Ruckstuhl 1986).

In the later years of the Swiss suffrage movement, even fewer sources of organizing and recruitment models existed. By the end of World War II, the suffrage movement had no strong ties to the interest groups that were utilizing national organizing strategies. If Swiss suffrage activists had any strong ties, they were to the political parties. However, Swiss activists were not likely to have acquired models of national organizing from the religious, middle-class, or socialist political parties. Although the division between socialists and middle-class suffrage activists lessened as the twentieth century wore on, even the socialists no longer provided a good organizational model. The Social Democratic party, now the major representative of socialists, became ensconced in the government coalition and grew to resemble other traditional parties.

As is the case in the United States, political parties in Switzerland were strongly decentralized. Local party organizations were more powerful than national parties and frequently contradicted national party decisions (Gruner 1977). Local parties issued their own platforms and recommendations concerning referenda that sometimes contradicted the national party platform. In several cantons, the local party even sported a different name from that of the national party organization. Thus, the entire structure of Swiss political parties accentuated cantonal autonomy. Even though many individual suffrage activists had some connections with political parties, these would only have reinforced, rather than reduced, the belief in local autonomy.

Consequently, the Swiss suffrage movement had no coalition beliefs and values that might have led to coordinated or national organizational activity. With little evidence to the contrary, Swiss suffrage activists clung to the belief in local autonomy. Although there were nationally organized interest groups that might have provided a different perspective, suffrage activists had few ties to these groups. It is, therefore, not surprising that they applied the principle of local autonomy to their recruitment tactics.

The Swiss suffrage movement's beliefs in decentralization limited its effectiveness in a second way. Some local suffrage activists occasionally organized other auxiliaries and engaged in effective recruiting tactics. However, information about the successful uses of organizational strategies by local Swiss suffrage activists never spread through the movement. Why did these tactics remain sporadic and local rather than resonate throughout the movement?

The answer lies in the absence of strong ties within the movement. The communication of information within the movement was hindered by attitudes of local autonomy and linguistic and political splits among activists. In interviews, strong feelings of local autonomy were often expressed when activists discussed how their canton differed from other Swiss cantons. To the extent that local autonomy developed into a feeling of "we are different from them," it may have hindered suffrage activists from adopting successful strategies from other cantons. Linguistic divisions between German-, French-, and Italian-speaking activists also probably reinforced the feelings of difference within the movement. Finally, the ties of suffrage activists to political parties, however loose, exacerbated the divisions within the Swiss suffrage movement, even within the same canton. For example, one activist with ties to the Social Democratic party argued that she felt cut off from activists with ties to Catholic political organizations (interview with suffrage activist, November 30, 1987). All of these divisions inhibited the creation of close ties and, hence, the transmission of information and values within the suffrage movement.

Conclusion

If the U.S. suffrage movement had an advantage over its Swiss counterpart, it was not the initial size of its membership, for the SVF attracted a higher proportion of the female population. Rather, it was the American movement's dynamic recruitment and organizing, which caused an explosion of support in the last twenty years of the movement. The Swiss suffrage movement began with relatively more members but never managed to expand their initial basis of support. The difference lies in the activities of the two movements. The American movement extensively utilized recruitment and organization strategies, while the Swiss movement largely did not. Although evidence from other movements and from isolated incidents in local suffrage associations suggest that American-style organizing and recruiting strategies would have been successful in Switzerland, they never became part of the movement's repertoire. Swiss suffrage activists felt public opinion favoring local autonomy limited what they could do. Yet, if disapproval of outside interference played a role, it was not in making organizing and recruiting tactics futile but in influencing the perceptions of suffrage activists.

American suffrage activists, although also products of a society with strong beliefs in local autonomy, had no problems realizing the usefulness of organization and recruitment. Early on, U.S. suffrage activists came into contact with political actors who demonstrated that national organizing, even in the face of great opposition, could produce results. Suffrage activists acquired this and other strategic information through their ties to the abolitionist movement and temperance organizations, among others. Moreover, new strategies for recruiting members picked up by a particular activist or tried in one state affiliate spread to other areas via the national association. While the centralized structure of the NAWSA was in part responsible for the diffusion of tactics, it was not so much the structure per se as the communal beliefs and values that permitted local innovations to spread. On the other hand, the Swiss suffrage activists had their closest bonds with other organizations, which only reinforced the prevailing belief that outsiders could not successfully intrude in local affairs. Moreover, these ties reinforced divisions within the Swiss suffrage movement, inhibiting the spread of the new techniques that were occassionally successfully used by individual activists or local organizations. Divided by language, politics, and feelings of uniqueness, Swiss suffrage activists never developed the bonds that facilitated the diffusion of new tactics and values within the movement.

4

THE IMPACT OF MOVEMENT RESOURCES

ON SUCCESS

ALTHOUGH American suffrage activists were much more cognizant of the importance of organization than their Swiss counterparts, money was a serious issue for both movements. In this chapter, I explore the role of two major resources—people power and money—in achieving woman suffrage in Switzerland and the United States. I find that these resources do not play a large role in determining the success or failure of the two movements. Just as membership levels were unrelated to success on the national level, Swiss cantons and American states with larger suffrage organizations were not more likely to introduce women's voting rights legislation, gain legislative support, garner voter support, or enfranchise women. While the Swiss suffrage movement lacked the financial resources available to its American counterpart, it also used the money it did have in fundamentally different ways. Tactical choices about the way monetary resources were spent may have been as important as the amount of resources in determining the success of the woman suffrage movement.

In order to examine the influence of these factors, "success" must be defined more explicitly. As suffrage organizations fought to achieve voting rights for women, they first had to achieve a number of intermediate victories along the way. It is useful, then, to consider success as a series of achievements. In this analysis, I examine the ability of suffrage organizations to accomplish four types of goals. First, woman suffrage movements in both countries sought government consideration of women's voting rights usually in the form of bills considered by legislatures. The introduction of women's voting rights legislation was an indicator of suffrage organizations' ability to put their issue on the political agenda. It was also often a difficult first step because legislators had few reasons to consider the opinions of constituents who could not vote against them. Second, suffrage activists strove for favorable votes on these bills from legislators. Although any level of legislative support below 50 percent meant defeat, 49 percent represents a considerable triumph compared to 15 percent and a unanimous victory may be viewed as more successful than winning by a single vote. Third, in Switzerland and most U.S. states, movements faced an additional hurdle after legislatures passed woman suffrage legislation: the referendum. In Switzerland, national and cantonal constitutional amendments cannot be adopted without a referendum. While the U.S. Constitution does not permit referenda on constitutional amendments, all U.S. states except Delaware and New Hampshire require them for state constitutional amendments. This meant that woman suffrage movements in both countries had to concentrate on increasing *voters*' support in order to win the vote. It is only after jumping these three hurdles—getting bills on the legislative agenda, gaining approval of legislatures, and raising the support of voters—that Swiss and American suffrage movements achieved their final goal: the enfranchisement of women.

Monetary Resources

While the effects of suffrage organization membership can be explored using statistical analyses, a lack of systematic information about the finances of local suffrage campaigns makes a definitive analysis of the influence of financial resources impossible. Even on the national level, my exploration of the Swiss archives unearthed only a few annual budgets of the Schweizerischer Verband für Frauenstimmrecht. Spotty historical records in Switzerland, as well as different methods of categorizing receipts and expenditures make it difficult to make systematic comparisons between the two countries.[1] As a result, I rely on multiple sources of evidence to explore how available funds were utilized by suffrage organizations. This information suggests that the National American Woman Suffrage Association (NAWSA) had more money to work with than the Schweizerischer Verband für Frauenstimmrecht (SVF), largely as a result of private donors. Nonetheless, there were differences in the spending habits of the two organizations that cannot be explained by the amount of money available in the budget.

Size of Budgets

Although the Swiss and American suffrage organizations were active in different time periods, the expenditures of the National American Woman Suffrage Association (NAWSA) far exceeded those of its Swiss counterpart (see Table 4.1 for a comparison of all available budget years). However, as with organization membership (see Chapter 3), absolute budget comparisons are biased against the Swiss movement. The smaller size of the Swiss population meant that the suffrage movement had fewer potential donors. In addition, the same activities probably cost less in

TABLE 4.1
Comparison of the Budgets of the Schweizerischer Verband für Frauenstimmrecht and
the National American Woman Suffrage Association

Switzerland

Year	Total Budget in Swiss Francs ($ equivalent)	Percent of Budget Saved	Total Budget Per 1,000 Population[b] (in U.S. $)	Number of Cantonal Referenda	Percent of Budget Spent in Cantons	Nonbudgeted Property
1946	2,058.40 SF ($596.64)	22.9	0.50 SF ($.12)	3	0	N.A.
1946/47	850.70 SF ($205.98)	25.6	0.20 SF ($.05)	1	0	N.A.
1947 (5 months)	1,245.47 SF ($301.57)	71.0	0.65 ($.16)[c]	1	0	N.A.
1948 (9 months)	11,460.70 SF ($2,872.36)	77.6	3.31 ($.83)[c]	1	7	N.A.
1948/49	6,044.10 SF ($1,405.60)	39.3	1.31 SF ($0.30)	1	0	20,577.11 SF
1956/57	11,559.62 SF ($2,697.69)	6.6	2.25 SF ($0.53)	1	3	17,965.11SF
1962	9,396.50 SF ($2,175.62)	38.8	1.70 SF ($0.39)	1	0	19,903.60 SF
1963	11,038.65 SF ($2,558.20)	0.0	1.94 SF ($0.45)	0	0	18,614.95 SF
1965	13,088.45 SF ($3,031.14)	0.0	2.24 SF ($0.52)	1	0	19,379.85 SF
1966	13,099.65 SF ($3,027.42)	0.0	2.21 SF ($0.51)	4	12	17,063.95 SF

United States

Year	Total Budget	Percent of Budget Saved	Budget Per 1,000 Total Population[b]	Number of State Referenda	Percent of Budget Spent on State Campaigns	Percent of Budget Spent on Organizers
1892	$4,347.31	1.5	$0.07	1	39.1	34.7
1893	$2,992.62	1.9	$0.05	1	6.1	0.0
1894	$5,820.24	6.0	$0.09	1	44.0	0.0
1895	$9,883.41	3.9	$0.14	0	0.0	36.8
1896	$11,823.30	1.4	$0.17	3	0.0	53.8
1897	$14,055.13	−2.6	$0.20	0	0.0	71.1
1898	$14,020.96	4.0	$0.19	2	0.0	30.0
1899	$10,344.71	9.0	$0.14	0	0.0	42.0
1900	$22,522.00	3.9	$0.30	1	2.0	7.3
1901	$18,290.24	54.0	$0.24	1	0.0	10.0
1902	$18,310.07	33.8	$0.23	0	0.0	19.1
1903	$27,311.29	51.0	$0.34	1	11.9	5.8
1904	$28,622.15	43.5	$0.35	0	0.0	7.2
1905	$28,333.92	41.5	$0.34	0	13.3	13.3
1906	$29,972.88	13.8	$0.35	1	38.8	25.8
1907	$19,072.22	9.5	$0.22	0	0.0	34.5
1908	$15,420.83	6.0	$0.17	1	0.0	22.3
1909	$21,466.08	7.7	$0.24	0	18.2	10.2
1910	$43,844.62	20.5	$0.48	3	15.8	2.7
1912[a]	$87,836.42	3.3	N.A.	6	20.7	0.0
1913	$45,597.79	6.7	$0.48	1	3.8	0.0
1914	$67,312.03	12.0	$0.69	7	36.5	0.0

TABLE 4.1 (cont.)

United States

Year	Total Budget	Percent of Budget Saved	Budget Per 1,000 Total Population[b]	Number of State Referenda	Percent of Budget Spent on State Campaigns	Percent of Budget Spent on Organizers
1915	$51,265.70	17.3	$0.52	4	23.6	0.0
1916	$90,731.84	20.1	$0.91	3	23.3	3.5
1917	$122,096.10	9.7	$1.21	3	23.0	9.2
1918	$119,610.12	18.0	$1.17	5	30.0	3.0
1919	$99,124.57	11.0	$0.95	1	13.5	13.5

Sources: In Switzerland, documents of the SVF available from the Gosteli Stiftung (Worblaufen, Switzerland) and from the Schweizerisches Sozialarchiv (Zürich, Switzerland). In the United States, proceedings of the twenty-fifth to the fifty-second annual conventions of the National American Woman Suffrage Association (1893–1920) and U.S. Censuses.

[a] In 1912, the organization shifted the beginning of its business year from January 1 to November 1. The budget for the ten-month interim period in 1911 (January 1, 1911, to October 31, 1911) was not reported in any proceedings.

[b] Population figures are derived from the U.S. and Swiss censuses. The population in a noncensus year is calculated as a linear interpolation of the preceeding and following census years.

[c] Because of shifting fiscal years, the 1947 and 1948 budgets cover five and nine months respectively. Per capita expenditures are adjusted for these years by multiplying by 12/5 and 12/9, respectively.

Switzerland; fewer people, a smaller geographical area, and fewer local governments meant that it was easier to publicize the cause, reach remote areas, and lobby local politicians. A fairer comparison requires examining how much money each organization could spend per inhabitant, which is reported in the fourth column of Table 4.1.

While the per capita spending of the SVF and the NAWSA was similar in some years, the U.S. suffrage organization still outspent its Swiss counterpart. In the ten budget years reported in Table 4.1, the SVF spent an average of $.38 per 1,000 inhabitants. While this compares favorably to the NAWSA's per capita receipts prior to 1912, once cost of living increases are included in the calculations, the U.S. suffrage organization still controlled more financial resources than its Swiss counterpart. Moreover, after 1915, the per capita income of the NAWSA increased steadily; from 1916 to 1919, the suffrage organization grossed an average of $1.06 per 1,000 inhabitants.

Only in 1948 does the SVF's per capita income approach these levels. In fact, SVF receipts remained constant, both in absolute and per capita terms, during the twenty years covered in Table 4.1. In 1948, the total operating budget of the SVF was 11,460 SF (for just nine months). In 1956, the SVF's total income was 11,560 SF (2.25 SF per 1,000); and in 1966, it equaled 13,100 SF (2.21 SF per 1,000). Given that prices rose 7 percent between 1948 and 1956 and another 30 percent between 1956 and 1966, the spending power of the SVF declined considerably. Thus, the SVF experienced stability or slight decline in both membership and financial resources over most of its history.

The budget of the national SVF was also small in comparison to the income of several local sections. For example, in 1946, the national SVF grossed only 2,671 SF ($619.00), while the Union für Frauenbestrebungen, the Zürich section of the SVF, earned 5,748 SF ($1,330.00). Even during the lean years of the depression (1931–1935) the income of the Basel section always exceeded 3,500 SF. Only in the 1950s and 1960s, when woman suffrage gained in popularity, did the income of the national SVF exceed that of its larger local sections. Even so, the largest national budget I could find (from 1966) only reached 13,100 SF or $3,027.50.

Unfortunately, the financial information of the SVF presented in Table 4.1 is highly skewed. Financial data for the two years when national referenda were held (1959 and 1971) were not found in any archive. Yet, these are likely to be the SVF's two highest grossing years, since referendum campaigns increased its national visibility. In this sense, the difference between the American and Swiss organizations is probably overestimated.

Despite the lack of expenditure data in these two referenda years, the archives yielded a few pieces of information that provide a rough sketch of the financial situation of the Swiss suffrage movement during the first suffrage campaign of 1959. A provisional budget for the 1959 national referenda estimated that 300,000 SF (about $67,000) would be necessary to run the campaign. This sum is only two-thirds of the amount that the NAWSA spent in 1919 during its campaign to ratify the Nineteenth Amendment. Once increases in the cost of living are considered,[2] the 300,000 SF was worth less than half what their American sisters spent. Moreover, a list of contributions to the 1959 referenda campaign committee implies that Swiss suffrage activists were overly optimistic in their expectations for the 1959 campaign. This document indicates that only a third of the provisional budget (106,492 SF) was raised. Thus, in absolute terms, Swiss suffrage activists were more financially strapped than their American counterparts.

Sources of Funds

The stability of both finances and membership in the Swiss suffrage organization is not coincidental. Both the Swiss and American suffrage organizations required that local affiliates pay a per member fee to the national organization. However, the SVF was very dependent on membership fees, while the NAWSA was not. Dues from local sections and members usually accounted for at least two-thirds of the SVF's income. On those rare occasions when additional monies were collected, they were a result of special SVF fund-raising activities. For example, in 1947 and 1948, Swiss suffrage activists sold picture postcards, raising over 12,000 SF. Private contributions, however, never became a significant source of revenue for the SVF, accounting for less than 5 percent of total receipts in the 1940s (2 percent in 1946; 1 percent in 1946/47; 1 percent in 1947; and 2 percent in 1948).[3]

The American suffrage organizations, on the other hand, received a large proportion of their operating budgets from individual donations. In most years, these donations raised three to five times as much income as membership dues. For example, in 1919, state association dues to the NAWSA equaled $5,894.20, while private donations amounted to $21,157.78. Bequests were particularly important to the NAWSA. Nearly every year, coffers were supplemented by the bequests of dying friends of suffrage, often in small amounts like $100. A few women made very large bequests: Mrs. Cornelia Collins Hussey left $10,000 in 1903 (NAWSA 1904); and in 1917, Mrs. Frank Leslie willed her entire estate (about $1 million) to the suffrage cause. Such bequests became an important source of funding, both for daily operations and special campaigns.

In contrast, Swiss women rarely contributed more than their membership dues to the Swiss suffrage organization. Interestingly, the single largest donation recorded in the budgets of the SVF (244 SF) came not from a Swiss woman but from an anonymous, sympathetic American (Schweizerischer Verband für Frauenstimmrecht 1948). Among suffrage activists, the idea of leaving money to the suffrage organization was foreign. "I've heard that the American women thought about the suffrage cause in their wills and such, and that helped the cause. Here people think of the environment and the protection of animals, but the women's movement is never or only seldom remembered" (interview of January 21, 1988). In fact, during the 10 years of SVF budgets listed in Table 4.1, only one individual, Anna Dück-Tobler, bequeathed money to the SVF.[4]

When individuals supporters of the SVF donated money, it was to finance referendum campaigns. Women or women's organizations constituted the majority of the contributors to the fund for the first national referenda in 1959, although they did not provide the largest donations.[5] In addition, local suffrage activists often financed many of the local costs incurred from national and cantonal referendum campaigns themselves. However, referenda on women's voting rights were rare; there were only two national referenda (in 1959 and 1971) and, on average, each canton had one referendum every thirty years, meaning that decades could pass between infusions of private donations.

The SVF's lack of financial resources probably constrained organizational activities. While the NAWSA spent a large proportion of its budget on propaganda and recruitment, Swiss suffrage organizations may have been forced to concentrate on infrastructure, such as maintaining a central office and financing meeting costs, leaving very little for propaganda and other activities. For example, in 1948/49, only 19 percent of the total budget was spent on activities and propaganda. In 1965, only 2,086 SF out of a total budget of 13,233 SF was spent on propaganda of all sorts. In contrast, 2,465 SF was spent on the annual convention; 4,329 SF on maintaining the general office; and an additional 1,290 SF was allocated for the meeting expenses of the national officers and some committees. These figures appear quite typical for the expenditures of the SVF.

Despite these constraints, the Swiss suffrage organization still had a fair amount of latitude. The spending habits of the SVF indicate that there was room to reallocate resources but that suffrage activists *chose* not to finance certain activities. There were vast differences between the allocation decisions of the Swiss and American woman suffrage organizations; the SVF preferred to save rather than spend its income.

Savings

One peculiarity of the Swiss suffrage organization was a tendency to vastly underspend its budget (see the third column of Table 4.1). The budgets I found in archives show that the organization actually increased its standing balance in eight out of ten years. During six of those years, the Swiss suffrage organization managed to save over 25 percent of its total income. In 1948 and 1949, the SVF saved over 75 percent of its total receipts. While the last two available financial statements (1965 and 1966) did show losses, these were relatively small compared to the total size of the budget (145 SF out of 13,233 SF total expenditures in 1965 and 2,315 SF out of 15,415 SF total expenditures in 1966).

Moreover, the operating budget underestimates the real wealth of the SVF, since it also possessed reserve funds not included in the normal operating budget. The reserves are first documented in 1949 (see column 7 of Table 4.1). Reserves greatly exceeded the annual budget of the organization. This property (*Vermögen*) does not appear to have been saved for important future actions such as referenda campaigns. These cash reserves remained relatively constant between 1948 and 1966, averaging close to 19,000 SF. While the suffrage organization occasionally drew money from these funds to pay for special actions, they rarely removed more than 1,000 SF. Because I was unable to locate budgets in 1959 and 1971, the years in which national suffrage referenda occurred, I cannot ascertain whether the property was utilized on these occasions. However, the budgets from 1956/57 and 1962 suggest that there was no significant drop in reserves during this time. Apparently, the SVF was not willing to spend these monies on either cantonal or national referenda campaigns.

In contrast, the NAWSA usually depleted its income and special fund monies. Year-end cash surpluses rarely exceeded 6 percent of the budget. In those years when the NAWSA chose to save more, it generally placed these extra monies (particularly bequests) into special funds to be used for later activity. However, in contrast to the Swiss organization, the NAWSA generally exhausted these accounts very quickly, even when it consciously tried to build a reserve. For example, although Susan B. Anthony worked very hard to raise a permanent endowment whose interest could be used for operating expenses (NAWSA 1904: 25), the monies collected for this purpose were quickly donated to special actions and campaigns. By 1909, the Susan B. Anthony Woman Suffrage Fund had received a total of $26,896 in donations, but over $18,500 had been spent during the same period.

Field-Workers and Local Campaigns

One reason the NAWSA saved so little is that it spent a large proportion of its budget on state campaigns. Until the organization focused its efforts on a federal amendment in 1916, a suffrage referendum in any state was viewed as an opportunity to further the suffrage cause. The national organization and other local organizations often contributed large sums of money to states with suffrage referenda on the ballot. Contributions from the NAWSA to state referenda campaigns (excluding contributions sent from one local section to another) often reached 40 percent of its annual budget, and rarely dropped below 10 percent.[6] These contributions usually took the form of paying for field-workers and propaganda materials rather than direct cash payments to state suffrage organizations. Indeed, while both the U.S. and Swiss suffrage organizations relied heavily on unpaid volunteers, a large proportion of NAWSA's operating budget went toward activists' salaries. Between 1895 and 1910, the amount allocated to paid organizers outside of the day-to-day operations in the central office averaged 24.5 percent of the NAWSA's total expenditures.

The SVF, on the other hand, provided little assistance to cantonal suffrage organizations and relied almost exclusively on volunteers. Although eight cantonal referenda occurred during the three budget years for which figures are available in the 1940s, the national SVF made only a single 800 SF donation to cantonal campaigns. After 1957, the SVF regularly budgeted monies for cantonal actions (usually 1,000 SF per year). However, these funds usually remained unspent even though cantonal referenda occurred in almost every year. In fact, only two other contributions were made to cantonal organizations—one in 1956 for 300 SF and one in 1966 for 1,517 SF. These two donations constituted less than 12 percent of the total operating expenses.

The SVF's only paid worker was the secretary in the central office, and she was first hired in the 1960s. However, volunteer lecturers may have been reimbursed for speeches or travel expenses in 1948/49, 1956/57, 1962, and 1963.[7] Financial statements in these years include a line under the general category of propaganda for trips and lectures (*Reisen, Vorträge*), although only a few hundred SF were budgeted for these endeavors. It is unclear how these funds were used; they may have been appropriated for outside speakers to attend national meetings or for suffrage activists to speak elsewhere. After 1963, the SVF apparently stopped reimbursement for trips or lectures since the budget line disappears. In any case, these expenditures, totaling only 1,600 SF over four budget years, could not have provided much support to volunteers.

The budgets of the SVF and the NAWSA indicate that the two organizations were very different. The Swiss suffrage organization received fewer funds and hence was more constrained than its American counterpart. It spent proportionately more money on infrastructure and donated less to cantonal work than the U.S. organization. Nonetheless, the frequent budget surpluses and unspent allocations to cantonal activities and propaganda indicate that there was room for reallocation within the budget. The American organization was wealthier, largely because of a tradition of private donations among woman suffrage supporters. While suffrage activists realized the importance of cash reserves, they did not develop large endowments, as their Swiss counterparts did, but rather spent all available monies on special actions and state referenda campaigns.

This analysis of financial resources suggests that resource mobilization theory cannot be refuted. However, since the analysis of their expenditures also indicates that U.S. and Swiss suffrage activists chose to spend their income in fundamentally different ways, an equally plausible theory is that the strategies of the two suffrage organizations determined their relative success and failure. Decisions on *how* available resources were used may have affected the final outcome more than the absolute level of resources. Unfortunately, incomplete information on the finances of the Swiss national organization and the lack of systematic financial data from local auxiliaries in both countries make it impossible to determine whether resources per se or spending decisions played a larger role in affecting the success of Swiss and American woman suffrage movements. Fortunately, membership data on the cantonal and state level permits a more rigorous analysis of the relationship between resources and success.

Analyzing Membership's Effect on Success

Before turning to the relationship between organizational membership and various forms of success, a few words on measurement and the statistical analyses are necessary.

Choosing the Unit of Analysis

In Chapter 3, I discuss how membership in several state and cantonal suffrage associations changed over time. To generalize beyond these few examples, however, we need techniques that "retain the attention to case . . . but that at the same time allow us to create narrative generalizations across cases" (Abbot 1992: 79). Pooled time-series cross-sectional analysis is one such technique (see Judge et al. 1985; Sayrs 1989). It combines time series from all states (or cantons) into a single data set, allowing researchers to utilize the maximum amount of information available (that is, both variation over time and across different places). In effect, state or cantonal time series are combined into a single statistical model and the unit of analysis becomes neither the state or canton nor a specific year but the state or canton in a particular year. For example, Georgia in 1915 constitutes a single datapoint, as do New York in 1915 and Georgia in 1916. The total potential sample size is, therefore, the number of states or cantons multiplied by the number of years for which data were collected (1893–1920 for the United States, and 1926–1980 for Switzerland). However, as we will see later, the actual number of datapoints will often be smaller than this maximum.

On the Swiss Membership Measure

In order to conduct this analysis, a new measure of Swiss organizational membership is introduced. Exact information about the number of dues-paying members in Swiss local suffrage sections is spotty, as Figures 3.4 and 3.5 illustrate. Because many indicators of success occurred only rarely in Switzerland, we need to have membership data from as many years as possible. To increase the amount of information available on the number of members in cantonal woman suffrage organizations, I utilize a membership index based on three measures—exact membership in the suffrage organization, number of delegates a section is entitled to have at the national convention, and the number of delegates who actually appear at the convention. Because all three measures rarely occur in the same year, the composite indicator is created by standardizing each measure and then averaging all data available for a particular year and canton. The intercorrelations among these items are extraordinarily high (the lowest pairwise correlation is .86) and so the index has high reliability. Creating this mobilization index (described in Appendix B) increases the number of years for which I have some measure of membership from 14 to 49.

Unique Country Characteristics

Although I have pooled data within both countries, I continue to analyze the United States and Switzerland separately. The statistical techniques used in this chapter assume that causal factors operate in the same manner (that is, they are fixed) for all cases in the analysis (see the LSDV model in Sayrs 1989: 26–32). Combining the United States and Switzerland into a single data set would likely violate these assumptions. Since the Swiss and American suffrage movements acted in different political opportunity structures and historical contexts, we cannot expect the same causal factors to operate in both countries. We also have no a priori reason to assume that the effect of suffrage organization membership on success was the same in both countries. Rather, I compare the two analyses to see if they present similar results.

It is also possible to argue that within a single country some regions (for example, the U.S. South) or time periods might also differ from one another. In the analysis that follows, I assume that suffrage movement success might be more or less likely in some regions and/or eras but that these effects are fixed and independent of membership. This assumption allows me to isolate the effects of membership on success by controlling for the variation connected to specific regions or historical periods.[8] For that reason I include sets of dichotomous variables (the coding of which are described in Appendix C) to denote time and place. While I report the estimates for these variables, my interest lies specifically with the effect of membership.

Classifying Different Types of Suffrage Legislation

Legislators and woman suffrage activists were creative in devising legislation to enfranchise women. Indeed, in both countries, some suffrage legislation was designed to create only small changes in women's voting rights. Some Swiss cantons adopted women's voting rights for members of the councils that governed church affairs. Others introduced legislation that permitted local communities to extend community suffrage to women. Swiss suffrage organizations often argued that partial voting rights would lead to greater gains, a strategy they named "Der Weg von unten nach oben," meaning woman suffrage from the bottom up.[9] A few local U.S. suffrage sections also attempted to acquire partial suffrage, particularly municipal or bond suffrage. However, this strategy was less prevalent than in Switzerland; most U.S. suffrage organizations focused on the right to vote in elections for the more significant political offices.

The analyses that follow are based only on full suffrage legislation in states and cantons (see Chapter 1 for the difference between full and partial suffrage). The type of legislation that is defined as "full suffrage" varies slightly according to country. In Switzerland, the only type of cantonal legislation where women received significant electoral power was that which authorized women's voting rights in cantonal elections. While this did not always include the right to vote in local communities (although it often did), the canton is the locus of most important political decisions. Consequently, cantonal voting rights gave women a significant voice in local affairs. Partial suffrage legislation in Switzerland included not only bills enfranchising women in specific areas of local government (for example, elections of church, school, or social welfare boards) but also legislation permitting local communities to extend community suffrage to women. Although local community option legislation created the potential for future voting rights for women, it actually enfranchised no one. Instead, these bills forced activists to campaign for suffrage in each local area.

In the United States, three types of woman suffrage bills are included in the category of full suffrage legislation. Legislation that granted women full voting rights in state elections is one form of full suffrage. In contrast to Switzerland, this "state suffrage" legislation enfranchised women in local elections as well. Second, presidential suffrage legislation, although enfranchising women for only one electoral office, gave women voters considerable influence in the political spectrum. Third, in southern states (as defined by Key 1977), which were dominated by the Democratic party, voting rights in party primaries ("primary suffrage") also provided women with a significant voice in state and national affairs.[10] Therefore, presidential suffrage legislation and, in southern states, primary suffrage laws are categorized as full suffrage legislation.

Introduction of Legislation and Suffrage
Organization Membership

For woman suffrage movements, the introduction of women's voting rights legislation was often a sign of progress, since it indicated that the issue had achieved a degree of legitimacy in the public debate.[11] This step was also a relatively easy one for woman suffrage movements. In Switzerland, women's voting rights could be introduced through an initiative petition, from a motion or postulate from a member of the cantonal parliament, or by the cantonal executive. In the United States, legislation could be submitted by individual legislators, by representatives to constitutional conventions, and, in a few states, through an initiative petition. Thus, in both countries, there were several paths by which such legislation could appear on the agenda. Nor did the introduction of woman suffrage legislation require a large constituency; within cantonal or state legislatures only a single supporter was needed to initiate this legislation.

Nonetheless, the states in the U.S. introduced more full suffrage legislation than did Swiss cantons. Between 1920 and 1980 only 87 bills for cantonal women's voting rights were introduced in Switzerland and 11 of the 25 cantons introduced only one or two such bills between 1920 and 1980.[12] In fact, in 22 of the 51 years between 1920 and 1971 (the year women were enfranchised on the national level), *no* canton considered full woman suffrage legislation. American legislators, on the other hand, initiated almost five times as many full suffrage bills between 1870 and 1920 (418 bills in all). The average American state introduced twice as much legislation, over a shorter period of time, as its Swiss counterpart (8.7 bills per state versus 3.5 bills per canton). State woman suffrage legislation was considered in at least one state every year between 1870 and 1920, and only four states introduced fewer than three woman suffrage bills in the 51 years. Two of these four states were Wyoming and Utah, where territorial woman suffrage legislation passed on the first attempt. Switzerland's relative paucity of cantonal suffrage bills is even more surprising since all Swiss cantons had to introduce at least one women's voting rights bill because the national amendment was limited to national elections only. On the other hand, women could be enfranchised in a U.S. state that never considered such legislation.

If Swiss suffrage activists had followed the bottom-up strategy many advocated, we might expect to find few full suffrage bills introduced and a plethora of partial suffrage legislation instead. However, only 20 such bills were considered between 1920 and 1980. More partial suffrage legislation (over 100 pieces) was introduced into U.S. state legislatures. Between 1830 and 1910, 20 states enfranchised women for school or municipal elections or for referenda on local tax or bond issues. Thus, by any measure, Switzerland lagged behind the United States in the introduction of women's voting rights legislation.

The Effect of Membership on the Introduction of Suffrage Legislation

To analyze whether differences in suffrage organization membership within each country can account for the variation in introductions, Ordinary Least Squares (OLS) regression analysis is conducted on the pooled time-series data discussed above. Introductions are measured here by a dichotomous variable coded "one" if any full suffrage legislation is initiated in the state or canton during the year whether through initiative petition, legislators, or constitutional convention. Otherwise, the state-year or canton-year is coded "zero."[13] Once a state or canton adopts full woman suffrage, data in future years are excluded from the analysis. After all, in states or cantons that have already enfranchised women, the lack of suffrage legislation introductions indicates not failure but success. Relatively few woman suffrage bills were introduced in Colorado, for example, because the state enfranchised women very early. Thus, states and cantons are included in the data set only until they adopt woman suffrage legislation.[14]

The first column of Tables 4.2 and 4.3 report the regression estimates and significance levels from the analyses of the introduction of suffrage legislation in the United States and Switzerland respectively. In neither case does the estimated effect of membership (.023 and .014, respectively) achieve statistical significance. States and cantons with large per capita suffrage organizations were no more likely to introduce suffrage legislation than those with relatively small groups.

On the other hand, voting rights legislation was more likely to be initiated during certain periods and, in the United States, in specific regions. In Switzerland, the probability of a woman suffrage bill being introduced increases in the 1960s and 1970s. In the United States, the last decade (1911–1920) was the period of greatest activity, and eastern and western states were more likely to introduce woman suffrage legislation than southern ones.

First Introductions of Suffrage Legislation

However, the analyses of all bill introductions may be misleading. There is a big distinction between the first time legislation is considered and later attempts. The initial introduction places the issue on the political agenda for the first time. Later introductions show that the issue has not disappeared from the public agenda, but they also signify failure. That is, multiple introductions indicate that woman suffrage organizations were unable to achieve voting rights during considerations of previous bills. Because high numbers of introductions can be interpreted as both failure and success, it is helpful to analyze first-time introductions.

Unfortunately, this is not possible in the United States, where many woman suffrage bills were first introduced between 1840 and 1870. In fact, 36 of the 48 states considered their first women's voting rights bill prior to 1893, the first year in which membership data are available. Since

TABLE 4.2

The Effect of Suffrage Organization Membership on Four Measures
of Success in the United States, 1893–1920

Variable Name	Introduction of Suffrage Bills	Support among Legislators	Support in Referenda	Adoption of Suffrage
	Regression Estimates (and Probability Values) for:			
Intercept	.012	.489	.450	.008
	(.816)	(.000)[a]	(.001)[a]	(.664)
Members in Suffrage Organization	.023	.025	.002	.040
per 1,000 pop.	(.251)	(.121)	(.803)	(.000)[a]
Period Dummies				
Years: 1896–1900	−.051	−.031	.104	−.015
	(.259)	(.643)	(.211)	(.328)
Years: 1901–1905	−.004	−.110	.094	−.019
	(.929)	(.082)	(.362)	(.229)
Years: 1906–1910	.059	−.122	.071	−.015
	(.189)	(.043)[a]	(.430)	(.324)
Years: 1911–1915	.313	.006	.064	.002
	(.000)[a]	(.909)	(.413)	(.887)
Years: 1916–1920	.261	.120	.167	.089
	(.000)[a]	(.040)[a]	(.052)	(.000)[a]
Region Dummies[b]				
Mountain Region	.189	.125	.126	.045
	(.001)[a]	(.104)	(.285)	(.027)[a]
West South Central	.093	.058	−.136	−.003
	(.105)	(.449)	(.271)	(.876)
Pacific Region	.193	.278	−.056	.048
	(.005)[a]	(.001)[a]	(.620)	(.041)[a]
New England	.251	−.016	−.201	−.021
	(.000)[a]	(.813)	(.095)	(.244)
South Atlantic	.061	−.114	−.337	−.022
	(.216)	(.103)	(.019)[a]	(.185)
East North Central	.274	.134	−.119	.022
	(.000)[a]	(.059)	(.286)	(.245)
West North Central	.253	.096	−.055	.017
	(.000)[a]	(.145)	(.601)	(.325)
Mid-Atlantic	.216	.080	−.079	−.011
	(.000)[a]	(.277)	(.483)	(.591)
F-Ratio:	13.232	6.071	3.258	9.750
	(p=.000)	(p=.000)	(p=.003)	(p=.000)
R-squared:	.144	.301	.611	.110
Adjusted R-squared:	.133	.252	.424	.099
N=	1114	212	44	1115

Note: Omitted categories for year and region dummy variable sets are 1893–1895 and East South Central states (Kentucky, Tennessee, Alabama, Mississippi) respectively.

[a] $p < .05$ in a two-tailed test

[b] For a description of which states are included in each region see Appendix C.

TABLE 4.3

The Effect of Suffrage Organization Membership on Four Measures
of Success in Switzerland, 1926–1980

Variable Name	Regression Estimates (and Probability Values) for:			
	Introduction of Suffrage Bills	Support among Legislators	Support in Referenda	Adoption of Suffrage
Intercept	.046	.815	.243	.013
	(.275)	(.001)[a]	(.057)	(.527)
Suffrage Organization	.014	.035	.010	.006
Membership Index	(.121)	(.184)	(.508)	(.173)
Period Dummies				
Years: 1931–1940	−.010	−.270	−.084	−.001
	(.692)	(.234)	(.600)	(.936)
Years: 1941–1950	.048	.015	.018	.002
	(.073)	(.940)	(.876)	(.902)
Years: 1951–1960	.041	−.015	.113	.015
	(.130)	(.940)	(.337)	(.276)
Years: 1961–1970	.146	.122	.294	.033
	(.000)[a]	(.532)	(.011)[a]	(.016)[a]
Years: 1971–1980	.451	.313	.433	.488
	(.000)[a]	(.207)	(.001)[a]	(.000)[a]
Region Dummies[b]				
Appenzell/Ausserrhoden	−.075	−.501	−.272	−.068
and Innerrhoden	(.094)	(.023)[a]	(.004)[a]	(.003)[a]
Eastern Mountain	−.070	−.299	−.023	−.017
Cantons	(.079)	(.057)	(.769)	(.387)
French-speaking	.018	−.050	.153	.006
Cantons	(.696)	(.716)	(.091)	(.789)
German Urban Cantons	−.019	−.242	.035	−.010
	(.641)	(.045)[a]	(.613)	(.623)
German/French Cantons	−.018	.044	.183	−.005
	(.693)	(.774)	(.062)	(.818)
Other German Cantons	−.020	−.095	−.026	−.010
	(.606)	(.414)	(.712)	(.599)
F-Ratio:	11.941	2.055	7.029	38.136
	(p=.000)	(p=.041)	(p=.000)	(p=.000)
R-squared:	.118	.359	.725	.298
Adjusted R-squared:	.108	.184	.622	.291
N=	1089	57	45	1089

Note: Omitted categories for year and region dummy variable sets are 1926–1930 and Ticino, the Italian-speaking canton, respectively.

[a] $p < .05$ in a two-tailed test

[b] For a description of which cantons are included in each region see Appendix C.

the measure of membership and the first introduction are separated by more than two decades in most cases, it is misleading, given the changes in membership and suffrage organizations during this time, to include those 36 states in the analysis. It is also deceptive to analyze only the remaining 12 states. For one thing, these states do not constitute a large enough sample to conduct an analysis. Nor can one determine the real relationship between membership and first introductions when all the early introductions are excluded from the analysis. For this reason, I examine the connection of first introductions with membership only in Switzerland, where data on membership and first introductions overlap.

First introductions are measured by a dichotomous variable coded "one" in the year a canton considers full woman suffrage legislation for the first time.[15] These data are also not without problems. Ten out of the 25 cantons introduced full women's voting rights for the first time before 1926, the first year in which the mobilization index can be calculated. However, in 9 out of the 10 cantons, the first suffrage motions were considered within a decade of 1926. The tenth canton, St. Gallen, considered its first suffrage motion in 1912, 14 years before my mobilization index begins. Although the difference in timing between the first introductions and the membership measure in these 10 cantons may still create some error in the analysis, the error will be smaller than in the United States for two reasons. First, on average, the first motion for full woman suffrage in these cantons was introduced in 1918, only 8 years before the first measure of membership. Second, as Chapter 3 notes, membership levels were very stable in Switzerland. It is unlikely that the membership index would be far off 8 years later. Therefore, in these 10 cantons, the first year in the analysis is coded "one" to indicate that the first introduction had already occurred.

The results of the Swiss analysis (presented in Table 4.4) suggest that the size of woman suffrage organizations did not significantly affect the timing of the first suffrage bills. The regression coefficient for the membership index is not statistically significant. On the other hand, both region and time period are significant. In Switzerland, significantly fewer first motions for woman suffrage were likely to occur in the 1930s while significantly more were likely to be introduced in the 1970s. Moreover, the German-speaking cantons, including those which were partially Francophone, were significantly less likely to put a motion for women's enfranchisement on the agenda for the first time than the French-speaking cantons or Ticino, the Italian-speaking canton.

Thus, the relative size of local suffrage associations did not influence whether woman suffrage made it into the political agenda—either for the first time or ever. Although we cannot be absolutely sure of the role of

TABLE 4.4

The Effect of Suffrage Organization Membership on the First
Introduction of Woman Suffrage Legislation in
Switzerland, 1926–1980

Variable Name	Regression Estimates	Significance
Intercept	1.006	(.000)[a]
Suffrage Organization Membership Index	.008	(.708)
Period Dummies		
Years: 1931–1940	−.066	(.013)[a]
Years: 1941–1950	−.032	(.238)
Years: 1951–1960	−.056	(.058)
Years: 1961–1970	−.050	(.120)
Years: 1971–1980	.461	(.000)[a]
Region Dummies[b]		
Appenzell / Ausserrhoden and Innerrhoden	−.966	(.000)[a]
Eastern Mountain Cantons	−.958	(.000)[a]
French-speaking Cantons	−.016	(.942)
German Urban Cantons	−.889	(.000)[a]
German/French Cantons	−.863	(.000)[a]
Other German Cantons	−.919	(.000)[a]
F-Ratio:	14.247	(p=.000)
R-squared:	.504	
Adjusted R-squared:	.254	
N=	516	

Note: Omitted categories for year and region dummy variable sets are 1926–1930 and Ticino, the Italian-speaking canton, respectively.

[a] $p < .05$ in a two-tailed test

[b] For a description of which cantons are included in each region see Appendix C.

U.S. suffrage organizations in the first women's voting rights bills, small organizations appear to have been able to wield enough influence to put their legislation on the agenda. It did not require large numbers of dues-paying members to convince a single legislator to sponsor a motion to enfranchise women, or to acquire the necessary signatures for the initiative. Instead, women's voting rights bills were introduced in both countries largely in waves. As woman suffrage became topical during the 1910s in the United States, and in the 1960s and 1970s in Switzerland, local governments responded by considering legislation.

Legislative Support and Suffrage
Organization Membership

In both countries, achieving women's voting rights usually necessitated working through legislative institutions, which meant suffrage activists needed the support of legislators. Indeed, in the United States, lobbying legislators became a major tactic toward the end of the suffrage movement (see Chapter 6). Were suffrage associations with large memberships more successful in convincing state and cantonal legislators to support women's voting rights? To answer that question we must examine the effect that membership size had on votes for woman suffrage in legislatures.

Measuring Legislative Support
for Woman Suffrage

Legislative support for woman suffrage is measured by the percent of the legislators voting yes on full women's voting rights legislation in a specific year and state or canton. In Switzerland, cantons have unicameral parliaments, so the percent voting yes is easy to calculate; it is simply the number of legislators voting for full woman suffrage legislation divided by all legislators voting on the bill. However, in the United States, every state except Nebraska has a bicameral legislature. In addition, most states convened constitutional conventions from time to time to rewrite their constitutions. In any one year, a state may have had one, two, or three legislative bodies voting on full woman suffrage amendments.

I combine the decisions in different legislative bodies into a single indicator by totaling up all the yes and all the no votes on final ballots (usually the third reading) from the different legislative bodies and calculating the percent supporting woman suffrage bills from these totals. Computing legislators' support in this manner weights individuals in all three institutions equally. Alternatively, I could have given each legislative body equal weight by averaging the percent yes vote from each institution. Since most state senates have fewer members than state houses, this calculation would have given more weight to legislators in smaller assemblies. However, since we are interested in the ability of suffrage movements to convince legislators, I elected to weight each legislator equally.[16]

Because legislative votes were gleaned from secondary sources, the exact vote was often unavailable. This occurred in about one-third of the cases (88 out of 296 total legislative votes) in the United States and in 13 of the 66 legislative votes in Switzerland. However, the degree of support for the bill was frequently indicated by certain phrases: legislation passed or failed "unanimously," "with an overwhelming majority," or "with a one- or two-vote margin." In the analysis that follows, the vote in the legislature is estimated where such language permits. Each of these phrases were defined as a specific percent support (unanimous for = 100 percent, overwhelming majority for = 80 percent, suffrage passed = 60 percent, close vote both for and against = 50 percent, suffrage failed = 40 percent, overwhelming opposition = 20 percent, and unanimous against = 0 percent). Then, the approximate number of votes for suffrage was calculated based on the average number of legislators in the institution participating in other suffrage votes.[17]

Explaining Legislative Support for Suffrage Legislation

Since there were many more bills introduced in the United States, it is not surprising that there were also many more legislative votes. On average, over the 50 years of the woman suffrage movement (1870–1920), a vote on full woman suffrage legislation occurred in each state about once every eight years.[18] In Switzerland, on the other hand, legislators rarely voted on women's enfranchisement during the period between 1920 and 1980. Each canton considered a suffrage bill, on average, only once every 25 years. However, when the issue arose, local (and national) Swiss parliamentarians were more pro-suffrage than their U.S. counterparts. When women's enfranchisement was considered in state legislatures, only 55 percent of the members on average voted for women's enfranchisement. On the other hand, when Swiss cantonal parliaments considered women's voting rights (which was infrequently), over 70 percent of them cast their ballots in favor. Thus, while legislators were polled on more full woman suffrage bills in the United States, they were less supportive of woman suffrage than local Swiss legislators.[19]

Can the amount of legislative support be explained by the relative size of local suffrage associations? The statistical analyses presented in the second columns of tables 4.2 and 4.3 suggest not. The coefficients for per capita NAWSA membership and for the Swiss membership index are insignificant. As with introductions, suffrage organization membership does not influence the percentage of yes votes on woman suffrage bills in either country.

There are, however, regional differences in the percentage of yes votes in both state and cantonal legislatures. In the United States, legislators in the Pacific region (Washington, Oregon, and California) were stronger supporters of woman suffrage bills than representatives in other regions. In Switzerland, the two Appenzell cantons and the German-speaking cantons with large cities elected cantonal legislators who were, on average, less supportive of the enfranchisement of women. In the United States, state legislators were more receptive to women's voting rights bills between 1916 and 1920 than at other times. The percent of representatives voting for woman suffrage increased by more than 11 percent during this period. On the other hand, local legislators were less likely to endorse bills enfranchising women between the years 1906 and 1910, as the negative coefficient for these years shows.

Thus, the size of woman suffrage organizations also made no difference in eliciting legislative support of full woman suffrage legislation. However, converting elected representatives to the cause is a different process from swaying the public. While large suffrage associations were not necessary to convince state legislators, were they better able to persuade an entire electorate to support women's voting rights? To answer this question, let us examine the role of membership size in affecting woman suffrage referenda results.

Referenda on Woman Suffrage Amendments and Organization Membership

Fifty-seven suffrage referenda occurred within the 48 U.S. states in the 50 years spanning 1871 and 1920, averaging 0.02 referenda votes per state per year, or approximately one state referendum every year. In Switzerland, a total of 56 cantonal referenda over full women's voting rights were held between 1919 and 1990, averaging 0.03 votes per canton per year, or about four cantonal referenda every five years.[20]

Although the number of referenda in the two countries seems comparable, these figures are somewhat misleading. Because the 1971 national suffrage amendment was limited to national elections only, all cantons in Switzerland were required to hold at least one referendum in order to enfranchise women at the canton level. In fact, 20 of the 56 cantonal referenda in Switzerland were held *after* the national amendment was adopted in February of 1971. These referenda introduced local voting rights in cantons where women already had national suffrage. In the United States, any further activity at the state level was superfluous once the Nineteenth Amendment was ratified. As a result, 17 states never held any referenda on the question of women's voting rights. A better comparison, therefore, is to examine the number of referenda that occurred before the national suffrage amendments were adopted in the two countries.

In Switzerland, limiting the analysis to cantonal referenda before 1971 does not alter the average number of referenda per canton-year (it remains .03), but it does slightly reduce voter support for woman suffrage. The average yes vote in all 56 cantonal woman suffrage referenda is 51 percent, implying modest support for the enfranchisement of women. On the other hand, in the 36 referenda held before the national woman suffrage referendum in 1971, an average of 44 percent of the voters favored enfranchising women. In contrast, 46 percent of the voters supported women's voting rights amendments in the referenda held in the U.S. states. Thus, when comparing similar types of referenda in Switzerland and the United States, there is little difference in the overall levels of public support for woman suffrage. Public support in cantonal referenda prior to 1971 was only slightly lower than in the United States.

What role does membership size play in determining whether the electorate of a particular state or canton will endorse the enfranchisement of women? Not much, according to the regression results from the United States and Switzerland given in the third columns of Tables 4.2 and 4.3. As in the previous analyses, the relative number of members in a suffrage organization does not significantly influence the support for women's voting rights in referenda. Large suffrage associations were no better at converting Swiss or American voters to the suffrage cause than small ones. Region again plays a role in determining suffrage movement success in Switzerland and the United States. Voter support for woman suffrage referenda in Appenzell-Innerrhoden and -Ausserrhoden was at least 24 percentage points lower than in the other regions. In the United States, the only significant finding is that voters in South Atlantic states were significantly less supportive of women's voting rights than voters from Kentucky, Tennessee, Alabama, and Mississippi (the omitted states).

While voter approval of women's voting rights did not change significantly over time in the U.S., Swiss referenda held in the 1960s or 1970s received significantly more support than referenda held in other years. In fact, the coefficient for the 1970s indicates that the percentage of yes votes on woman suffrage amendments increased by over 40 percent. Since most of these referenda occurred simultaneous with, or immediately after, the 1971 national referendum, it is not surprising that voters in cantonal referenda voted in favor of enfranchising women.

Thus, as with the previous measures of success, voters' approval of women's enfranchisement is not affected by membership in suffrage organizations in Switzerland and the United States. Regional differences in both countries and the 1971 national referendum in Switzerland explain much of the variation in public support for suffrage referenda.

The Adoption of Woman Suffrage and
Suffrage Organization Membership

The previous analyses provide little support for the theory that size of the suffrage association's membership made a difference in the success of woman suffrage legislation. However, in the end, only the final goal—the enfranchisement of women—mattered. If membership influences the adoption of woman suffrage, then it is less important that it had no effect on these intermediate steps. For this reason, in this last section, I explore whether the passage of full woman suffrage legislation was associated with the size of suffrage organizations.

The timing of full women's voting rights adoption varied greatly within both countries. Wyoming, while still a territory, was the first to enfranchise women in 1870. When it became a state in 1890, it included woman suffrage in its state constitution. In contrast, when the Nineteenth Amendment was ratified in 1920, 17 states still had not adopted full voting rights for women. The average year of adoption of full woman suffrage legislation in the 48 American states was 1915. In Switzerland, the first canton passed full voting rights for women in 1959, with the majority of cantons adopting suffrage around 1971. Women in Appenzell Ausserrhoden and Appenzell Innerrhoden were the last to win cantonal voting rights for women (1989 and 1990 respectively). The average year for the adoption of full woman suffrage legislation in Swiss cantons was 1971.

For this analysis, the adoption of full woman suffrage is coded as "one" in the year in which the state or canton first adopted full woman suffrage legislation. After that year, I remove the state or canton from the data set as I did in the analyses of the introduction of legislation. In the United States, those states that still had not enfranchised women in 1920 are coded "zero" in every year.[21] Because the data only run up to 1980 in Switzerland, two cantons—Appenzell Innerrhoden and Appenzell Ausserrhoden—also are coded as never adopting women's voting rights.

In the United States, the results of these analyses (reported in the fourth column of Table 4.2) indicate that a relatively large per capita membership significantly increases the likelihood of a state suffrage association winning the vote. If an average-sized state organization (31 members per 100,000 inhabitants) could triple its membership (that is, increase to 93 members per 100,000), it would more than double its chances of achieving suffrage. However, the average probability of success is low to begin with; the average state had a 2 percent chance of achieving suffrage in a typical year. In absolute terms, the model suggests tripling an average suffrage organization's membership would only increase the probability of winning the vote from about 2 percent to 4.5 percent, other factors being equal.

Suffrage association membership continues to make no significant difference in the achievement of Swiss women's voting rights, as the results in the fourth column of Table 4.3 show. As before, the time and region dummy variables affect the likelihood of full suffrage legislation being passed. The two Appenzell cantons were significantly less likely to adopt full suffrage legislation. In addition, the analysis shows that the probability of women being enfranchised was stronger in the 1960s and 1970s than at other times. Some year and region variables also have a significant positive effect on the adoption of full woman suffrage in the United States. The mountain states—Colorado, Idaho, Montana, and Arizona—were significantly more likely to adopt women's voting rights than other states, as were states during the last five years of the suffrage battle.

Conclusion

These results suggest that resource mobilization—at least in terms of finances and followers—may not be as important as some theorists have suggested. While I was unable to rigorously analyze the effect of financial resources on movement success, the budgets of the SVF and the NAWSA differed in two ways. First, the United States suffrage organizations had a larger budget than their Swiss counterparts, suggesting that they were better able to succeed because of the financial resources available to them. Second, the spending priorities of the two organizations also differed; Swiss suffrage organizations saved more and spent less on cantonal campaigns or propaganda (even though they often budgeted for these things). Thus, even if resources do affect success, the tactical choices of the movements may mediate their effect.

Moreover, the size of cantonal suffrage organizations is unrelated to every measure of success. In the United States, the strength of organizational membership plays a role in the probability of the final achievement of full women's voting rights; yet, it makes no difference on the intermediate steps to woman suffrage. However, these intermediate steps are not merely indicators of partial success. As we explore in later chapters, the introduction of bills, the ensuing legislative action, and referenda may also be opportunities for suffrage organizations to engage in activities that will affect the final outcome. In particular, Swiss suffrage organizations undertook few activities unless a referendum was approaching or a motion was being considered. Thus, I argue in Chapter 7 that organizations that constantly initiated referenda on woman suffrage amendments were able, even in an otherwise hostile environment, to speed the passage of such legislation.

Why should the size of suffrage organizations affect the final outcome in the United States and not in Switzerland? One possibility is that Switzerland differs in some way that negates the effectiveness of suffrage organization resources. If this were true, Swiss suffrage activists would have little reason to utilize recruitment strategies like those of their American counterparts. Swiss suffrage organizations may have *chosen* not to invest efforts in increasing their numbers because they knew that the size of membership had no effect on their future success.

There is, however, little evidence from my interviews with Swiss suffrage activists to support this theory. The activists I interviewed rarely volunteered information about recruitment techniques, but when the topic was raised, almost all of them discussed recruitment as one of their goals and mentioned that their activities, such as the educational courses for women, facilitated this objective. Not one activist argued that the number of members was irrelevant. In fact, several activists complained that there were not enough new members to fill organization offices or to engage in propaganda activities.

The answer, I believe, is that recruitment tactics and not membership per se are driving this result. The statistical models presented above test only whether membership size is a resource that increases the likelihood of success. However, the recruitment activities in the United States had a number of additional intended and unintended effects. These included the reorganization of the state suffrage organizations and increased professionalism among state activists. Since these (and other) changes accompanied increases in membership size in the United States, membership and success may be only indirectly connected. Or, the relationship could be spurious: The tactics of suffrage organizations may have affected *both* the number of members and success. Since Swiss suffrage activists engaged in few, if any, of the same recruiting activities, membership size in Switzerland is *not* connected to success in the same manner.

In the next chapters, I focus more closely on some of the differences between the two countries as I explore the importance of political opportunity structures to the success and failure of both movements. In so doing, we will return as well to the influence of tactics, information, beliefs, and values on the achievement of women's voting rights in Switzerland and the United States.

5

BUILDING SUFFRAGE COALITIONS

S UFFRAGE MOVEMENTS did not act alone but in concert with, or opposition to, other organizations concerned with the politics of women's rights. Political opportunity structure theorists emphasize the role these other political actors can play in determining movement success and failure. Divisions among elites, the availability of potential allies, and the composition of ruling alignments may determine the character of pro- and anti-suffrage coalitions and, thereby the speed with which women were enfranchised. This chapter examines how the pro- and anti-suffrage alliances shaped the battle for woman suffrage in the United States and Switzerland.

The reaction of political actors to the woman suffrage issue varied with their influence in governmental institutions and their dependence on electoral support. The U.S. woman suffrage movement had numerous supporters who endorsed suffrage legislation and occasionally gave resources to the suffrage cause. The most important allies—temperance organizations, Populists, and the Progressive party—were groups that challenged the political system. While none of these groups were consistent in their support for the women's voting rights, their assistance provoked anti-suffrage activities among their opponents. In Switzerland, very few organizations besides opposition political parties were active participants in the suffrage debate. For this reason, the pro-suffrage alliance did not engender great opposition. Although women's organizations also allied with the Swiss suffrage movement, they were not as strong as their American counterparts. Nonetheless, they still influenced the timing of women's voting rights, especially in regions where the suffrage movement itself was weak or nonexistent.

In both countries, political parties in power were largely unwilling to shoulder the cause of suffrage. However, where pro-suffrage opposition parties became an electoral threat, ruling parties reacted by embracing woman suffrage as well. Because of the stability of Swiss voters and the nature of ruling coalitions, Swiss political parties were not as threatened by challenging parties and hence were slower to accept women's voting rights. However, the Swiss suffrage movement's allies did not generate an anti-suffrage coalition, thereby generally helping the suffrage cause. In brief, suffrage coalitions in both countries were different in their composition and possible influence on the timing of suffrage success. Therefore, this aspect of the political opportunity structure merits closer examination.

The Pro-Suffrage Coalition in the United States

In the United States, the pro-suffrage coalition included actors from the entire political spectrum: Republicans and Democrats, agriculture and labor, Mormon church leaders and Catholic priests. Women's groups of many types—including labor movement organizations and the Federation of Women's Clubs—became advocates of women's voting rights.

Nonetheless, these groups cannot be counted as staunch supporters. First, few of these organizations consistently supported women's enfranchisement. Within an organization, a few state sections might advocate suffrage while others would oppose it. The Arkansas and Florida sections of the Federation of Women's Clubs, for example, publicly endorsed woman suffrage legislation, while Georgia's auxiliary refused to support comparable measures (Stapler 1917). Similarly, teachers' associations in California and New York supported voting rights for women, while similar organizations in other states refused to take a stand on the issue (Harper 1922b). Other associations varied their stance over time, endorsing woman suffrage only in specific situations. For example, the Farmers' Alliance of South Dakota initially asked national suffrage leaders to run a campaign for a woman suffrage amendment in 1889 promising to do "all in our power to aid in woman's enfranchisement" (Reed 1958: 22). One year later, the Farmers' Alliance decided support of suffrage was inopportune and refused to endorse the suffrage amendment they had helped to place on the ballot.

Second, few organizations were sufficiently devoted to the enfranchisement of women to contribute substantial material resources to the suffrage battle. Some organizations occasionally contributed money to referendum campaigns, helped collect signatures on a woman suffrage petition, or lobbied government officials for a specific piece of legislation. Mostly, groups merely lent their name to the cause. For example, several labor unions, like the National Association of Letter Carriers and the Brotherhood of Locomotive Engineers, officially endorsed woman suffrage (Stapler 1917), but did not actively campaign or lobby for women's voting rights legislation or make financial contributions to the suffrage effort.

While none of the organizations supporting suffrage provided complete and unrestricted support for women's enfranchisement, three groups can be labeled stronger supporters. Temperance and prohibition activists (particularly the WCTU), Populists (particularly the Grange and the People's party), and the Progressive party were more consistently pro-suffrage and backed their endorsement with tangible resources. The public and, most importantly, their enemies perceived them to be inextricably linked to the suffrage movement. As a result, the liquor, railroad, and business interests aligned themselves with the anti-suffrage coalition.

Temperance Activists and Suffrage

The suffrage and temperance causes were intimately bound together from the beginning of the women's rights movement. While most of the literature on the connection between prohibition and suffrage focuses on the women's temperance organizations of the 1870s and 1880s (Blocker 1985a; Kraditor 1981), the connection between woman suffrage and prohibition began in the 1840s. During this early period, temperance work was accomplished mainly through associations headed by men, with women forming women's auxiliaries (Blocker 1985a). Indeed, Susan B. Anthony's organizing skills were first employed in trying to create additional women's auxiliaries—Daughter of Temperance lodges (Harper 1898, 1: 62). The first independent women's temperance organizations appeared in 1873 with the formation of the Women's Temperance Crusade (Blocker 1985a, 1985b).[1] Its successor, the Women's Christian Temperance Union (WCTU), was created the following year.

Despite the male-dominated leadership of early temperance organizations, a large minority of temperance activists advocated women's rights. Indeed, the issue of women's rights was hotly contested within temperance organizations as early as 1848 (see, for example, Stanton et al. 1881a: 472–513). Support for woman suffrage may have reflected the importance of women to the temperance movement; Blocker (1985a: 460) estimates that women constituted a third to a half of the movement's supporters. Moreover, even at this early date, Susan B. Anthony and other women temperance activists were turning to women's rights (Harper 1969, 1: 53).

By 1874, when the WCTU was created, woman suffrage was already associated with the temperance movement in the minds of many. The goals and ideas expressed within the WCTU coincided with the ideology of the women's rights and woman suffrage movement. The early Women's Crusaders and the early WCTU believed women should take an active role in the public sphere and promoted their formal political participation through demonstrations, petition drives, and lobbying (Blocker 1985b). Frances Willard, president of the WCTU from 1879 to 1897, developed the specific principle of "Home Protection": Temperance women must seek the ballot to protect their homes from "Demon Rum" (Earhart 1944). In 1880, the national WCTU endorsed the Home Protection Ballot. By 1883, the organization chose to advocate women's enfranchisement without specific reference to Home Protection.

The WCTU went well beyond mere endorsement and actively devoted itself to the achievement of woman suffrage legislation. Starting in 1880, the WCTU directed significant resources in the fight to enfranchise women. The national WCTU and many of its state sections had separate franchise departments that undertook suffrage propaganda work such as lectures, pamphlets, press work, and petitions (Baker 1991; Women's Christian Temperance Union ca. 1900). Earhart (1944) argues that the Franchise Department became the leading department within the national WCTU in the 1880s.

The WCTU became a major actor in the passage of suffrage legislation where suffrage organizations were weak or nonexistent. Between 1880 and 1890, the WCTU aided woman suffrage organizations in many states and fought alone for women's voting rights in others. Larger and better organized than the suffrage organizations, the WCTU of the 1880s was uniquely equipped to carry out suffrage campaigns or lobby legislatures. For example, the South Dakota WCTU spearheaded all woman suffrage campaigns from 1885 until the state suffrage organization was firmly in place in 1909 (Reed 1958). Even afterwards, the suffrage organization continued to be closely tied to the WCTU. Buechler (1986: 149) credits the Illinois WCTU with being the first to push a piece of women's voting rights legislation (a school suffrage measure) through the state legislature in 1891; the local suffrage organization backed a full suffrage bill in the same year, but it was defeated.

Finally, part of the bond between the two movements derived from the extensive overlap in the personnel of the WCTU and the woman suffrage organizations at the national and state levels (Blocker 1985a; McBride 1993; Paulson 1973; Rosenthal et al. 1985). Anna Howard Shaw, for example, had served as the head of the Franchise Department of the national WCTU in the 1880s before she became president of the National American Woman Suffrage Association (Earhart 1944). In Michigan, Iowa, Ohio, and West Virginia, woman suffrage and women's temperance organizations shared the same leaders (Blocker 1985a). Many suffrage activists with no organizational connection to the temperance movement publicly expressed sympathies with temperance goals. Even Abigail Scott Duniway, a well-known adversary of the WCTU who argued that temperance should be separated from the suffrage issue, had herself been active in the earlier temperance movement (Moynihan 1983: 139–47).

Despite intense support for women's voting rights by the national and many state WCTU's, not all state temperance organizations advocated the enfranchisement of women. In fact, during the WCTU's first five years (1873–1878) the suffrage cause was still recovering from the connections between Elizabeth Cady Stanton and Victoria Woodhull, who championed the cause of "free love," and the publicity surrounding the Beecher-Tilton affair (and the subsequent law suit). Conservative, Christian women were unable to support a cause associated with such scandal and "ridiculed by pulpit and press alike" (Earhart 1944: 148). Even as these controversies faded, temperance organizations in some southern states continued to oppose women's voting rights.[2] Because southern temperance activists believed woman suffrage would bolster arguments for the enfranchisement of blacks and give black women the vote, they refused to support women's voting rights. Indeed, in the South, arguments for prohibition were combined with disparaging remarks about African-American voters; for example, southern prohibitionists claimed that alcohol was used to buy black votes (Timberlake 1963). Within the Prohibition party, the strength of the suffrage plank vacillated with the relative importance of southern temperance supporters: "A weak suffrage plank indicated frenzied courting of white southern prohibitionists; a strong suffrage plank signaled rejection of white southerners in favor of reformist northern voters" (Blocker 1989: 87).

Although southern temperance activists spurned suffrage efforts and many suffrage and temperance activists attempted to disassociate the two causes, both proponents and opponents continued to link the two issues. The overlap in leaders, the extensive suffrage activities of the WCTU, widespread temperance sentiment among suffragists, and the WCTU's emphasis on women's political participation all helped to cement the causes together in the mind of opponents of both suffrage and prohibition.

Populists and Suffrage

Woman suffrage was also "long important in the [populist] reform movement and . . . inextricably linked in the minds of both their supporters and opponents" (Argersinger 1974: 162). Early Populist groups such as the Grange, Farmers' Alliances, and the Greenback party endorsed the enfranchisement of women (Marti 1991). In fact, the Farmers' Alliance and the Grange admitted women as full members in their organizations (Earhart 1944; Marti 1991), and the populist Kansas People's party even nominated a woman as one of its candidates at its first convention in 1890.

In several states, Populists played a crucial role in the battle for woman suffrage. In Colorado, a newly-elected Populist governor and Populist-

TABLE 5.1

Average Year of Adoption of Woman Suffrage in States by Populist Vote in 1892
and Populist/Democratic Fusion Vote in 1896 Presidential Elections

States with a Populist or Populist/Democratic Fusion Vote of:	1892 Election: Year Suffrage Adopted (Number of States)	1896 Election: Year Suffrage Adopted (Number of States)
Less than 30%	1918.3 (33)	1918.0 (6)
30% or more	1911.0 (9)	1917.1 (37)

dominated legislature voted overwhelmingly to hold a referendum on women's voting rights (Catt and Shuler 1926: 117). All local People's party organizations endorsed the enfranchisement of women in that campaign (as did a number of local Republican groups), and those districts where the People's party was strong also supported the woman suffrage amendment (Catt and Shuler 1926). In Kansas and Washington, Populist legislators introduced and passed woman suffrage constitutional amendments.

Table 5.1 provides additional evidence that Populists aided the suffrage cause. The table displays the average year in which woman suffrage was adopted in 42 states, broken down by party vote in the 1892 and 1896 elections.[3] In those states where the People's party received more than 30 percent of the vote in the presidential election of 1892, the average year in which women are enfranchised is 1911. In comparison, states where Populists received less support adopted women's voting rights, on average, in 1918.

However, Populist support for woman suffrage was not universal, particularly within the People's party. Southern Populists opposed the enfranchisement of women, in part because they believed that a suffrage plank would ruin the People's party's chances in the South (Shaw 1984). In addition, the fusion faction of the People's party was averse to committing to the suffrage battle for tactical reasons. Between 1890 and 1896, the People's party sent several representatives to Congress and won a large proportion of seats in the legislatures of several midwestern and western agricultural states. It posed a real challenge to Republican control in Colorado, Kansas, and Washington. However, its real power lay in being a spoiler party, splitting the vote and reducing Republican control in these areas. Fusionists' argued that the only hope for becoming a major political force lay in fusing with the Democratic party. However, this put the People's party in a weak bargaining position vis-à-vis the Democrats who demanded that the Populists abandon many of their original reforms. The movement was not strong enough to force the Democrats to yield to other platform changes, particularly those threatening to the Democratic South. As a result, fusionists tried to rid the People's party platform of many reforms—such as woman suffrage, prohibition, and black voting rights—that were repugnant to elements within the Democratic party. Conversely, the anti-fusion wing strongly held to the conviction that women's enfranchisement was an important tenet of Populist ideology, and could not be so easily abandoned.

The tactical strategy of the fusionists explains why the national and many state populist parties abandoned woman suffrage in the 1890s. The South Dakota People's party, created by the Farmers' Alliance and the Knights of Labor, repudiated its earlier stance supporting women's voting rights when it appeared detrimental (Catt and Shuler 1926). In California, where the People's and Democratic parties were fused, woman suffrage "was kept out of sight as much as possible" (Anthony and Harper 1902: 492) although many individual populists supported the cause. Similarly, after the Populist-dominated legislature in Kansas passed a woman suffrage constitutional amendment in 1894, the issue resurfaced at the People's party state convention: "Among the opponents of a supporting [suffrage] resolution were some . . . who believed an endorsement unnecessary and unwise, who may or may not have supported the right of women to vote, but who were certain an endorsement would cost the party badly needed Democratic support" (Clanton 1969: 153). In the end, the fusionists' attempt to reject the suffrage resolution or pass a compromise failed, but many Kansas Populists avoided visible activism during the referendum campaign.

Indeed, the relationship between the vote for the People's party and the timing of woman suffrage disappears when one looks at the Democratic fusion ticket of 1896 (see the second column in Table 5.1). States where 30 percent or more of the electorate voted for the Democratic fusion party in 1896 enfranchised women in 1917, while states where fusionists received less than 30 percent of the vote adopted woman suffrage in 1918. Compared to the difference in the first column of Table 5.1, this finding suggests that the People's party fusion with the Democrats in 1896 certainly did not aid the suffrage cause. In the end, Populist support of woman suffrage was more tentative than that of the temperance movement. Although early Populist organizations like the Grange urged the enfranchisement of women, fusion with the Democrats attenuated the connection between populism and woman suffrage, as many fusionists de-emphasized women's voting rights (sometimes in spite of their personal beliefs) in order to champion populism by allying with a stronger political party.

Progressives and Suffrage

Like the early Populists, the Progressive party, many progressive organizations, and their leaders advocated woman suffrage.[4] Working to improve social conditions in the cities, increase the health and safety of working women and children, and control political corruption, they argued that the enfranchisement of women could help their cause. Organizations like the National Purity Congress and the Women's Trade Union League endorsed, and in many cases fought for, voting rights for women (Schneider and Schneider 1993; Stapler 1917). Woman suffrage was particularly important to the Progressive party. When the Progressive party developed in California in 1910, it included a pledge to submit a woman suffrage amendment to the voters of California on its platform. Later, the 1912 platform of the national Progressive party endorsed voting rights for women (Johnson and Porter 1973). Progressive senators and representatives uniformly advocated women's voting rights in the U.S. Congress. Unlike the People's party, the Progressive party showed no inclination to reduce its official support for suffrage in order to garner more votes.

Several suffrage activists also played a prominent role in the Progressive party campaign of 1912. The party allowed women to serve on national committees and as delegates to party conventions. Jane Addams, a vice-president of the National American Woman Suffrage Association (NAWSA), gave the speech seconding Theodore Roosevelt's nomination as the Progressive party's presidential candidate. Although the NAWSA continued to claim nonpartisan status during this election, numerous suffrage officers on the state level campaigned vigorously for the Progressive party in 1912 because of their suffrage plank (although many also favored other aspects of their platform, such as direct democratic reforms, child labor laws, and government regulation of industry). The connections between the Progressive party and individual suffrage leaders were so strong that some members of the NAWSA attempted to pass a resolution requiring officers of the organization to remain strictly nonpartisan. However, delegates at the annual convention decided that nonpartisanship could be maintained without restricting officers' political freedom (Harper 1922b: 342).

The connection between the progressive and woman suffrage movements also translated into support for woman suffrage legislation on the state level. For example, the adoption of the 1913 presidential suffrage bill in Illinois resulted from the central role Progressive representatives played in the state legislature's balance of power (Harper 1922b). The success of suffrage amendments in the states of Washington, California,

TABLE 5.2

Average Year of Adoption of Woman Suffrage in States by Progressive Vote
in Presidential Election of 1912

States with a Progressive Party Vote of:	Year Suffrage Adopted	Number of States
Less than 25%	1919.0	23
25% or more	1917.1	19

Oregon, Arizona, and Kansas was due in large part to progressive influences in their state legislatures (Harper 1922a). Table 5.2 verifies that the adoption of woman suffrage was quicker in progressive states; states where the Progressive party received more than 25 percent of the vote in the 1912 presidential election were two years earlier in enfranchising women than their nonprogressive counterparts.[5]

The Progressive party also exercised greater influence on the platforms of the two major parties than the populist People's party. Progressive activists initially worked within the two major political parties, although most well-known progressive leaders were connected to the Republicans.[6] Even before the Progressive party was established, progressive factions within the existing parties managed to significantly alter the face of state politics by focusing on the election of progressive candidates. For example, in California progressive Republicans organized a campaign for progressive candidates within the G.O.P. before a separate party was founded (Mowry 1951). Once the Progressive party was created, it held the balance of power in several states and won a number of seats in the U.S. Congress. More importantly, the Progressive party proved that its platform and candidates could break the two major parties' dominance in a presidential election. In the election of 1912, the Progressives split the Republican party and ended over 15 years of Republican control of the presidency, a feat the People's party never managed.

The Progressive party's success led to changes in the two major parties. Catt and Shuler (1926) argue that the suffrage plank of the Arizona Progressive party in 1912 compelled state Republicans and Democrats to endorse a suffrage amendment. After the 1912 presidential elections, Democrats and Republicans tried to counter the third-party threat by including on their 1916 platforms such progressive policies as the regulation of business, civil service reform and, for the first time, woman suffrage (albeit based on a states rights principle). Even long-time suffrage activists like Catt and Shuler interpreted the platform changes as a consequence of the Progressive electoral menace: "The Republican machine was broken or out of repair in most of the States where campaigns were pending and the strong attitude of the new minority party presented a warning to both old parties to treat the suffrage question with fairness" (1926: 239–40).

While many other organizations and movements participated in the battle for woman suffrage during its more than 70-year history, these three groups—temperance unions, populist organizations, and Progressives—were the most vocal and visible, and their participation is linked to the timing of women's enfranchisement. However, they also produced a backlash from several wealthy and powerful interests.

The Anti-Suffrage Coalition in the United States

The anti-suffrage coalition in the United States largely consisted of groups reacting to these suffrage allies. The temperance organizations' support spurred liquor and beer manufacturers to oppose women's enfranchisement. Manufacturing and railroad interests, concerned about suffrage connections to the anti-monopolistic and socially concerned progressive and populist movements, objected to women's voting rights legislation. Political machines feared the progressive governmental reforms, which were endorsed by many suffrage activists. The contributions of suffrage allies were not only positive but also negative to the extent they provoked their enemies into the anti-suffrage camp.

The development of this powerful anti-suffrage coalition occurred mainly after 1885. Prior to this, anti-suffrage sentiment was widespread. Early suffrage opponents were not just against women voting, they were amazed that people would even consider such a thing. By 1885, however, suffrage was a legitimate issue; two territories had enfranchised women and numerous states were considering some sort of suffrage legislation. Suffrage opponents now seriously contemplated the consequences of women voting. Fearing that the pro-suffrage alliance indicated women's future voting trends, adversaries of temperance, populism, and progressivism mobilized.

Anti-Temperance Actors

Prior to 1885, liquor and brewing interests engaged in little anti-suffrage activity. In fact, the first three volumes of the *History of Woman Suffrage* (Stanton et al. 1881a, 1881b, 1886), which cover the period until 1885, do not even mention the liquor and beer industry, although later volumes emphasize the role of these groups especially in state referenda campaigns (Anthony and Harper 1902; Catt and Shuler 1926; Harper 1922a, 1922b). Thus, according to the suffrage activists' own history, the liquor and brewing industry only entered suffrage battles after the WCTU began to support women's enfranchisement. While these accounts must be read with a critical eye, activists' claims about the role of alcohol-related industries are often verified in the press accounts of the time and a few state and Congressional investigative committee reports (see Catt and Shuler 1926: 135, for some of these sources).

The liquor lobby was well organized and had considerable resources at its disposal. Almost all businesses connected to the manufacture and sale of alcoholic beverages were members of one of the associations of liquor dealers or brewers, allowing them to quickly mobilize to battle suffrage legislation. These organizations controlled large sums of money, which were often used in anti-suffrage campaigns. Thus, a 1918 Senate Judiciary Committee investigation reported that state and national Brewers' Associations normally taxed member brewers about 1 cent for each barrel produced. During political campaigns brewers often paid additional dues, up to 65 cents per barrel (cited in Catt and Shuler 1926: 138).

Suffrage activists also claimed that liquor and brewing interests were able to control a large number of votes. For example, in the 1906 Oregon woman suffrage referenda, the Brewers' and Wholesale Liquor Dealers' Association sent cards to all retailers instructing them to "take twenty-five friendly voters to the polls on election day" (Catt and Shuler 1926: 125). In several state campaigns, particularly those in Michigan and Ohio, suffrage activists accused liquor interests of buying votes and fixing election returns (Harper 1922b).

In addition, the brewing and liquor interests mobilized immigrant populations to vote against woman suffrage amendments. One immigrant organization, the German-American Alliance, was specifically linked to anti-temperance forces. Formed in 1901 and largely concentrated in Midwestern states, this organization numbered 2.5 million members in over 10,000 branches at its peak. Catt and Shuler (1926) argue that the organization's most influential members were German brewers and that much of its finances came from the liquor and brewing interest groups. In several referenda, including those in Michigan, Nebraska, and Ohio, the German-American Alliance actively encouraged its members to vote against woman suffrage. Catt and Shuler (1926) claim that the Alliance mobilized its members to become naturalized and register to vote in order to cast their ballots against women's voting rights. They even suggest that the organization, financed by anti-temperance groups, paid the costs of naturalization and registration for immigrants.

Much of the anti-suffrage literature of the German-American Alliance emphasized the connection between suffrage and prohibition. In Michigan, for example, the circular issued by the German-American Alliance spelled out the evils of woman suffrage: "If the suffrage would be laid into the hands of the native-born American woman . . . prohibitionists and their refuse, the Anti-Saloon League, will easily set up for dictators in the State of Michigan" (quoted in Catt and Shuler 1926: 184–85). Similarly, the German-American Alliance in the Nebraska campaign of 1913 argued: "Our opponents desire the right of suffrage mainly for the purpose of saddling the yoke of prohibition on our necks" (quoted in Harper 1922b: 377). Thus, the German-American Alliance perceived a link between the suffrage and the temperance movement which inspired, at least in part, their anti-suffrage stance.

In the end, Catt and Shuler (1926) blame the liquor interests for the loss of many state referenda on woman suffrage amendments and for the inability to get such amendments to a vote in other states. They estimate that just one of the anti-temperance interests, the United States Brewers' Association, contributed millions of dollars to anti-suffrage campaigns. Regardless of whether immigrant organizations like the German-American Alliance were fronts for the liquor and brewing industry as suffrage activists believed, or independently rejected the enfranchisement of women, their hostility to prohibition motivated their anti-suffrage activities.

Anti-Populist and Anti-Progressive Actors

If suffrage activists claimed liquor and brewing interests were the main impediment in their struggle for the vote, they also noted the presence of anti-populist and anti-progressive interests in the anti-suffrage coalition.

Some railroad companies, the main targets of the populists anti-monopoly efforts, publicly opposed woman suffrage legislation. During a 1913 Nebraska referendum, the wife of an attorney for the Northern Pacific Railroad appealed to Catholics to vote against the suffrage amendment because it was backed by Socialists and feminists (Harper 1922b: 376). In New Hampshire, an Investigating Commission found that the Boston and Maine Railroad spent a considerable amount of money to prevent the inclusion of woman suffrage in the 1912 revision of the state constitution (New Hampshire Public Service Commission Report of 1916, cited in Catt and Shuler 1926: 153).

Similarly, manufacturing interests found reasons to fight against suffrage legislation. Not only had woman suffrage activists played an extensive role in the Progressive party, local women's organizations also endorsed laws limiting women's working hours, restricting child labor, and setting minimum wages for women (McDonagh and Price 1985; Ryan 1992; Skocpol 1992). Given the activity of women's organizations in these progressive causes, manufacturing interests had reason to fear what women would do once they were allowed to vote, even though manufacturing interests approved of prohibition because it improved the quality and efficiency of the workforce (McDonagh and Price 1985).

The result was that manufacturing and business interests often opposed woman suffrage legislation. After the 1913 Montana referendum, one activist reported that "The Amalgamated Copper Company, striving to defeat the workmen's compensation act . . . had put on the petticoat and bonnet of the organized female anti-suffragists" (Harper 1922a: 421). An appeal against suffrage signed by the men who formed the Nebraska Men's Association Opposed to Woman Suffrage also indicates that opposition was heavily concentrated among railroad and business interests. The 30 signatories included eight men associated with railroads, seven in the banking industry, and eight who owned or managed businesses (Harper 1922b). In contrast, of the 21 national organizations run by men which endorsed woman suffrage in 1917, 20 were labor groups; only one, the National Street Railway Association, could be construed as representing business or manufacturers (Stapler 1917).

Leaders of urban political machines also sought to deny women the vote. Many suffrage activists claimed their opposition stemmed not so much from their fear of women voters' potential role in governmental reform as from the influence of liquor interests in their area. Hence, Catt and Shuler (1926) claim that bosses of urban political machines worked in concert with liquor interests to defeat suffrage legislation. For example, they blame New Jersey's James Nugent and New York's Tammany Hall for defeating state women's voting rights amendments in 1915. They also attribute New York's successful referendum campaign in 1917 to Tammany Hall's decision to end its fight against woman suffrage.

Republicans and Democrats

Given the powerful interests, including urban political machines, opposing women's voting rights, one wonders why the two major political parties were not more active in the anti-suffrage coalition. As already mentioned, the national Republican and Democratic parties did not explicitly endorse woman suffrage until 1916. The closest thing to a suffrage plank occurred in the Republican party platforms of 1872 and 1876, which praised the work of women and argued that demands for additional rights "should be treated with respectful consideration" (quoted in Johnson and Porter 1973: 47). However, this ambiguous plank did not compel support for women's rights, and after 1876 it disappeared from the platform.

This left individual politicians and local parties free to determine their own stance on the issue. Both Republicans and Democrats tended to endorse woman suffrage in states where the Progressive or People's parties made electoral gains. Republican party support was generally stronger since it was at greater risk of losing activists to populist (and later, progressive) parties. However the party contained both pro-suffrage and anti-suffrage factions. Enemies of populist and progressive activists also had standing within the Republican party and often controlled party leadership. Progressive and populist activists' potential departure from the party was one piece of leverage that countered the influence of the more powerful and better endowed railroad, business, and political machine interests in deciding about a suffrage plank. Thus, despite differing opinions within the Republican party, in states where the People's or Progressive parties successfully challenged Republican dominance, it was persuaded to endorse women's enfranchisement.

However, Republican party endorsements of women's voting rights rarely translated into active assistance. For example, California Republicans recommended passage of the 1896 woman suffrage referendum but did little to mobilize its voters. Aggregate data suggest that Republican voters did not necessarily follow the party line; Republican counties voted against woman suffrage in the 1896 California referendum despite the party's endorsement (Catt and Shuler 1926).

The Democrats were less threatened by division on the woman suffrage issue. Anti-suffrage sentiment was more widespread in the Democratic party because of the strong Southern bloc that remembered the suffrage movement's historical tie to abolition. More importantly, the southern faction feared women's enfranchisement would lead to greater scrutiny of southern institutions that disenfranchised blacks. Given its southern constituency, it is not surprising that no state Democratic party endorsed suffrage before 1912. Even the electoral threat of populism did little to alter the Democratic party's stance. While several southern states, like Alabama, Georgia, and Mississippi, were strongholds of populism, southern populism took on a very different character. The farming interests of the rural south which joined the Grange and supported the People's party were attracted by populism's economic reforms and did not advocate voting rights for women. Thus, not only were populist (and later progressive) factions less numerous within the Democratic party, they also were not advocates of woman suffrage. Widespread defection to third parties could not, therefore, be reduced by adding a suffrage plank to the Democrat's platform.

Democratic party stances on suffrage changed slightly after 1912. In states where the Republican party supported the enfranchisement of women, the local Democratic parties followed suit. Yet, even after the national Democratic party added a suffrage plank to its platform in 1916, some southern state Democratic parties refused to sanction voting rights for women.

In the end, it is probably inaccurate to categorize the major parties as political actors which joined pro- or anti-suffrage coalitions. Rather, the parties served as battlefields upon which specific factions fought for control. The Republican party, and to a lesser extent, the Democratic party had no overarching reasons to endorse or oppose women's voting rights. Rather, they followed the prevailing winds. Electoral threats from third parties might lead them to adopt a suffrage plank. Local parties that actively opposed women's voting rights were often controlled by interests that were hostile toward abolitionist, temperance, populist, or progressive groups. Thus McDonagh (1989), analyzing Congressional roll-call votes, finds partisanship played a much smaller role in determining support for the Nineteenth Amendment than state-level constituencies. Only when pro-suffrage minor parties threatened Democratic or Republican hegemony did they endorse women's enfranchisement.

The Pro-Suffrage Coalition in Switzerland

The pro- and anti-suffrage coalitions in Switzerland differed considerably from those in the United States. None of the political actors engaged in the Swiss battle proved to be as zealous as the allies and opponents of suffrage in the United States. Instead, other women's organizations, opposition parties and organizations, and center/right political parties provided limited or occasional support for woman suffrage. However, for a number of reasons, the activities of these groups did not inspire a vehement counterreaction among other organizations. Thus, the anti-suffrage coalition in Switzerland, unlike that in the United States, was not a conglomeration of groups worried about the effect of woman suffrage on their particular interest. The Swiss woman suffrage movement suffered from a lack of strong allies but benefitted from the resulting dearth of strong enemies as well.

Women's Organizations

The Schweizerischer Verband für Frauenstimmrecht (SVF) was not the only women's organization that fought for woman suffrage. In fact, almost all of the Swiss women's organizations participated in at least one woman suffrage referendum campaign. Even those organizations that were officially devoted solely to charitable causes or social functions occasionally gave money to a cantonal woman suffrage action committee or endorsed a cantonal suffrage amendment. For example, the Luzern section of the Schweizerischer Gemeinnützige Frauenverein, a charitable women's organization, joined a cantonal action committee for woman suffrage although other local sections were known for their refusal to take stands on women's political issues (Vonwyl 1988). Nonetheless, three types of women's organizations—federations of women's groups such as cantonal women's centers and the Bund Schweizerischer Frauen-organisationen, women's associations within political parties, and women's religious organizations—were strong advocates of women's enfranchisement in both national and cantonal struggles.

On the cantonal level, the shape of a pro-suffrage coalition depended on whether an active suffrage organization existed. In cantons that lacked suffrage organizations, these other women's organizations created and staffed pro-suffrage action committees during referenda. In Graubünden, where only a few individuals were members of the SVF, the Frauenzentrum actively fought for woman suffrage; in Zug, the main proponents were the women's sections of the Freisinnig-Demokratische Partei (FDP) and the Sozialdemokratische Partei (SP). Where suffrage organizations existed, other women's organizations sometimes united with them in order to build public support. However, these united fronts do not appear to have helped the suffrage cause much. To understand why, we need to explore the goals of these other women's organizations and the nature of their participation.

BUND SCHWEIZERISCHER FRAUENORGANISATIONEN

On the national level, most women's organizations were united in the Bund Schweizerischer Frauenorganisationen (BSF), created in 1900 (Woodtli 1983).[7] The BSF actively endorsed women's enfranchisement from the time of its founding until the late 1920s and then again after World War II. Although the BSF donated money to the two national referenda campaigns and to some cantonal campaigns, its most important contribution in the later years was probably the creation of the Arbeitsgemeinschaft der schweizerischen Frauenverbände für die politischen Rechte der Frau.[8] The BSF's 1957 commission on woman suffrage recommended that the various women's organizations consolidate their activities. The Arbeitsgemeinschaft, which united 40 groups in this effort, provided much of the propaganda in the 1959 national suffrage campaign and coordinated the activities of individual organizations. After this first referendum was defeated, the Arbeitsgemeinschaft continued to serve as a clearinghouse for pamphlets, brochures, and other information utilized by pro-suffrage organizations.

While BSF championed women's rights in its first two decades, its pro-suffrage activities in the 1950s were more reactive than proactive. For example, the BSF established the Arbeitsgemeinschaft only after the Bundesrat proposed a suffrage referendum. The actions that the BSF took on its own—endorsements of suffrage motions and contributions to referendum campaigns—were responses to legislative proposals in the Nationalrat (1919 and 1945), the Bundesrat, or the Governing Councils of cantonal governments.[9] When women's voting rights were not being considered in federal or cantonal governments, the BSF did not raise the issue or engage in pro-suffrage activities. As a national organization with no local auxiliaries, the BSF also did little at the cantonal level beyond encouraging and aiding existing local groups.

WOMEN'S PARTY ORGANIZATIONS

The women's auxiliaries of Swiss political parties were unanimous in their endorsement of women's voting rights. Yet, this unanimity is less impressive when one considers that not all parties had women's auxiliaries. Those parties opposed to woman suffrage, such as the Schweizerische Volkspartei (SVP), did not encourage the formation of women's auxiliaries. In contrast, the Communists and Socialists had incorporated women into their parties in the 1920s. The Landesring der Unabhängigen (LdU), a small reform party that always supported the enfranchisement of women, had women's groups from its creation in 1935. The Freisinnig-Demokratische party (FDP), an occasional advocate of suffrage, also organized some local women's groups as early as 1940, although in many cantons they were first created in the 1960s.

Since the political parties that developed women's groups tended to favor women's participation in politics, it is not surprising that their women's organizations endorsed women's voting rights. As one suffrage activist noted: "Most of the FDP women's group would have found it strange if the members had been anti-suffrage since the purpose of the group was to participate in politics" (interview of June 27, 1988).[10] In encouraging women's participation in politics, these groups also strengthened public support for women's enfranchisement. Women's party organizations usually joined cantonal action committees and contributed money in support of woman suffrage referenda. In most cantons, women's party organizations participated in suffrage activities initiated by other women's groups.

However, in a few cantons, women's party organizations became a leading influence in the suffrage battle. For example, pro-suffrage activity in Zug started in the 1960s when some FDP leaders encouraged their wives to form a women's party organization. Prior to this, there was very little debate over whether women should vote, and during the 1959 suffrage referendum, no pro-suffrage cantonal action committee was organized. It was the FDP women's association which, after 1969, sponsored lectures on woman suffrage and women in political life, organized the cantonal action committee in the 1971 referendum, and sponsored the only street action in Zug: the distribution of chocolate hearts with stickers asking men to vote for suffrage.

This example illustrates the limitations of women's party organization. These groups were primarily party auxiliaries, formed at the behest of male party leaders. As a result, many women's party auxiliaries appeared relatively late in the suffrage movement, and then only when the parties themselves were already willing to support women's participation in politics. Once on the scene, their purpose was to convince women to become active in party politics. The organizations promoted all forms of political activity for women, especially participation in commissions, community politics, and the development of policy. Women's enfranchisement was only a small part of their larger purpose, and often suffrage activity was subsumed within education encouraging women's participation in the public sphere.

WOMEN'S CENTERS

If women's party organizations' main interests lay elsewhere, that was even more true for local women's centers (*Frauenzentrum*). In 18 cantons, local women's organizations joined together in cantonwide women's centers, almost all of which predate the 1959 suffrage referendum. These cantonal women's centers incorporated social clubs, like sewing circles and associations for young mothers, and political women's organizations, like SVF sections and women's party auxiliaries. Tension about whether and how actively the center should endorse women's voting rights was common, and, consequently, the stances of these centers varied widely.

Some cantonal women's centers (including those in Basel, Genève, Graubünden, and Luzern) were at the forefront of campaigns for woman suffrage referenda. They not only endorsed suffrage but also contributed money, joined action committees, and organized events to publicize the cause. The Basel-land women's center, for example, set up streetside tables to distribute free apples and suffrage propaganda. Women's center leaders also lectured and wrote newspaper and magazine articles advocating women's voting rights. Thus, some women's centers promoted women's enfranchisement as actively as many suffrage organizations. However, many other women's centers preferred to shun politics and refused to take a stand on woman suffrage, although individual members might disagree. Thus, in one small canton: "The leader of the women's center was worried if she did something too political. . . . Although the head of the center was in a commission [to work on woman suffrage legislation], she always required that the minutes show that she was representing only her personal opinion, and not that of the organization" (interview of April 22, 1988). As a result, this center never supported local suffrage efforts.

Women's centers' support of suffrage depended on the politics within the organizations and whether member groups were interested in women's voting rights or politics in general. When internal politics allowed, a women's center could be active in the battle for woman suffrage, although usually the issue created internal strife. When the member groups were apolitical, the women's centers refused to support woman suffrage. As one suffrage activist sympathized: "I also understand why it was difficult for them to support suffrage since they were an organization of very different groups—singing and athletic groups—people that were absolutely not interested in politics" (interview of May 19, 1988).

Like women's party organizations, women's centers had a much wider mission than the enfranchisement of women. Women's centers were created to coordinate the activities of the member associations; inform women on social, economic and political problems; and represent women's interests to cantonal and national government (Nanchen 1985). Because they engaged in this wide variety of educational, charitable, and emissarial activities, and because women's enfranchisement was controversial, women's centers only became involved (if they became involved at all) after suffrage legislation was already being considered by national or local governments. Even then, their pro-suffrage activity consisted mainly of education for women or small propaganda efforts, like the tables with free apples in Basel-land.

WOMEN'S RELIGIOUS ORGANIZATIONS

Women's religious organizations differed from women's centers and women's party organizations in that their official agendas did not include women's incorporation into political life or the representation of women's political interests. Nonetheless, several women's religious organizations participated in the campaigns for woman suffrage. The Catholic women's organization, the Schweizerischer Katholischer Frauenbund (SKF), joined the Arbeitsgemeinschaft in 1957. In 1958, it passed a resolution supporting women's enfranchisement despite the objections of the bishop assigned to act as its spiritual advisor. Protestant women's organizations also appear on the rosters of cantonal action committees for suffrage legislation. The Protestant Women's Federation and the Federation of Jewish Women's Clubs were both members of the 1959 national action committee.

Of the women's religious organizations, the SKF was perhaps the most important to the suffrage battle for a number of reasons. First, it was the largest and oldest of the women's religious organizations (Nanchen 1985). Second, it played a very prominent role in the Catholic mountain cantons of eastern Switzerland. These cantons never developed women's centers; instead, different Catholic women's groups united under the umbrella of the SKF, making it the largest women's organization. Because these cantons also lacked sections of the SVF, Catholic women's organizations, mainly the SKF and STAKA, became the only potential locus for women's support of suffrage.

On the other hand, the SKF was even less able to integrate support of women's voting rights into its organizational goals than other women's groups. The SKF, which included all Catholic organizations from sports clubs to professional women's groups, sought to coordinate and facilitate women's activity in religious life as well as to represent their interests in public life. Thus, like women's centers, cantonal SKF organizations were only marginally concerned with women's political participation. However, the SKF faced an additional obstacle: For much of its history the church itself exercised considerable influence, in large part through the bishop assigned to provide spiritual guidance to the organization (Mesmer 1988; interview of December 15, 1987). Given the formal role of the church in the SKF, it is not surprising that the national SKF only became more supportive of woman suffrage in the 1950s after the Catholic church accepted women's active participation in politics. A clear change in the Catholic church's attitude occurred in October 1945, when Pope Pius XII met with leaders of Italian women's organizations and told them that it was their duty to engage in politics (Ruckstuhl 1986). Many of the Catholic activists I interviewed noted that this was a turning point for the Swiss church as well.

While some cantonal women's centers or women's party auxiliaries led the fight for women's voting rights in their areas, cantonal SKF sections did not. In Fribourg/Freiburg and Luzern, the local SKF worked with other organizations in action committees and endorsed woman suffrage legislation. In others, the SKF remained silent on the issue. The closest the SKF came to championing the suffrage cause was in Uri. Overwhelmingly Catholic, Uri lacked a suffrage organization, a women's center, or women's party organizations. There were simply no other women's organizations to lead the battle for women's enfranchisement. Nonetheless, the SKF did not organize an action committee or actively endorse the cantonal suffrage amendment considered in 1972. In fact, its only action was to sponsor courses educating women about politics after women were enfranchised.

The Effect of Other Women's Organizations on the Pro-Suffrage Coalition

Although women's party groups, women's centers, and women's religious associations all engaged in the suffrage battle at various times, they never became as influential as the WCTU in the United States. For one thing, woman suffrage never played a major role in the activities or goals of these associations. While the WCTU had very large and active national and local Franchise Departments, woman suffrage activity was a small portion of the activities of the Swiss groups, which were, for the most part, active only during referenda. Since referenda were infrequent, these groups never became linked to the cause of woman suffrage. Moreover, pro-suffrage action committees were always carefully designed to represent as many interests as possible. In addition to increasing monetary resources and womanpower, building large action committees "was also a matter of building public opinion. . . . The point is that when a number of organizations unite they have greater weight than a single organization. If the newspapers report that the woman suffrage organization handled a problem together with other organizations, that is not only educational but says something to the public. It counters the argument that it is only a minority who support suffrage" (interview of January 21, 1988). For that reason, if an organization would not officially join the action committee, suffrage supporters attempted to recruit at least one prominent individual from the organization to include on its list of supporters. Because action committees included many different interests, other women's organizations were never linked to the suffrage cause in the eyes of the public or other political organizations.

Surprisingly, where other women's organizations were heavily involved in the suffrage issue, the result was not always positive. To examine the effect these organizations had on the timing of suffrage, I begin with the German-speaking Swiss cantons because some organizations were only active there. I classify the cantons according to the characteristics of the pro-suffrage coalition: (1) cantons where no women's organization worked for woman suffrage before 1972, (2) cantons where the SVF was nonexistent but other women's organizations were active, (3) cantons where other women's organizations provided little or no aid to the local SVF section, and (4) cantons with alliances between the local SVF section and other women's organizations (see Table 5.3).[11]

In those cantons where there were no suffrage organizations, woman suffrage was adopted earlier if other women's organizations advocated the enfranchisement of women. However, the activities of other women's organizations do not completely compensate for the lack of a woman suffrage organization. Cantons with a local SVF section enfranchised

TABLE 5.3

Type of Involvement of Women's Organizations by Year Cantonal Woman Suffrage Legislation Passed (in German-speaking Cantons Only)

	Canton	Year Passed
No organization before 1972	Appenzell Ausserrhoden	1989
	Appenzell Innerrhoden	1990
	Uri	1972
Average Year of Passage		**1983.7**
No Suffrage Organization	Schwyz	1972
in Canton: Other Women's	Obwalden	1972
Organizations Active	Nidwalden	1972
	Glarus	1971
	Zug	1971
	Graubünden	1972
Average Year of Passage		**1971.7**
No Coalition Formed Between	Solothurn	1971
SVF and Other Women's	Basel-stadt	1966
Organizations	Schaffhausen	1971
	St. Gallen	1972
Average Year of Passage		**1970.0**
Coalition Formed Between SVF	Basel-land	1968
and Other Women's	Bern	1971
Organizations	Luzern	1970
	Zürich	1970
	Aargau	1971
	Thurgau	1971
Average Year of Passage		**1970.2**

women a year and a half before those cantons with no SVF section but where other women's organizations were active. Given that these groups had other goals, it is to be expected that their active support was only a partial substitute for the presence of a suffrage organization.[12]

What is surprising is that the combined efforts of women's organizations and the SVF did *not* speed the adoption of women's voting rights. Those cantons where other women's organizations actively worked with the woman suffrage organizations enfranchised women at the same time (on average) as those where woman suffrage organizations acted alone. Thus, Table 5.3 suggests that the organizations' contributions of resources and as opinion leaders were less important where the SVF existed, despite their significance elsewhere. Before we can explain this puzzle, we need to examine the role of several other organizations in the pro- and anti-suffrage coalitions.

Political Parties and Organizations

In Switzerland, political parties were much more active in woman suffrage referenda than parties in the United States, notwithstanding the activities of the Progressive and People's parties. Swiss political parties often initiated referenda on their own accord, and in many cantons they became the driving force behind woman suffrage. Swiss parties similarity to U.S. parties (and differences to most western European parties) was important in this respect. The freedom to issue their own programs allowed cantonal party organizations to contradict the national party on the question of votes for women, as state parties did in the United States. Moreover, since Swiss parties did not exercise discipline over party members, individual politicians were free to oppose their parties' program. For example, Dr. Peter von Roten introduced a motion for woman suffrage in 1949 even though his Catholic Conservative party's platform consistently opposed women's enfranchisement (Ruckstuhl 1986).

As in the United States, oppositional parties were the first to embrace suffrage. The Swiss Social Democratic and Communist parties advocated woman suffrage from the beginning of the suffrage movement (see Chapter 1). On the other hand, few center and right parties endorsed suffrage prior to 1959. Only after the 1959 national referendum did center and right political parties begin to alter their stance, so that by 1971 no political party officially opposed women's enfranchisement. However, a few center and right cantonal parties were even quicker to embrace suffrage.

OPPOSITIONAL POLITICAL PARTIES

Oppositional political parties and oppositional groups within party organizations were the strongest supporters of woman suffrage legislation. During the era of the suffrage movement, the opposition political parties were the two left parties—the Swiss Communist party called Partei der Arbeit (PdA) and the Sozialdemokratische Partei (SP)[13]—and the Landesring der Unabhängigen (LdU), a small, reform party of the center. In addition, during the turbulent 1960s, youth organizations of the governing parties functioned as internal oppositional groups, urging reforms in party policies.

The role of these political organizations is clear when one examines the initiatives and motions made for full suffrage on the national and cantonal level. The LdU and the SP are responsible for introducing two-thirds of the motions for woman suffrage in the Swiss Parliament. Of the 50 motions or initiatives for cantonal voting rights that occurred before 1970 (and where the sponsoring party could be identified), 34 originated from the oppositional groups listed above. Prior to 1950, the connection between left parties and cantonal motions and initiatives is even more striking. Fourteen of the 16 motions and initiatives launched during this period came from the SP and the PdA.

Opposition organizations not represented in legislatures used different means for raising the suffrage issue than those which held seats. The SP and the LdU, which usually held at least a few seats in cantonal legislatures, tended to introduce woman suffrage motions in Parliament. On the other hand, the PdA and the youth groups of political parties were more likely to sponsor initiative drives. Of the 14 initiatives launched by identifiable groups other than the woman suffrage organization, 10 emanated from either the PdA or youth organizations. Youth groups often acted without the approval of their parent political parties. For example, one suffrage activist in Italian-speaking Ticino noted that the initiative managed by youth organizations from the four major parties "was not supported by the political parties. They [the party organizations] said that the young people should not go over their heads" (interview of May 19, 1988). For these groups, initiatives were the only means of advancing the suffrage cause.

THE EFFECT OF OPPOSITIONAL POLITICAL PARTIES

If the SP and the PdA were important advocates of woman suffrage, we would expect that women would become enfranchised earlier where they were strongest. In fact, Table 5.4 illustrates that the strength of the SP within a canton had little effect on the timing of woman suffrage. Cantons where the SP received an average of 30 percent or more of the vote in Nationalrat (lower house of Parliament) elections were no more likely to adopt women's voting rights than those where the SP played a lesser role. These data imply that the Social Democrats may not have supported woman suffrage as strongly as they were able, particularly where they were a major force in cantonal politics.

Indeed, although the SP was an active proponent of woman suffrage, anecdotal evidence suggests that its support for woman suffrage may not have been wholehearted. True, the SP consistently endorsed all woman suffrage referenda, even during the earliest years of the suffrage movement. During many cantonal referenda it also contributed money, served on action committees, and otherwise tried to influence public support for woman suffrage. However, many suffrage activists, including a number of its own party members, gave two reasons for doubting the extent of SP support. First, while party leadership may have advocated suffrage, many of the rank-and-file members did not. According to many suffrage activists, SP party endorsements of woman suffrage did not always translate into positive votes by SP members at the polls. Second, even though the SP

TABLE 5.4
Average Year of Adoption of Woman Suffrage in Cantons by Average
Social Democratic Party (SP) and Average Communist Party (PdA)
Vote in Nationalrat Elections between 1920 and 1975

		Year Suffrage Adopted (Number of Cantons)
Cantons with an Average SP Vote of:	Less than 30%	1970.8 (17)
	30% or more	1970.7 (8)
Cantons with an Average PdA Vote of:	Less than 5%	1972.8 (20)
	5% or more	1963.0 (5)

advocated woman suffrage, other issues often took higher priority. Since the party had to spread its resources over all the issues in an election, woman suffrage referenda rarely took precedence. As one socialist suffrage activist described it: "They would lecture a bit on woman suffrage, and they always endorsed it in the Social Democratic party, but otherwise they did not do much" (Interview of February 1, 1988).

The Partei der Arbeit (PdA), on the other hand, launched four initiatives on their own, gathering the signatures and doing the necessary publicity work without the aid of other organizations. In addition, the Zürich PdA proved its dedication to women's voting rights by conducting a suffrage referendum campaign on its own in 1954 (as noted previously, even the SVF did not campaign for this suffrage amendment). Of the 62 suffrage activists I interviewed, none complained about a lack of support from the PdA organization or their supporters. Indeed, as Table 5.4 indicates, even where the PdA was only a minor party in cantonal politics, there was a greater likelihood that woman suffrage would be adopted. Cantons where the PdA received 5 percent or more of the electoral vote enfranchised women almost 10 years before cantons where the PdA was small or nonexistent.[14]

OTHER POLITICAL PARTIES

If the SP was an equivocal ally of women's voting rights, the other major parties in the Swiss political scene were even more reluctant supporters. The three major center and right political parties—the Freisinnig-Demokratische Partei (FDP), the Christlichdemokratische Volkspartei

(CVP), and the Schweizerische Volkspartei (SVP)—did not begin to advocate suffrage until the 1950s.[15] Prior to 1950, only a few prominent individuals in these parties advocated full woman suffrage, although some cantonal center parties were willing to endorse partial voting rights legislation. At best, these parties would give out *Stimmfreigabe Parole* (literally, Vote Release Endorsement) for full woman suffrage referenda, which permitted members to decide the issue themselves. Usually, however, they recommended voting against referenda that would have enfranchised women in both the canton and the community.

After 1950, and especially after the first national referenda in 1959, these political parties began to endorse woman suffrage legislation and to participate in the pro-suffrage coalitions. On the cantonal level, these changes can be documented by examining party endorsements over several referenda. For example, in a 1951 optional community suffrage referendum in Vaud, only the SP, PdA, and Liberal (FDP) parties supported the bill. However, when a referendum on full cantonal and community voting rights was held in 1959, the other political parties including the Agrarian Party (SVP), Radical party, and the religious parties, added their endorsements. While cantonal parties often endorsed suffrage before their national organization, some lagged behind: "Before 1959, the national parties began slowly to say yes to suffrage, but . . . the Zürich FDP said no even after the national party had begun to say yes" (interview of January 15, 1988).

As center and right political parties modified their attitudes toward woman suffrage, they also began to play a major role in the introduction of legislation, referendum campaigns, and action committees. For example, both the Liberale Partei (FDP) and the Konservative Volkspartei (CVP) opposed the first referendum in Luzern in 1960. However, by the 1970 referendum, these parties had altered their position; they helped to organize the action committee and run the referendum campaign. Indeed, they became so active in the pro-suffrage coalition that few women played a public role in the 1970 campaign, although they had been the driving force in the previous campaign (Vonwyl 1988). In several eastern mountain cantons, particularly Uri and Obwalden, women's rights activity began after 1968 when the CVP, the major party, decided to shoulder the cause.

Thus, the pro-suffrage coalition was headed mainly by women's organizations and political parties. At first, only opposition parties endorsed suffrage. Later, a few prominent individuals and the youth groups within the center and right parties, as well as some cantonal parties, also became champions of women's voting rights. Finally, around 1970, the remaining anti-suffrage parties converted to the cause. What is surprising is the extent to which support from some pro-suffrage allies, specifically other women's groups and the Social Democratic party, did not affect the pro-suffrage coalition's ultimate success. One possibility is that, as in the United States, by endorsing the enfranchisement of women, these groups inspired other powerful actors to join the anti-suffrage alliance.

The Anti-Suffrage Coalition in Switzerland

Other political actors were never drawn into the Swiss suffrage battle by the pro-suffrage allies in the way that the temperance movement caused the liquor interests to join the anti-suffrage coalition in the United States. No issues that might have convinced political actors they should oppose women's voting rights became linked with woman suffrage. Even the Swiss action committee for woman suffrage, in discussing the 1959 campaign, noted: "In contrast to other national referendum issues . . . the grouping of supporters (with exception of the Social Democrats and unions) is not identical with parties, interest groups, Swiss organizations, or other existing groups or communities of eligible voters on the national level. The same—perhaps to an even higher degree—holds for the opponents of the bill."[16] Similarly, when I asked activists about opponents to woman suffrage, very few suggested that opponents could be associated with a particular interest group or association.

In fact, the only identifiable opposition occasionally mentioned by these activists were voters in agricultural and rural areas. However, these activists did not claim that farmers were an organized force against women's voting rights; rather, they thought that voters in rural areas were more conservative and hence more likely to oppose enfranchising women. Nor did they argue that conservative attitudes were limited to the male voting population in rural areas. One activist from a rural canton explained: "We have here a more conservative thinking population, . . . mainly because the population is farmers, although it is especially in the farm that a woman is integrated into the man's work, and stands equal to him. She doesn't have the feeling of suffering, since a farmer cannot exist without his wife. So they can influence their men and they are happy with their condition" (interview of May 16, 1988). Like anti-suffrage feeling in the U.S. prior to 1885, rural opposition was based more on amazement that women thought they needed the vote, than on a fear that women's voting rights would harm their specific interests.

Anti-Suffrage Organizations

Two types of organizations opposed women's voting rights prior to the early 1960s. First, during pre-1960 cantonal suffrage referenda anti-suffrage action committees often surfaced. Like their pro-suffrage counterparts, these groups usually tried to include prominent men and women from a range of political parties and organizations. However, while anti-suffrage activity increased over time in the United States, by the 1960s and 1970s, more and more campaigns for woman suffrage referenda in Switzerland were conducted in the absence of anti-suffrage action committees. Moreover, few members of these action committees were stalwarts of the anti-suffrage cause. Indeed, several suffrage activists I interviewed named politicians who had been members of anti-suffrage action committees and later changed their position.

More prominent than the anti-suffrage action committees, especially after 1950, was a second type of organized opposition: anti-suffrage organizations headed by women.[17] These groups appeared during woman suffrage referendum campaigns or when the suffrage issue arose on the public agenda for other reasons (for example, suffrage motions or initiatives). Many of my informants expressed doubts that these were actually full-blown organizations since they vanished when the suffrage issue was dormant. Like their U.S. counterparts (see, for example, Harper 1922a: xix), Swiss suffrage activists argued that women's anti-suffrage organizations were really created and controlled by men. These claims rested mainly on the fact that many leaders of the women's anti-suffrage organizations were wives of well-known elected officials and business leaders: "the Minister sent his wife . . . and a few other prominent people sent their wives into this [anti-suffrage] committee" (interview of February 1, 1988). Despite the widespread impression that men managed many cantonal women's anti-suffrage groups, Swiss suffrage activists did not believe that these accomplices were linked by mutual interest. "The anti-suffrage people came from all sorts of circles, some were intellectuals but there were also farm women in these groups" (interview of January 21, 1988).

Nor do the arguments used by these two types of anti-suffrage organizations reflect any connection to particular interest groups. Anti-suffrage organizations generally did not state that specific groups would be hurt by women's enfranchisement. Rather, most reasons for opposing votes for women fell into one of three categories. First, anti-suffragists claimed that women's enfranchisement would force them out of the home and thereby destroy family life. Second, they argued that Switzerland was unique and that woman suffrage could not be successfully integrated into the age-old direct democratic institutions with their bond between voting and military service. Third, in later years, opponents of suffrage claimed that this unwanted reform was being forced upon them by the national government, politicians, the press, and foreign influences. For example, one anti-suffrage pamphlet from the 1960s emphasized that several suffrage activists were not native Swiss.

While many anti-suffrage arguments in the United States mentioned the negative effect voting women would have on specific groups, I found only three similar claims made by Swiss anti-suffragists. First, one lone letter to the editor in a 1960 Luzern newspaper argued that suffrage should be opposed because consumer organizations objected to raising milk prices (Vonwyl 1988).

Second, anti-suffrage activists tried to link women's enfranchisement to temperance during the 1947 cantonal suffrage campaign in Zürich. They distributed a letter and circular arguing that suffrage activists supported closing bars and dancing clubs. By the time this propaganda appeared, however, these arguments were so ludicrous that the Action Committee *for* Woman Suffrage publicized the document as evidence of the disreputable arguments used against them. While early Swiss women's right groups had been associated with temperance before 1920, by the 1940s, temperance was a dead issue.

The third anti-suffrage argument focused on the negative effect women's voting rights would have on the support for specific political parties. While these statements did not appear in public propaganda, some woman suffrage activists argued that anti-suffrage sentiment developed among center and right parties because they were concerned that women's voting patterns would disadvantage them: "Their main argument [was] that all the working class women would then go and vote socialist" (interview of May 28, 1988). In another canton, "The FDP was afraid that the Conservatives [CVP] would gain because of woman suffrage, and the Conservatives were very worried that the opposite would occur" (interview of June 27, 1988). However, I could find no evidence of these fears in the anti-suffrage literature. Moreover, suffrage activists' statements suggested that many different parties shared this perception; sometimes socialists, sometimes conservatives, and sometimes liberals predicted they would be disadvantaged by women's voting rights. While center and right political parties may have been concerned about women voting socialist during the 1920s, that threat disappeared by the 1940s when the Social Democratic party became more mainstream and evidence from other countries indicated women favored conservative and religious parties. Hence, it seems unlikely that center and right parties opposition to suffrage stemmed from concerns about how the enfranchisement of women would affect them.

Despite the existence of anti-suffrage action committees and women's organizations, the organized Swiss anti-suffrage coalition was never very strong. By the late 1960s the anti-suffrage coalition had wasted away to nothing. Even those center and right parties which previously opposed women's voting rights easily abandoned this position.

Political Parties

We are left with the question of why center and right parties converted to the suffrage cause. One possibility suggested by the U.S. analysis is that they altered their stance in response to electoral threats from pro-suffrage opposition parties. However, in Switzerland the Communist and Social Democratic parties did not alter voter support for center and right political parties. The Partei der Arbeit (PdA), for example, achieved only 4 percent of the seats in the Nationalrat, the lower house of the Swiss parliament, at its peak in 1947 and they never won a seat in the Ständerat. In 23 of the 25 cantons, the PdA was either nonexistent or a minor political party. The two exceptions were Basel-stadt and Genève. In Basel-stadt, there was a "red" coalition government between 1935 and 1949. In Genève, the PdA received over 20 percent of the vote in several elections between 1950 and 1970, while the center and right parties simultaneously lost voter support. In both cantons, cantonal woman suffrage was adopted before national suffrage legislation was passed and local center and right political parties generally endorsed women's voting rights before their national parties. Thus, where the PdA threatened center and right party support, the reactions of those parties resemble those of Democrats and Republicans to third-party challenges in the United States.

Although the Social Democratic party (SP) was much larger than the PdA, it also was not perceived as a threat to the center and right parties. Between 1919 and 1971, the SP never exceeded 30 percent of the seats in the Nationalrat and at its peak (1943) managed to procure only 10 percent of the seats in the Ständerat. On the cantonal level, the SP fared no better. In nine cantons, the SP drew less than 10 percent of the vote; elsewhere, the SP is a mid-sized party procuring between 10 and 30 percent of the vote in elections. In contrast, the CVP received more than 50 percent of the vote in nine cantons (Faganini 1978).

Moreover, a few characteristics of the Swiss political system also reduced the SP's ability to pose a threat to center and right parties. First, Swiss voting patterns were very stable in both national and cantonal elections. Between the introduction of proportional representation in 1919 and 1975, no party lost or gained more than 10 percent of the seats in the Nationalrat; in most elections, the change was as little as 2 or 3 seats (Gruner 1977). In 22 of the 25 cantons there was also little change in party control of cantonal governments. In fact, Gruner (1977) notes that the vote for the major Ticino parties in the elections of 1922 and 1975 varied by as little as 1 percent. Because voting patterns were so stable, center and right political parties had little reason to worry about oppositional parties support for woman suffrage.

Second, the Swiss system of decision making and extra-large governing coalitions reduced the SP's ability to present itself as a true opposition party. While governments in the United States are headed by a one-person presidency or governor, the national executive in Switzerland is a seven-seat Federal Council elected by Parliament. There is little competition between parties for the Federal Council (Bundesrat) since the distribution of seats according to political party, language, and region is predetermined. The "magic formula" that decides the makeup of the Federal Council rarely changes; the last modification occurred in 1959 when the Social Democratic party gained an additional seat. Similarly, the cantonal executives are five-to-nine–member Governing Councils (Delley and Auer 1986). Although elected by the people of the canton using a majority voting system (except in Zug and Ticino which use proportional representation), these generally reflect the distribution of all the major parties in the canton. Since incumbent members are usually reelected, it is rare for a seat to change parties. Thus, there is little competition between parties for control of the government.

Decisions in these Governing Councils are not based on competitive groups vying for the majority but on the creation of consensus—be it by amicable agreement (Steiner 1974) or by accretion (Steiner and Dorff 1980). Within the Bundesrat and cantonal Governing Councils, the consensus system translates into a norm of collegiality which states that all members must support and are responsible for the decisions of the executive (Faganini 1978). Once a decision has been made, the parties represented in the Bundesrat or Governing Council are expected to support the government's position.

Although the SP presents itself as an opposition party (Kriesi 1995), it has been a part of the Bundesrat since 1943, and was represented in all but six of the cantonal Governing Councils. In every case, the SP had less than a majority of the seats, usually making it a minority partner of center or right parties. The unique status of the SP as both an opposition party and part of the governmental coalition may explain why SP support did not significantly affect the timing of suffrage or other parties stances on the issue. It is true that the SP periodically introduced woman suffrage legislation. Yet, once the government coalition decided on the issue, the collegiality principle prohibited the SP members of the executive from publicly expressing dissent. As a result, the SP could not act solely as opponents of government decisions or complain about its inactivity. Although it did not control a large enough number of seats to impose its policy preferences on national and cantonal executives, neither could it divorce itself completely from their (in)actions.

Both electoral stability and the SP's inability to be solely an opposition party left the other major parties free to decide the issue of woman suffrage without electoral pressure. However, as we have already seen, center and right political parties converted from opponents to supporters of women's voting rights between 1959 and 1971. What was the catalyst that altered the stances of these parties?

The two factors that encouraged their acceptance of woman suffrage can be found within the parties themselves. Suffrage activists argued that the parties became convinced that suffrage was inevitable. Center and right political parties thought their opposition to woman suffrage would hurt them once women joined the electorate. Particularly in the eastern, German-speaking mountain cantons, there were few, if any, woman suffrage proponents before 1970. As it became clear that national suffrage would pass in 1971, center and right parties in these areas endorsed woman suffrage referenda. After the 1971 referendum gave women the right to vote on the national level but not on the cantonal level, even party leaders who had recently opposed suffrage used their influence to push through cantonal suffrage legislation. The fact that women were already voting for the Nationalrat increased the importance of being an active member of the pro-suffrage coalition.

The new pro-suffrage stance also resulted from the activities of party youth organizations, which supported women's enfranchisement even when their parent parties opposed it. Party youth organizations sponsored approximately one-quarter of the cantonal suffrage initiatives, all of which were introduced in the late 1960s and early 1970s as the student movement was developing. While few members of the party's youth organizations participated in that movement, they represented a new generation of party leadership. Given the political context and the youth groups' strong support for women's voting rights, party leaders may have feared that inaction would repel younger members away from the party.

Center and right political parties were not responding, therefore, to the opposition parties when they changed their attitudes on woman suffrage. Except perhaps in Basel-stadt and Genève, they had little reason to do so since these parties posed no threat to their political power. The PdA was never a strong electoral challenge and the SP participated in the power-sharing arrangements that gave stability to the rule of the center and right political parties. Indeed, it was the threat from within—from youth organizations and women themselves—that provided the impetus for change.

Conclusion

The archival and interview evidence shows that there were large differences in how U.S. and Swiss suffrage alliances were created. In the United States, a few organizations had enormous impact on the formation of pro- and anti-suffrage coalitions. The strong alliance of prohibitionists, progressives, populists, and woman suffrage organizations inspired an aggressive anti-suffrage bloc of liquor, brewing, railroad, and manufacturing interests.

National and state political party organizations reacted somewhat differently as they were only threatened by the pro-suffrage policies of the People's and Progressive parties when those policies reduced their electoral support. Thus, the connection between prohibition and woman suffrage did little to alter the official stances of political parties, although individual politicians who relied on the support of liquor interests may have been motivated to join the anti-suffrage coalition. On the other hand, where the populist People's party captured some state governments and when the Progressive party made significant inroads into national politics, the Republicans and, to a lesser extent, the Democrats yielded to suffrage demands.

Switzerland distinguishes itself from the United States by the absence of strong alliances on either side of the suffrage cause. Suffrage organizations were supported by a number of women's groups. However, these groups were not particularly devoted to the suffrage cause and their activity in the suffrage battle did not inspire any negative reaction. The only other long-term supporters of women's enfranchisement were leftist parties. Yet, Switzerland's electoral stability and power-sharing institutions limited the left's influence. Only when suffrage advocates, in the form of youth groups and newly enfranchised women voters, emerged *within* center and right parties were the parties inspired to endorse women's voting rights.

Comparisons between these two countries, the histories of state suffrage battles, and the analysis of coalitions in Switzerland all suggest that larger pro-suffrage coalitions speeded the consideration of suffrage legislation as well as the chances that women would be enfranchised. Even where the larger pro-suffrage alliances inspired a negative reaction, strong alliances appear to pay off in terms of greater success. Thus, Switzerland's late adoption of women's rights can in part be attributed to the lack of strong allies in the suffrage cause. However, this analysis also suggests that care must be taken in how the actors in a political opportunity structure are defined. In Swiss and American suffrage politics, parties were not simply actors that joined pro- and anti-suffrage alliances; they were also battlefields within which other groups clashed for control. As such, a complete discussion of the development of alliances must focus on attempts to sway important actors within the major parties and the consequences for the party policy.

Moreover, the ambiguous effect that other women's organizations had on the timing of suffrage in Switzerland suggests that the shape of pro-

and anti-suffrage alliances cannot completely explain local differences. The data in Table 5.3 show that the addition of allies in the Swiss context may have accelerated the adoption of women's voting rights in some cases, but not in others. There is nothing in the political context to suggest why women's organizations should be effective when suffrage organizations are absent, but ineffective when they are present.

The explanation lies, I believe, not in the structure of political opportunities but in the perceptions and tactical choices of the various groups. Many of these women's organizations eschewed public tactics, preferring to remain behind the scenes. They endorsed woman suffrage legislation and conducted citizenship courses, but they generally shunned the term "suffrage" in their activities. In those cantons that lacked a suffrage organization, other women's organizations may have still had a positive impact because their activities, however meager, at least gave a voice to the suffrage cause. On the other hand, in cantons where SVF sections existed, these groups may have delayed the enfranchisement of women by altering the tactical decisions of suffrage associations. This explanation rests on two assumptions: (1) suffrage organizations were influenced by the values of allied women's organizations, and (2) strategic decisions can influence outcomes. To explore these assumptions more closely, we need to focus on the tactics of the pro-suffrage coalitions.

6

LOBBYING THE GOVERNMENT

IN AN OVERWHELMING MAJORITY of cases, women's voting rights legislation in the United States and Switzerland required action by national or local legislatures. For this reason, suffrage movements in both countries attempted to influence the opinions and actions of legislators and other government officials. Their techniques for doing so constitute the topic of this chapter.

Strategies for influencing legislators' opinions varied over time, between Switzerland and the United States, and among the local movements within each country. During the early phases of the two suffrage movements, activists emphasized petitions as a means of swaying the government. While the U.S. suffrage movements moved in later years to a more aggressive and organized use of lobbying tactics, the Swiss movement generally eschewed these techniques even though they were effectively used by other Swiss interest groups. In part, the dearth of lobbying is a result of the structure of political opportunities in Switzerland, which excluded suffrage activists from the realms where decisions were made. However, historical and anecdotal evidence also suggest that Swiss suffrage activists lacked information about lobbying tactics.

Local movements differed in their tactics for influencing legislators. Movements in some states and cantons were quick to innovate, others less so. In the United States, the differences between states were muted, particularly after 1900, by the National American Woman Suffrage Association (NAWSA), which encouraged local suffrage groups to use similar strategies. By training local sections how to lobby and coordinating state and federal action, the NAWSA reduced the variation in state strategies. In Switzerland, most local movements, like their national counterpart, did not engage in lobbying activities. In a few, rare cases a local suffrage section attempted these techniques, usually with success, but these tactics did not spread to other local suffrage groups or to the national organization. Their diffusion was impeded by linguistic, political, religious, and regional divisions among activists and by the strong belief in local autonomy, which made the national suffrage organization unwilling to disseminate tactical information.

The Tactics of Woman Suffrage Movements
in the United States

Early woman suffrage organizations in the United States relied on three basic tactics in trying to build legislative support.[1] Several of these also generated publicity among the voting public. First, activists would testify at federal and state hearings on woman suffrage. When state legislatures and the U.S. Congress considered suffrage bills or petitions, they often invited supporters and opponents to present their arguments. In some states, committee hearings were heavily publicized as local activists were accompanied by famous suffrage personalities like Susan B. Anthony (for an extended example, see Stanton et al. 1886: chap. 29).

A second major tactic of suffrage organizations, at least until about 1900, was to petition legislatures. Petitions were intended to demonstrate widespread public support for the suffrage cause and hence required that suffrage activists conduct statewide (or national) campaigns to gather signatures. The petitions were usually presented to the legislature by a sympathetic representative in a staged public ceremony. The resulting press coverage and the signature campaign thus also served a second function of stimulating public interest. In the late 1800s, petitions were a major part of suffrage activists' legislative strategy; for example, the 1867 New York Constitutional Convention received over 40 petitions, each from a different locale, asking that women be enfranchised (Stanton et al. 1881b: 283–84).

The third suffrage tactic involved attempts to influence individual legislators and party platforms. While suffrage activists lobbied individual politicians and political parties throughout the movement's history, the techniques suffrage activists used before and after 1910 differed. Early attempts to influence legislators were typically small, informal, and unorganized. Activists wrote letters to or conversed with individual legislators. To achieve endorsements for women's voting rights in party platforms, small delegations of women attended party conventions and spoke to the delegates. In contrast to later years, however, these activities were unsystematic, rarely coordinated by the organization, and undertaken largely on the initiative of individual activists.

By the last decade of the suffrage movement, however, the techniques for persuading legislators had changed. Activists still testified and presented petitions, but they no longer placed much weight on these activities as a means of swaying legislators' opinions. This change in emphasis is clear when one compares the discussion of the U.S. Congress in the third

(1876–1885) and the fifth (1900–1920) volumes of the *History of Woman Suffrage* (Stanton et al. 1886; Harper 1922a). The third volume's discussion of the U.S. Congress focuses primarily on the testimony of suffrage activists before congressional committees. In the later volume, however, there is only passing mention of this activity.

The overall numbers of petitions also declined after 1910,[2] and the petition's intended target changed from national and state legislatures to individual politicians. When utilized, petitions were usually delivered to a particular legislator and were signed by voters from his district in an attempt to sway his vote. However, petitions were rare. "This method of agitation had been abandoned many years before, not only because petitions seemed to produce no direct result, but as it was no longer the custom to present such petitions publicly and with speeches" (Catt and Shuler 1926: 234). On the few occasions when larger petition drives were undertaken, suffrage activists emphasized their effect on the public more than on elected representatives. Thus, signatures gathered in a 1917 New York drive were placed on placards and featured prominently in the propaganda of the ensuing referendum campaign (Harper 1922b: 480–81). Overall, however, suffrage organizations favored other forms of influence.

The largest change in suffrage tactics involved informal contacts with legislatures. After 1910 suffrage activists focused more on lobbying than any other tactic; they carefully planned and orchestrated their informal contacts with legislators. One important development occurred around 1910 when state suffrage activists reorganized their sections to correspond with electoral districts in the state. A clear hierarchy was established to keep track of legislators and to assure that attempts to influence elected officials came from their own constituents. The chairwomen in each electoral district spurred constituents to flood the offices of legislators (particularly those wavering on the suffrage issue) with letters, telegrams, and telephone calls. They would also arrange for a number of influential people from the legislator's district to contact him and insist that he support voting rights for women.

State and national organizations also carefully trained the women who served as lobbyists in national and state capitols (see Taylor 1987 and Catt 1940). They were taught to keep careful dossiers on all legislators, record all relevant roll-call votes, and focus their efforts on those few individuals who could make the difference between passage and failure. Activists were also instructed to use a legislator's social circle to influence his opinion; lobbyists were taught to befriend the office secretary and uncover information about family and friends (Catt 1940: 170). Suffrage activists even assumed the role of legislative whips, assuring that supportive legislators were present for important votes. As a result, U.S. woman suffrage associations reached new heights of organization. In Illinois' push for presidential suffrage, for example,

> Messages had been sent to every friend of the measure urging him not to fail to be present for the vote. On the floor of the house itself were "captains," each a friendly member in charge of a certain number of men. In the gallery sat Mrs. Booth and Mrs. McCormick with the list of members, and Mrs. Trout stood guard at the entrance to the floor of the house to see that no friendly member left his seat, and to prevent any unfriendly lobbyist from violating the law by entering after the session opened. (Brown 1940b: 90)

Lobbying tactics were also carefully coordinated with public tactics designed to show massive public support and, to a certain extent, intimidate political elites. While early attempts to have suffrage planks included on party platforms largely consisted of sending a few suffrage leaders to party conventions, later activists began to hold suffrage parades at the convention sites of the major parties. They also organized gallery and floor demonstrations within the convention hall.

In all these activities, suffrage activists coordinated their efforts with supporters in legislatures and political parties. Sympathetic party leaders provided valuable information to suffrage lobbyists. In many states, legislators would inform suffrage activists which of their colleagues were most likely to be swayed and what sort of arguments would be most effective (see Catt 1940: 88). For this reason, new lobbyists were advised: "If the member is known to be in favor . . . ask him for advice and help with the rest of the delegation. This point is *very important* (cited in Catt 1940: 170, emphasis in original). Such information helped the suffrage activists build an effective lobbying structure.

An additional tactic was attempting to defeat anti-suffrage candidates. Between 1914 and 1920, the Woman's party worked to defeat Democratic candidates especially in states where women were already enfranchised. Woman's party leaders Lucy Burns and Alice Paul argued that the party in power (the Democrats) should be held accountable for the lack of a national woman suffrage amendment (Ford 1991). Their results were mixed. Ford notes Democrats did poorly in the 1914 midterm elections but very well in 1916; in both cases the Woman's party's activities "made woman suffrage a campaign issue" (1991: 74).

While the National American Woman Suffrage Association (NAWSA) rejected the strategy of targeting Democrats, preferring to remain nonpartisan, it also tried to defeat candidates opposed to women's enfranchisement. The Texas association was one of the first to suggest this electoral strategy; in its 1894 "Plan of Work," it issued the following instructions:

"If the nominee of the dominant party refuses to pledge himself in writing to vote for equal suffrage in the legislature, then the county committee shall secure an independent candidate who is an equal suffragist . . . and elect him if possible" (quoted in Taylor 1987: 99). In 1918, after the Nineteenth Amendment was defeated in the Senate by two votes, the NAWSA decided to fight the reelection of four anti-suffrage senators. In keeping with their nonpartisan stance, they targeted two Democrats and two Republicans, defeating two of them—Weeks of Massachusetts and Saulsbury of Delaware.

Regional Differences

Although there is a clear evolution in legislative tactics in the United States, state organizations differed in the degree and speed with which they adopted well-organized, aggressive lobbying tactics. As the discussion of Texas' early election strategies shows, some states embraced the new techniques very early. Others, however, adopted only a few of the new lobbying methods and then only in the last years of the suffrage battle. To convey a sense of the variation in state tactics, it is helpful to look at examples of the two extremes—suffrage associations that were quick to innovate and those that lagged behind.

One state that adopted strong legislative lobbying tactics relatively early was New York. In 1894, Susan B. Anthony and other New York suffragists planned a careful campaign to advance a woman suffrage amendment during the New York state constitutional convention. Like most early suffrage work, the campaign focused mainly on petitions to the convention. Nonetheless, a report on suffrage activities in New York notes that a Lillie Devereux Blake formed a legislative committee that "managed" bills of interest to women (Anthony and Harper 1902: 839–73). The section maintained this committee until 1917 when women were enfranchised in New York. Many lobbying techniques that later became prevalent were utilized by Blake's committee in the 1890s. For example, members of her legislative group polled state legislators and focused their appeals on individual politicians using local sections to "influence their representatives" (Anthony and Harper 1902: 861).

Although the New York suffrage association employed these tactics relatively early, their use increased during the last decade of the suffrage movement. In 1910, the New York woman suffrage association organized a Woman Suffrage party by political districts which formed the basis for later lobbying efforts. For example, after the first suffrage referendum was defeated in 1915, these local groups lobbied legislators to reintroduce the bill in the next legislative session. An entourage of Woman Suffrage party leaders converged on Albany and continually pressured legislators to support a new bill while others called suffrage leaders in different precincts to make sure that "a senator would be called up by the most influential men of his district, demanding that he stand firm" (Brown 1940a: 117). Some members of the legislative lobbying committee even made headlines with their vigilance in standing watch outside of the Senate Judiciary Committee to make sure that a new suffrage bill would be reported out (Harper 1922b: 477). Suffrage activists argued that these tactics were responsible for the state legislature's decision to permit a second woman suffrage referendum just two years after the first.

If New York was an early innovator, Georgia represents the opposite extreme. Even during the last decade of the suffrage movement, the Georgia suffrage association conducted very little direct lobbying. The first attempts to personally contact legislators occurred in 1915 and 1916: Suffrage activists set up a literature table in the capitol building and testified at a legislative hearing (along with suffrage opponents). In 1917, the association notified state legislators in writing that suffrage bills would be introduced and sent them a copy of the national suffrage publication, the *Woman Citizen* (Harper 1922b: 130). In 1919, the state organization pressured state legislators to ratify the Federal Amendment by mailing "a personal letter with copies of letters from . . . the Democratic Executive Committee woman from Georgia, and the eminent clergyman, Dr. J. B. Gambrell, urging the members to ratify the Federal Suffrage Amendment" (Harper 1922b: 131).

The only additional lobbying tactics used by the Georgia section were petitions or letters from the organization to various legislative bodies. In 1916 and 1918, long after most other state associations had reduced their reliance on petitions, the Georgia sections continued to circulate and present petitions to the state legislature and city councils asking for the franchise. However, the Georgia section never polled representatives, applied systematic informal pressure, or amassed helpful information (for example, legislators' biographies or voting records) as their New York counterparts did.

Despite the local differences in lobbying tactics, every state suffrage organization, even the most quiescent, had some contact with their state legislatures. Relatively inactive state organizations, for example, always participated in committee hearings when suffrage legislation was being considered. This differentiates them from their Swiss counterparts, who did not have many contacts with legislators. However, states differed in the extent to which they adopted the later innovations in pressure tactics: recording roll-call votes, polling elected officials, organizing pressure from home districts, and orchestrating activities on the floor of the legislatures.

The Effectiveness of Lobbying Tactics

Did the early adoption of these innovations make a difference to the success of woman suffrage movements? Many U.S. suffrage activists seemed to think so. They argued that the new breed of lobbyists were better able to push women's voting rights legislation through hostile or indifferent legislatures. The adoption of presidential suffrage in Illinois and the passage of the second New York woman suffrage referendum in 1917 were credited to the organization and careful lobbying of suffrage activists.

With 48 states (and 25 cantons), I can systematically explore whether such tactics are correlated with success although this task is complicated by a number of practical difficulties. First among these are the challenges of consistently coding the tactics of suffrage movements in all states and cantons over a period of 70 years. In particular, the primary sources on suffrage organization activities are spotty and incomplete. To solve this problem, I limit the period to be studied to between 1900 and 1919 in the United States and 1951 to 1970 in Switzerland. In these years, relatively accurate organizational reports are available.

A second analytical consideration is that such actions do not have an instantaneous impact. Indeed, the lag between a tactic and its effect could vary greatly. In Switzerland, for example, legislation had to undergo a lengthy pre-parliamentary process often taking years for a motion to result in a bill. In the United States, where many state legislatures met biannually and constitutional amendments might require passage by two consecutive legislatures, successful tactics might yield results several years later. Because the lag between tactics and their effects varied between localities and even between different events within the same state or canton, the method of pooled time-series in which state-years and canton-years are the units of analysis is inappropriate. In its place, the simpler but less powerful method of cross-sectional analysis must be employed. In this method, all movement actions during the time period under consideration are aggregated.

The use of lobbying techniques in a particular state is measured by the number of legislative sessions in which suffrage activists employed at least one of the following techniques: setting up suffrage headquarters in the state capitol, polling legislators, attempting to influence legislators' opinions or votes, endeavoring to marshal votes within the legislature, or striving to elect pro-suffrage or defeat anti-suffrage legislators.[3] The number of legislative sessions is measured by an ordinal variable with three values (0=never used, 1=used once, 2=used more than once). I then examine the association between this measure and three indicators of success: the number of suffrage bills introduced in the decade, the percentage of

TABLE 6.1

Correlations between Lobbying Tactics and Three Measures of
Success in the United States, 1900–1919

Type of Success	Use of Lobbying Tactics (in 0, 1, or 2 and More Legislative Sessions)	N
Full Suffrage Adopted during Period[a]	.48[b]	42
Number of Bills Introduced	.31[b]	42
Percent Legislators Who Support Suffrage in Most Recent Legislative Vote	.32[b]	41

[a] Full woman suffrage legislation is defined as the right to vote in all state offices, the right to vote for presidential electors, or, in southern states, the right to vote in primaries.

[b] $p < .05$

legislators favoring woman suffrage in the last legislative vote during the period, and whether or not suffrage was achieved in the state prior to ratification of the Nineteenth Amendment. To facilitate comparisons across different outcomes and with similar analyses for Switzerland (below) I report Pearson correlation coefficients in Table 6.1.[4]

Before describing them, however, I should note that because the data begin in 1900, the four states that had already enfranchised women (Colorado, Idaho, Utah, and Wyoming) are excluded from the analyses. In addition, in examining the correlations between lobbying and legislative votes, routine regression diagnostics showed that Montana and Washington were outliers, radically reducing the correlation between legislative vote and lobbying tactics.[5] As a result, these states are also excluded from the analyses in Table 6.1.

This analysis corroborates the anecdotes of activists; Table 6.1 indicates that the measures of success correlate with lobbying tactics. Lobbying techniques are significantly related to all three measures of success. In states where suffrage activists used these organized, aggressive lobbying techniques, more suffrage legislation was introduced, women were more likely to be enfranchised before the Nineteenth Amendment was ratified, and state legislators were more likely to support women's voting rights bills.

One way of illustrating how the use of lobbying techniques increased the chances that women's voting rights would be adopted on the state level is to compare the eighteen states that employed these well-organized, more aggressive tactics in none or only one legislative session with those where suffrage activists applied them more often. While three-fourths of the 24 states where suffrage activists lobbied extensively enfranchised women before the Nineteenth Amendment took affect, only five (28 percent) of the other states did so. Organized attempts to garner legislative votes were clearly associated with the early adoption of women's voting rights.

Spreading Innovations in Lobbying

Given the success of organized pressure tactics, it is not surprising that the national woman suffrage association was eager to disseminate information. While many of the tactics were first attempted by state organizations, their wide diffusion among the states after 1910 was largely due to the efforts of national suffrage organizations. Both the NAWSA and the Woman's party prodded state organizations to utilize more extensive lobbying. The Congressional Union, the predecessor to the Woman's party, encouraged the formation of local organizations by electoral district in order to pressure congressmen for a federal amendment (Ford 1991: 55). Unlike NAWSA activists, Woman's party leaders were less interested in recruiting a large membership or building lasting organizations. They were also unconcerned about lobbying state legislatures since they believed in the necessity of a federal amendment. The Woman's party did send organizers into states but did so in order to build lobbies focused on pressuring congressmen into the pro-suffrage camp (Irwin 1921: 327–35) or to stir up anti-Democratic feeling in western states, where women already had the vote, in the hopes of forcing the Democratic party to become pro-suffrage (Ford 1991).

The National American Woman Suffrage Association, particularly under the direction of Carrie Chapman Catt, also urged state organizations to adopt certain lobbying techniques albeit for slightly different reasons. The business meeting of the 1908 NAWSA national convention recommended that state societies do "systematic legislative work" focusing on state legislatures (Harper 1922a: 240). The "Winning Plan" developed by Catt in 1916 argued that each state and local organization, by pressuring their local governments, could contribute to the drive for a federal amendment. Thus, pressure on elected officials was to proceed at both the national and the state levels.

The NAWSA encouraged legislative work by its state auxiliaries in a number of ways. First, the NAWSA urged state affiliates to reorganize state and local clubs to correspond with electoral districts. While many states had already reorganized along these lines, the NAWSA only began to advocate this policy in 1914, under the leadership of the future Woman's party activists. However, NAWSA activists who abhorred the militant tactics of the Congressional Union and Woman's party appreciated the power of congressional district organization. Even Anna Howard Shaw, in her presidential address in 1915, argued that the pursuit of women's voting rights required "Congressional District organization, such as has been set in motion by our National Congressional Committee and which has proved so successful during the past year" (quoted in Harper 1922a: 446).

Second, the NAWSA's annual conventions were used as opportunities to train state delegates in lobbying techniques. Convention symposia included topics such as state legislative work, polling candidates on their stands on suffrage, defeating anti-suffrage candidates, and organizing by political district. In later years, such practical workshops dominated the NAWSA annual conventions. Harper noted that by 1915 "it was felt that the general public needed no further education on this subject; the association had become a business organization and the woman suffrage question one of practical politics" (1922a: 441).

Third, national suffrage leaders also found it necessary to go into the states to train local suffrage activists. In 1913, the NAWSA established Suffrage Schools, instruction for local suffrage activists in the various aspects of suffrage work like parliamentary law, publicity, suffrage arguments, and organization. Originally, NAWSA asked state auxiliaries to reimburse them for at least part of the costs of these schools. Yet, by 1917, the NAWSA chose to pay the entire costs of the training, stressing the importance of well-trained state activists to the cause. At the 1917 NAWSA convention, suffrage leaders conceded "our failure many times had not alone been due to the fact that numbers of women would not work but that those who were willing were untrained and inefficient" (Harper 1922a: 538). According to the minutes of the NAWSA convention, 19 different Suffrage Schools were held in that year. Many were in states where the suffrage organization had not yet actively lobbied for suffrage legislation. This training was reinforced by NAWSA publications like the *Headquarters Newsletter*, which included specific suggestions on how to influence elected officials.

Finally, the NAWSA organized visits from state suffrage activists to their congressional delegation. Between 1913 and 1920, NAWSA annual conventions convened biennially in Washington, D.C., to provide activists with the opportunity to pressure Congress. During the 1917 convention, the NAWSA promoted state lobbying by hosting receptions for Washington politicians and by asking senior senators from unenfranchised states to host a meeting of their congressional delegation with suffrage delegates (Harper 1922a: 516). At the same time, NAWSA delegates passed a resolution to target anti-suffrage representatives and senators if the federal amendment did not pass Congress in that session. The targets were selected by both state and national boards.

Thus, while increasing national and state legislators' support of women's voting rights was always a focus of the U.S. suffrage movement, the form of this strategy evolved. National woman suffrage organizations in the United States encouraged this change and reduced the variation between states. Innovations, such as organization by political district, spread quickly throughout the United States. Beginning in 1910, and especially after the introduction of the Winning Plan in 1916, these changes were aided by the NAWSA's deeper involvement in the education and coordination of local state activists. As a result, state suffrage activists adopted political district organization, created legislative committees in state capitols, polled local candidates and elected officials, and pressured individual politicians to enfranchise women. Even relatively inactive states like Georgia benefitted from the national organization's intervention. Although some local suffrage activists did not implement lobbying on the scale of the New York or Illinois associations, most tried to comply as much as possible with the national organization's plans for state work. Voting rights for women on the state level and on the national level resulted in large part from the legislative strategy of American suffrage movements (see McDonagh 1990: 10).

Lobbying Techniques of Woman Suffrage Movements in Switzerland

While the historical evidence in the United States indicates organizations frequently pressured elected representatives to increase support for woman suffrage legislation, Swiss historical documents rarely mention any legislative tactics. In numerous annual reports, anniversary reviews of past work (for example, *Die Staatsbürgerin*, November 1968), and programs of action, legislative lobbying always took a backseat to public education and propaganda. For example, in its 1948 Program of Action, a two-page, single-spaced document, the Schweizerischer Verband für Frauenstimmrecht (SVF) places most of its emphasis on the education of women, publicizing the need for woman suffrage, and representing women's viewpoint in every election and referendum. The only reference to influencing government officials alludes to the goal of continuing "incessant cultivation of the public through the press, visits to officials and party people" (translated by the author).

Nor is this absence unusual. In a publication chronicling the first 25 years of the suffrage organization, SVF President Anne Leuch-Reineck mentioned only three activities that could broadly be construed as attempts to influence elected officials: petitions from organizations, letters to members of the Nationalrat, and a vague reference to "actions to the Federal Council" (SVF 1934: 20; translated by author). Twenty-five years later in a similar publication, the only such references were to one petition to the Swiss Parliament and an official visit with a member of the Federal Council (SVF 1959: 20–21). The latter visit was prompted not by a concern about woman suffrage but about the citizenship rights of Swiss women married to foreigners.

My interviews with 62 Swiss suffrage activists also provide little evidence that suffrage organizations engaged in any pressure tactics. When asked to recall the organizations' activities, activists' responses centered almost exclusively on referenda for woman suffrage and highly visible public events like demonstrations. The lack of discussion of parliamentary activities in both historical accounts and in the interviews indicates their marginality in the Swiss struggle for the vote.

The few legislative tactics employed by Swiss suffrage associations paralleled those of the early U.S. suffrage movement. These consisted almost entirely of circulating petitions and presenting them to cantonal and federal legislatures and Governing Councils. For example, in 1928, the major legislative tactic of the SVF was a national petition drive. The petition, which was officially received by the presidents of both houses of parliament, asked the national government to enfranchise women. In contrast to their U.S. counterparts, Swiss activists never developed the strategy of using petitions from constituents to influence the opinions of particular legislators. Suffrage petitions were always presented to entire parliaments or to the executive branch.

While American suffrage activists were constantly testifying before state and federal legislative committees, their Swiss counterparts were rarely called upon to do so. The first time any parliamentary commission received a delegation of women was in 1951 (Ruckstuhl 1986: 66–67). In that year, representatives of the SVF testified before a parliamentary committee charged with responding to a Federal Council report on woman suffrage. However, there is no mention of any further testimony on the national level and only one reference to testimony before cantonal parliaments or parliamentary committees (in Zürich in 1946).

More common was the letter of appeal (*Eingabe*) to national and cantonal officials declaring the official position of the organization. After petitions, this appears to be the main lobbying tactic of every Swiss woman suffrage organization. Many such letters, covering a variety of issues, were written every year by suffrage groups. For example, the early Swiss suffrage organization wrote letters supporting the signing of the international opium convention, the addition of a woman to the Swiss delegation to the International Conference on Work, and, of course, woman suffrage (SVF 1934: 75–78). The early Basel suffrage organization asked for women's voting rights in the Protestant church, women representatives on the labor union court of arbitration, and the hiring of a female police assistant (Villard-Traber 1984). Requests for the enfranchisement of women were, thus, a small proportion of the letters of petition a suffrage organization might write. And even when these letters of petition addressed women's enfranchisement, they were often limited to appeals for partial suffrage.

Letters urging that new legislation be considered were usually sent to the entire Parliament or Federal Council, and not to individual politicians. In this respect, these letters were no different from petitions except that they carried only the weight of the organization and not of any mass support. When women's organizations wanted to increase the influence of a letter of appeal, they arranged for the letter to be signed by a number of different organizations. For example, a 1919 letter of petition was signed by leaders representing 158 different organizations (SVF 1934: 20). Fifty years later, the SVF coordinated with other women's organizations to send a letter of petition to the Bundesrat (Federal Council) opposing its decision to write exceptions into the European Declaration of Human Rights.

Simply because historical documents did not record contacts between government officials and the suffrage activists does not necessarily mean that such contacts did not occur. Certainly suffrage activists or leaders of other women's organizations associated informally with national and cantonal members of Parliament. Some suffrage activists were even married to elected cantonal officials. What suffrage activists lacked was not the contact per se, but the information to make those connections a useful means of lobbying for women's voting rights.

The private correspondence between woman suffrage organization leaders reveals that they had little experience in using informal connections to lobby. One lengthy letter to leaders of the Swiss Action Committee for Woman suffrage in 1948 discussed the advice of a pro-suffrage member of the Federal Council. In the letter, two suffrage activists recount their visit to the Federal Council member where they asked for advice about how to further the suffrage cause. The politician advised the activists "to get in touch with the political parties as well as the party organizations within the legislatures" (translated by author). In addition, he felt it necessary to explain in great detail exactly how the contact should be made (with a personal letter not a printed circular), when to plan a meeting of representatives (not during the day when Parliament was meeting), and even where to hold such a meeting (at a nice restaurant and not at the Parliament building). This advice is significant for two reasons. First, it indicates that activists were not in contact with their representatives at that point in time; rather, they required the advice of a politician to get them to undertake such legislative action. Second, the activists did not have much knowledge about how best to approach their elected officials; leaders in the suffrage movement felt it important to transmit these exact details in a letter to other activists, indicating that they placed value on this advice.[6]

Other forms of formal contact with elected officials were also unusual. The historical record chronicles few accounts of formal meetings with members of Parliament or the executive except when suffrage activists delivered petitions. Nor was it common for suffrage organizations to send suffrage propaganda to members of cantonal or national parliaments unless they were specifically asked to do so. The only mentions I found of this sort of activity were among records of the early suffrage movement. In 1920, the SVF sent letters to members of the Nationalrat (SVF 1934: 20), and in 1917, suffrage activists from the canton Vaud sent copies of their organization's newspaper to all the members of the cantonal parliament. In the United States, even relatively inactive suffrage associations, like the Georgia section, engaged in this sort of legislative activity. Yet, in Switzerland, even this basic contact with government officials placed a suffrage organization in the category of extremely active.

The Swiss suffrage organization occasionally utilized public actions in the legislature. For example, one suffrage activist noted that the threat of a women's action in the Nationalrat encouraged legislative action on a suffrage motion: "Mr. von Roten's motion for us was always being delayed on the minutes. . . . So finally when it was put on the end of the list of future business, I sent a letter saying women would be in the balcony and would not leave until the postulate was handled. And that day it was handled in a late-night session" (interview of May 9, 1988). However, while such demonstrations occurred once or twice, they were rare in comparison to similar efforts by American suffrage activists. Moreover, legislative demonstrations were never staged in cantonal parliaments. When women suffrage activists attended cantonal parliamentary sessions, they usually acted only as passive spectators. They did not use any means to influence politicians' opinions beyond the symbolic effect of their silent presence. Indeed, on such occasions, they did not even gather information about legislators' opinions or voting habits.

Finally, it is worth noting that some American tactics were completely missing from the Swiss suffrage movement. For example, the national Swiss suffrage association never attempted to elect legislators friendly to their cause. Indeed, the national and the cantonal suffrage organizations (with one exception) did not participate in the election of parliamentary candidates at all. Since suffrage activists almost never polled legislators on their opinions of women's voting rights, they could not even publicize the positions of the various candidates on women's voting rights. The historical documents on suffrage organization activities indicated only three cantonal organizations (Genève, Schaffhausen, and Zürich) that ever systematically asked legislators or candidates their positions on woman suffrage. And each of these cantons report having used this tactic only once in the 70 years of the movement. There is no evidence of the national suffrage association engaging in these activities.

In general, then, woman suffrage organizations did not utilize lobbying techniques to develop legislative support. Instead, their activities focused on public education and propaganda. The emphasis on education stems partially from the implicit belief of many suffrage activists that tactics affecting public support also influenced elected officials. When a motion was to be considered in Parliament, activists tended to engage in building public opinion. For example, when motions were presented for suffrage legislation in Appenzell Ausserrhoden in 1989 and Schaffhausen in 1964, the national suffrage organization held its annual meeting in these cantons to give the suffrage issue added publicity there. However, there were no *explicit* attempts to convert increased public support for women's voting rights into pressure on the Parliament to pass suffrage legislation.

Cantonal Differences

As in the United States, all Swiss cantons did not act alike; some local suffrage organizations focused more explicitly on influencing cantonal parliaments than others. In fact, Swiss cantons developed their strategies largely on their own because the national organization did little to encourage legislative techniques in cantonal activities. The SVF and national action committees provided press information and propaganda to cantonal organizations but not technical assistance on legislative tactics. While the American suffrage organizations conducted numerous Suffrage Schools on legislative techniques, only one canton reported that the national SVF conducted a class for activists: In 1944, the SVF president instructed Schaffhausen activists on how to run an organization. However, the course focused on organizational aspects and was open to all women's organizations. Hence, the course did not deal with political techniques. Nor was there a Swiss equivalent of the "Winning Plan" to coordinate the activities of cantonal suffrage organizations. Local suffrage organizations were left on their own to learn and innovate.

Two cantons distinguished themselves in their use of American-style lobbying techniques. Genève suffrage activists twice attempted to elect candidates who were supportive of woman suffrage: once prior to 1920 and once in 1954, when they actually started their own party. In a pamphlet describing their activities between 1907 and 1917, the Association genevoise pour le suffrage féminin reports asking political parties to put suffrage in their platforms and supporting candidates sympathetic to suffrage. In 1954, it ignored the existing political parties and chose to support a candidate from a new party, Vrai democratie. Nonetheless, reports on the Genève association's activities mention no other election where it supported candidates.

Vaud was another exceptionally active canton; here suffrage activists utilized informal connections to politicians to affect the timing of a suffrage referendum. While the early suffrage organization engaged in some legislative tactics (for example, see SVF 1934: 57), both interviews and historical documents suggest that one activist, Antoinette Quinche, was particularly adept at using these pressure techniques. Suffrage activists from several other cantons mentioned her unique belief in the importance of political parties: "Quinche always said that if we were to get suffrage we must get the parties involved" (interview of May 19, 1988). When the first national referendum was announced in 1957, Quinche convinced the suffrage organization in Vaud to urge the cantonal government to introduce a cantonal referendum at the same time. In addition to direct lobbying, she utilized her ties to the La-Tour-de-Peilz city council to encourage them to pass a resolution supporting the idea. The Governing Council of Vaud acquiesced, ultimately resulting in Vaud being the first canton to enfranchise women.

However, these two suffrage associations are unique; most cantonal groups used few, if any, legislative tactics. In fact, in 12 cantons, there appears to have been absolutely no attempt to influence cantonal legislatures, even through letters of petition. The most active suffrage organizations relied heavily on petitions and letters to cantonal legislatures. For example, the suffrage section in the canton Aargau, one of the more active suffrage organizations, sent one petition and three letters to the cantonal parliament asking for woman suffrage between 1919 and 1969. Their only other legislative action involved sending women to observe (but not record any information about) sessions of the cantonal parliament.

Cantonal suffrage activists, like their national counterparts, rarely talked to members of cantonal parliament about woman suffrage. In Schaffhausen, for example, suffrage activists who were planning an initiative were surprised to learn that a member of the cantonal parliament had introduced a motion for suffrage. Interestingly, Ruckstuhl, herself a long-time suffrage activist, implies that the politician should have informed the suffrage activists of his actions; she complains that the motion's introduction "occurred without the briefing of the women who had worked on woman suffrage for decades" (1986: 199; translated by author). In the United States, regular contacts with legislators avoided such duplication of effort and suffrage activists believed the onus was on them to notify legislators of their activities.

The Effectiveness of Lobbying Tactics

The relative lack of legislative strategies raises a question about the Swiss political opportunity structure. Is it possible that lobbying tactics were generally ineffective in Swiss legislatures? If true, we would expect suffrage activists to ignore such techniques. We need to know, therefore, whether legislative tactics affected the adoption of woman suffrage in Switzerland.

To explore this, I classify cantons on the basis of their lobbying tactics using the same criteria applied to U.S. suffrage movements above. The 25 Swiss cantons are divided according to how often they used American-style lobbying tactics such as polling legislators, running candidates in elections, or trying to pressure elected officials. Twenty cantons never utilized these tactics. The other five cantons each utilized these more aggressive lobbying techniques only once in the 51 years between 1920 and 1971. Because so few suffrage organizations employed these sorts of tactics, I also coded cantons into categories according to the frequency with which pro-suffrage organizations used typically Swiss legislative tactics, particularly petitions and letters from organizations (one year, two or more years, or never). Even using this criterion, 12 cantons employed no legislative techniques.

Legislative tactics appear to be related to measures of suffrage organization success. In Table 6.2, I correlate these two indicators of lobbying with three measures of success—the number of suffrage bills introduced, whether cantonal suffrage was adopted before 1971, and the percent of Parliament voting for the most recent pre-1971 suffrage bill. While statistical significance with such a small number of cases is difficult to achieve, the Pearson correlation coefficients between both types of lobbying techniques and the measures of success are all positive and all except one exceed .25. Both types of legislative tactics, it appears, were connected to increased success. However, aggressive tactics are more strongly associated with the early success of cantonal woman suffrage legislation and support for suffrage in cantonal parliaments than the typical Swiss tactics of petitions and letters of appeal.

Indeed, all five cantons where suffrage organizations attempted to influence individual legislators by informal contact, polling political candidates, or endorsing pro-suffrage candidates, adopted women's voting rights before 1971. On the other hand, only 4 of the other 20 cantons enfranchised women before 1971. Even the use of petitions and letters of appeal to cantonal parliaments or Governing Councils increased the chances of woman suffrage, albeit less dramatically than these more aggressive tactics. Among those Swiss cantons where suffrage organizations petitioned—by organizational letter of appeal or collecting signatures—

TABLE 6.2

Correlations between Lobbying Tactics and Three Measures of
Success in Switzerland, 1920–1970

Type of Success	Use of Petitions and Letters	Use of More Aggressive Tactics	N
Cantonal Suffrage Adopted	.37	.67[a]	25
Number of Bills Introduced	.37	.32	25
Percent Legislators Who Support Suffrage in Most Recent Parliamentary Vote	.19	.38	19

[a] $p < .05$

cantonal governments in two or more years, 57 percent adopted cantonal women's voting rights. The percentage is similar where suffrage organizations petitioned only once; three of these six cantons enfranchised women before 1971. On the other hand, of the 12 cantons where women had no contact with legislatures, only two (17 percent) had woman suffrage when national voting rights were adopted in 1971.

Assessing Lobbying Tactics

This analysis raises an additional question. If legislative techniques were successful in Switzerland, as Table 6.2 suggests, why did Swiss suffrage activists not lobby more often? Swiss suffrage activists argued that delays in getting the vote emanated not from elected officials but from the lack of public support for the issue. As one activist said, "In Parliament there are people who think a bit more and are an elite group, and are more likely to be for suffrage. That is also true in Switzerland. We would have had suffrage much earlier if only the Parliament needed to vote on it" (interview of February 12, 1988). Indeed, both national and cantonal parliaments were more supportive of the enfranchisement of women than the general public: Numerous suffrage referenda were approved by cantonal legislatures but defeated in the general election.

Although few elected officials actively opposed suffrage, the dearth of suffrage activity in Swiss parliaments may have allowed most to avoid taking specific steps leading to women's voting rights. While suffrage activists believed that most politicians were pro-suffrage, indifference was also widespread. As one cantonal legislator noted, "The other people in the Catholic-Conservative Party viewed my support of woman suffrage as a curiosity. They didn't actually occupy themselves with woman suffrage. They would say, sure we are for woman suffrage, but it will eventually come with patience. I never saw a person directly opposed to woman suffrage" (interview of June 22, 1988). Even suffrage activists occasionally noted this problem. Ruckstuhl observed that "in most cantons the influential middle-class politicians dealt with the problem of how to obtain woman suffrage only immediately before a referendum in the context of an action committee and once it lost, [they] let the thing lie" (1986: 194; translated by author).

In fact, the image of supportive national and cantonal parliaments facing unsupportive and intransigent voters is belied by the history of suffrage legislation in Switzerland. As Chapter 4 notes, relatively few women's voting rights bills were considered by cantonal parliaments. The lack of suffrage legislation cannot be attributed to cantonal parliaments being dissuaded from introducing new bills by the low public support expressed in referenda. Eight cantonal parliaments did not submit women's voting rights legislation to the electorate until 1969. In all of these cantons, woman suffrage legislation passed on the first try.

Moreover, as the correlations in Table 6.2 suggest, legislative techniques may have other effects besides encouraging a legislative majority. They can also assure that the issue reaches the political agenda and is dealt with in a timely manner. In New York, for example, suffrage organizations lobbied their state legislature heavily to convince them to reintroduce a suffrage amendment immediately after a referendum had failed. In Switzerland, one problem that the suffrage movement repeatedly faced was the pocket tabling (*Schubladesierung*) of suffrage legislation. Suffrage motions and petitions would disappear for long periods without any action by the Federal Council. Could lobbying have made it more difficult for elected officials to ignore the suffrage issue for years at a time?

The answer depends in part on whether suffrage activists were limited by the structure of political opportunities. Another potential explanation for the lack of lobbying techniques in Switzerland is that the specifics of the Swiss political system—its electoral system and voting patterns, its stable government coalitions, the lack of conflict between political actors, and the decision-making process (which occurred largely outside of parliamentary politics)—limit the usefulness of these legislative tactics. If true, it is possible that the results in Table 6.2 are spurious; perhaps other factors related to legislative tactics produced these correlations. Alternatively, Swiss suffrage activists may have failed to employ these tactics because they are absent from the repertoire of Swiss social movements or interest groups (see Tilly 1978). If there were no examples of these sorts of tactics among *other* Swiss political actors, suffrage activists may not have had the opportunity to learn them. To examine the validity of these explanations, we need to explore the political context of the Swiss suffrage movement in greater detail.

The Influence of the Political Context in Switzerland

Despite strong similarities in federal structure and weak political parties, the Swiss political opportunity structure differed from that of the United States in several ways which may have made legislative and electoral tactics less useful to Swiss suffrage organizations. In particular, the nature of interest group mediation, the secrecy surrounding political decisions, and the representation of interests by elected politicians may have decreased the efficacy of U.S.-style lobbying tactics. To explore this possibility, let us examine how formal and informal political institutions and procedures affect the activities of *other* Swiss groups.

Swiss interest groups are able to influence legislation at many points in the political process. However, a consensus on most issues is usually reached long before votes are cast in Parliament (Höpflinger 1984; Linder 1994). Decisions are usually wrought in two institutions. First, legislation introduced in the national or cantonal parliaments is usually hammered out in expert committees. Created by the government, these committees include nongovernmental experts, interest group representatives, and civil servants (Linder 1987). They resolve disagreements between different interests, eventually resulting in a consensus on the legislation. As the deliberation process and decision making of extra-parliamentary committees are secret (Tschäni 1987), groups outside the committees are generally unable to influence the decision at this stage.

While women have generally been underrepresented on expert committees (Linder 1987: 33), a few large women's organizations—the Federation of Women's Clubs (Bund Schweizerischer Frauenorganisationen or BSF) and the Swiss Catholic Women's Federation (SKF)—occasionally had representatives on national expert advisory committees. Indeed, women had been included on national expert commissions since 1907, and BSF was represented on commissions for revising health insurance in 1921 and the penal code in 1925 (Bund Schweizerischer Frauenvereine 1950). The SVF was never considered large or important enough to be involved in these committees, although suffrage activists who were members of other women's organizations served on such committees. Thus, Lotti Ruckstuhl, one president of the Swiss suffrage organization, served as the SKF's representative to the expert commission on marriage law.

Representation on these national committees, however, did little to further the cause of woman suffrage. There were no national expert committees on women's voting rights, only on other women's issues. Woman suffrage activists also played little role in drafting suffrage legislation in cantonal advisory committees. Only Appenzell Ausserrhoden officially included the woman suffrage organization on advisory committees and then only for the last (1989) bill.[7] Thus, while representation on national and cantonal advisory committees helped women's organizations affect many women's rights issues, it was inconsequential in dealing with woman suffrage.

In addition to going through expert committees, once a bill has been drafted it must also undergo a consultation process (known as *Vernehmlassung*) before it can be considered by Parliament. In this process, interest groups and local governments are given the opportunity to submit comments on the proposed legislation to the Federal Council or cantonal Governing Councils. The input of the larger interest groups is considered particularly important since they have the ability to collect enough signatures to force legislation into a referendum (Höpflinger 1984). An influential interest group might use the referendum threat in expert committees and/or during the *Vernehmlassung* process to force amendments in a bill. At the end of the process of expert committees and *Vernehmlassung*, the bills introduced into Parliament represent a careful balancing of different interests. As a result, few are amended in Parliament since this might disturb the compromise painstakingly hammered out in the pre-parliamentary process (Werder 1978). Indeed, roll-call votes in the Swiss Parliament are rare because the fate of most bills is already determined by the time the vote occurs (Hertig 1978; Kerr 1978).

The pre-parliamentary process of expert commissions and *Vernehmlassung* also made it difficult for suffrage organizations to push women's voting rights legislation through parliaments. As one of many interest groups, and a minor one at that, the SVF could not have a major effect in the pre-parliamentary process. Moreover, because expert commissions and the consultative process are secret and slow, it was difficult for the Swiss suffrage movement to distinguish procedural delays from rejection. In the United States, legislation had to be handled within a single legislative session. In contrast, petitions to cantonal governments and motions from cantonal parliaments for woman suffrage often seemed to disappear for years. Because Swiss suffrage activists could not be certain if the cantonal and national governments were working on legislation or ignoring their motions and petitions, it may have been difficult to determine whether lobbying was the appropriate strategy.

In addition to the pre-parliamentary process, Swiss interest groups also play a large role in parliaments through the system of multiple mandates (known generally as *Amtkumulierung*), where representatives often hold several political offices and/or leadership roles in interest groups simultaneously. For example, Tschäni (1987: 207) notes that one member of the Nationalrat during the 1983–1987 session was a member of the cantonal government, on the governing boards of two firms, and official representative of the Swiss milk producers association and the Swiss cattle organization. This is not unusual. Steiner (1974: 122) estimates that half of the Nationalrat and 79 percent of the cantonal parliament of Bern could be considered representatives of specific interest groups. Moreover, 18 percent of the Swiss Nationalrat of 1975 listed their profession as full-time functionary of an interest group (Gruner 1977: 170). As a result, interest groups have direct representation in parliaments and cantonal Governing Councils.

The multiple mandates of parliamentarians and cabinet members were an important source of influence for other Swiss interest groups. Steiner (1974) and Tschäni (1987) both argue that the pre-parliamentary process and multiple mandates constitute interest groups' best means for affecting a legislative decision. The elected officials with connections to interest groups could informally affect the composition of expert committees. In addition, these representatives provided a wealth of inside information and contacts that helped interest groups decide who, when, and how to lobby other governmental officials.

Excluded from *Amtkumulierung*, woman suffrage activists lacked this source of influence. Although some men belonged to suffrage organizations, most members and almost all officers were women. Since women could not be elected to office, suffrage organizations could not be represented in government positions through multiple mandates. As a result, Swiss women suffrage activists were disadvantaged; they lacked inside knowledge about whom to lobby, could not influence the composition of expert committees, and were often in the dark as to the status of legislation.

Although other Swiss interest groups and social movements relied heavily on their multiple mandates and extra-parliamentary decision making to influence legislation, they also engaged in legislative lobbying. Tschäni (1987) notes that interest groups regularly utilize the same techniques as American suffrage activists including organized lobbying of members of Parliament and encouraging members to write and call their representatives. When the Swiss government considered eliminating the Swiss cavalry, for example, the cavalry club organized its members to contact members of Parliament. Members who were part of the social circle of a particular representative were specifically asked to contact their friends about the bill (see Tschäni 1987: 72). Nor was the example unusual. The largest interest group for the Swiss construction industry, the Schweizerischer Baumeisterverband, regularly contacts different federal government offices and individual members of the Governing Council (Farago 1986). Thus, despite the existence of other, more important means of influencing political decisions, lobbying was (and is) a significant part of the strategies of Swiss interest groups.

The participation of Swiss interest groups in the parliamentary process does not end with the lobbying tactics discussed above. Like the American woman suffrage movement, many Swiss groups utilized electoral politics to influence the stances of their elected representatives. On first glance, one might think that the stability of voter preferences in Switzerland might reduce the effectiveness of such strategies. As I noted in Chapter 5, political parties could generally count on receiving approximately the same electoral support as they had previously. The lack of volatility among voters decreased the ability of suffrage activists to influence party policy. Since parties had little fear of losing votes, they did not need to respond to suffrage movement demands.

However, the Swiss electoral system permits Swiss voters to choose individual representatives and not just political parties. This is unusual since the Swiss utilize a proportional representation electoral system, which, in most countries, means that political parties and not voters determine which candidates will represent them. In most proportional representation systems, political parties have considerable power over individual politicians because they create the list of candidates, thereby reducing interest groups' ability to target individual candidates on specific policies. However, the Swiss electoral system is a modification of proportional representation that allows voters to affect the order of candidates on the party list. Voters may strike candidates from a party list or vote for an individual twice. They may even place a candidate from one party on another party list. The order of the party list is determined by how many votes each candidate receives. This system allows different interests, even those without representation in party institutions, to affect the electoral prospects of individual candidates.

Because of the modified proportional representation system and the lack of party discipline (see Chapter 5), electoral politics actually plays a significant part of the repertoire of *other* interest groups and social movements. Swiss interest groups, even those not engaged in politics, recommend particular candidates based on their issue stances. Steiner (1974: 66) notes that sports, motoring, and travel groups (even the Sports Fishing Club of Bern) have recommended candidates during elections. To avoid appearances of partisanship, these groups usually endorse candidates from several parties. Nor is the practice of endorsing candidates just a tactic of the larger interest groups. Even the Vereinigung zum Schutz der kleinen und mittleren Bauern, an organization for small farmers numbering less than 2,000 members, published a list of election recommendations (Engeler 1986).

Many voluntary associations go even further and provide resources (such as volunteers, propaganda, or money) to the candidates they endorse (Hertig 1978; Steiner 1974; Tschäni 1987). Moreover, because the largest interest groups control more resources than political parties, parties and individual candidates rely heavily on the support of interest groups during campaigns (Gruner 1977). Hertig notes that "interest groups provide money and campaign assistance in return for places on the ballot" (1978: 73) thereby translating resources directly into representation. By concentrating on electing those candidates who explicitly and actively support their goals and by defeating outspoken opponents, interest groups are able to influence the stances of elected officials. Thus, electoral strategies are an important part of the tactics of both big and small interest groups.

Although suffrage activists could not vote, they were not prohibited from campaigning for or against candidates. Even if they could not alter the total vote received by a particular party, Swiss suffrage activists might have altered the rank order of candidates on the party list by encouraging double voting for candidates who supported suffrage and the elimination of anti-suffrage politicians from a party list. Moreover, like their American counterparts and other Swiss interest groups, the Swiss suffrage organization could have endorsed candidates without abandoning its nonpartisanship merely by campaigning for pro-suffrage candidates regardless of their party affiliation. However, they chose not to do so.

What can we conclude about the effect of the Swiss political opportunity structure on the legislative tactics of the Swiss suffrage movement? On the one hand, Swiss woman suffrage organizations were clearly cut out of some aspects of the decision-making process. Suffrage activists did not participate in the pre-parliamentary decisions nor were they represented by parliamentarians with multiple mandates. In that sense, the special characteristics of the Swiss political system may have constrained the activities of Swiss woman suffrage organizations. On the other hand, Swiss suffrage activists did not take advantage of two key opportunities—campaigning for pro-suffrage candidates and lobbying officials.

The disadvantages caused by the Swiss system cannot explain the lack of other lobbying tactics in the movement's repertoire. Although Swiss suffrage activists were more disadvantaged by their political process than their U.S. counterparts, American suffrage activists were also excluded from many informal arenas of decision making. American activists complained about the political decisions being made in smoke-filled back rooms where women had no entrée (see for example, Brown 1940a: 107). Nonetheless, woman suffrage activists in the United States reacted differently to their lack of access to informal decision making, choosing to increase their emphasis on legislative lobbying and electoral strategies. Although suffrage activists in both countries could not vote, American suffrage activists still conducted campaigns for pro-suffrage candidates while their Swiss counterparts did not.

Moreover, suffrage associations are not the only interests disadvantaged by the Swiss political process; many Swiss groups are not represented in the extra-parliamentary decision-making process. Usually only the larger powerful interest groups are granted a seat at the bargaining table (Linder 1987: 33). Nonetheless, even smaller interest groups and social movements, which work primarily outside of formal institutions, have utilized lobbying techniques. For example, Engeler notes that even many new social movements in Switzerland have chosen to use traditional legislative tactics including "seeking, creating, and, if already existing, strengthening very specific contacts to elected officials" (1986: 241; translated by author). Thus, although the Swiss system of pre-parliamentary decision making and multiple mandates limited the influence of the suffrage movement, that alone is insufficient to account for the almost complete absence of lobbying tactics by Swiss suffrage activists, especially since their occasional use was so effective.

Conclusion

There is a stark contrast between the Swiss and the American suffrage movements' attempts to win the vote by influencing the government. Swiss suffrage activists rarely even considered employing the techniques that had such great success in the United States. The sporadic attempts at polling candidates or pressuring officials never spread beyond a few innovative cantons. Local suffrage organizations that used these tactics did so only once, never making them a part of their routine. These aggressive lobbying techniques seem to be almost random events in a legislative strategy otherwise filled with petitions and organizational appeals to the government. Random or not, these very same tactics appear to have been highly successful in convincing cantons to formally consider and finally adopt women's voting rights.

The documentary and interview evidence in Switzerland give no indication that polling, supporting candidates, contacting officials, or pressuring parties were considered but then rejected by the national and cantonal suffrage movements. While Swiss suffrage organizations deliberated carefully about the form that public propaganda and campaigns for suffrage referenda should take, they generally assumed that legislative support was unproblematic and would automatically follow from increasing public support for suffrage. When legislative tactics were considered, they focused on highly public petitions or letters of appeal to parliaments but almost never on more practical, but less visible, lobbying.

In contrast, the American suffrage movement had a wealth of information about legislative tactics. The national suffrage organization was constantly disseminating advice on tactics, some of which originated from the experiences of local sections. In fact, the suffrage organization developed specific institutions—Suffrage Schools, workshops at annual conventions, and publications—to spread this knowledge to local groups. The result was that information about tactics and strategies spread quickly in the United States.

Although Swiss suffrage activists were largely excluded from a formal pre-parliamentary process of influence and could not be represented by legislators with multiple mandates like other interest groups, that alone cannot account for the total absence of legislative strategies. Yet, before we consider the reasons for this absence by examining the role of information, values and beliefs, we must explore one other alternative explanation—that Swiss suffrage activists did not employ these strategies because they chose to work outside the system. Swiss suffrage activists even more than their American counterparts had other possible courses of action open to them. They could use disruption in the hopes of forcing the government to accede to their demands or bypass elected officials and initiate legislation using available direct democratic institutions. The latter possibility meant that Swiss suffrage activists were not totally dependent on national and cantonal legislatures to achieve suffrage.

7

RAISING SUFFRAGE DEMANDS:

CONFRONTATION VERSUS COMPROMISE

BOTH THE UNITED STATES and Switzerland offered opportunities to bypass legislatures altogether. In several states and all cantons, initiative rights permitted suffrage activists to circumvent the decisions of elected officials and bring suffrage directly to a vote of the (male) electorate. In addition, suffrage activists in both countries also hoped to enfranchise women by legal challenges. Both Swiss and American suffrage activists attempted to register to vote and took their cases to court when they were prohibited from doing so. Suffrage activists also engaged in extra-governmental challenges to the system that differed from more "conventional" political means in their tone and activities. Extra-governmental challenges *demanded* the vote and they did so in a public manner involving parades, demonstrations, picketing, and strikes. In a few instances in the United States, these led to the arrest of suffrage activists and to more extreme actions such as hunger strikes.

Each of these—initiatives, litigation, and extra-governmental challenges—also helped to develop public support for women's voting rights. Initiative petition drives not only allowed suffrage organizations to bypass the legislature but also served an educational function as suffrage activists crisscrossed the state drumming up the required number of signatures. Most initiative petitions received considerable media coverage, further increasing public consciousness of the issue, even when they failed to acquire a sufficient number of signatures (Cronin 1989; Magleby 1984). Legal challenges, as a tactic for gaining the vote, were generally unsuccessful. Except for the Swiss lawsuit in 1990 giving women the right to vote in Appenzell Innerrhoden, none of the court cases in either country resulted in an extension of the franchise. Nonetheless, even when suffrage activists were sure they would not win, they were happy about the publicity the legal challenge created. Similarly, parades, demonstrations, and strikes gave the suffrage cause notoriety, even though not all activists were happy about it. When American activists burned President Wilson in effigy or Basel teachers struck to protest the rejection of the national woman suffrage amendment, the public debated the propriety of their actions for weeks.

In addition to these tactics, suffrage organizations in both countries conducted educational campaigns. In nonreferenda years, these varied from "quiet" campaigns where the specific issue of suffrage was de-emphasized to vociferous crusades designed to draw attention to the suffrage cause. Suffrage organizations sponsored lectures and courses on suffrage or a related topic, and took their educational campaigns to public spaces by setting up information booths at state fairs, town squares, or wherever an opportunity existed.

Public education in both countries increased dramatically during suffrage referenda. Indeed, these plebiscites not only had the potential to enfranchise women but also were preceded by campaigns designed to mobilize public opinion. Thus, Mary de Vou, describing the woman suffrage movement in Delaware bemoaned the fact that "the advocates of woman suffrage have continued to suffer from the handicap peculiar to Delaware—no referendum to the voters possible on constitutional amendments—and therefore it never has had the advantage of a State-wide educational campaign" (Harper 1922b: 86).

This chapter explores the different use of these four types of tactics—educational, legal, electoral, and extra-governmental—by local and national suffrage organizations. As was the case with lobbying, the tactics of national suffrage organizations differed significantly, even though both movements saw an increase in confrontational strategies toward the end of their suffrage campaigns. Although there was variation within each country, the American suffrage movement employed more confrontational tactics than those of the Swiss suffrage movement, which relied heavily on education and referendum campaigns. The choice of tactics was significant in both countries; when local organizations increased their use of confrontational tactics, they were more likely to have suffrage legislation considered in legislatures, suffrage amendments supported in referenda, and voting rights for women adopted. Yet, in spite of the connection between these tactics and success, few Swiss suffrage movements took advantage of them.

The Role of Confrontational Tactics

The effectiveness of disruptive and violent tactics in allowing movements to achieve their goals is hotly debated (Astin 1975; Gamson 1975; Piven and Cloward 1979; Snyder and Kelly 1976; and Welsh 1975). In fact, violent or disruptive tactics were rare in western suffrage movements; only the British suffrage activists used violence to achieve women's enfranchisement. The American and Swiss suffrage movements are no exception. With one minor exception, the two movements initiated no events involving violence, strikes, or boycotts which might have disrupted society. The strongest tactics used were demonstrating, picketing, and civil disobedience, none of which were violent or disruptive in Piven and Cloward's (1979) sense of interfering with the process of government.

Nonetheless, suffrage tactics varied in the degree of confrontation. Activists within both the Swiss and the American suffrage movements debated whether confrontational tactics were helpful in achieving suffrage. In Switzerland, the disagreement divided the women's liberation movement (*Frauenbefreiungsbewegung* or FBB) from longtime suffrage activists. Activists in the newer women's liberation movement argued that their confrontational and militant tactics were the impetus that finally forced the government and public to support woman suffrage. In contrast, many of the suffrage activists I interviewed argued that their years of careful preparation and the resulting slow evolution of public opinion made the enfranchisement of women possible.

A similar debate raged in the United States. There, members of the Congressional Union, later called the Woman's party (WP), copied the militant strategies of the British suffragettes, while leaders of the National American Woman Suffrage Association (NAWSA) found these tactics extreme. When the battle was over, supporters of the WP claimed that the government had "yielded under gunfire" (Doris Stevens cited in Ford 1991: 244). According to Carrie Chapman Catt, however:

> The Woman's Party claims that its . . . anti-Wilson demonstrations, including the constant picketing of the White House, and the burning of his book "The New Freedom" and his effigy, were the source of his [President Wilson's] change in attitude. The National Suffrage Association credits him with yielding to the momentum of the movement . . . *which grew in spite of and not because of these demonstrations.* (Catt and Shuler 1926: 259–60; emphasis added)

While the most vehement debate occurred between different women's rights groups (the WP and the NAWSA in the United States, and the FBB and the SVF in Switzerland), both arguments were also voiced within suffrage organizations. In Switzerland, some SVF activists advocated more confrontation and symbolic acts of protest while others argued that these would be counterproductive. In the United States, the NAWSA, despite its passive rhetoric, adopted more confrontational tactics like the suffrage parade in later years, although some local sections continued to shun these techniques. Thus, while the Woman's Party in the United States or the Frauenbefreiungsbewegung in Switzerland engaged in substantially different activities from the NAWSA and SVF, they were not the only source of confrontation.

An examination of the efficacy of such techniques therefore requires that we define "confrontation" so that we can measure its use within each organization. For the purpose of this study, tactics are considered confrontational to the extent to which they: (1) make explicit demands on the political system, (2) show an unwillingness to compromise on these demands,[1] and (3) force the intended audience to face the issue by raising it in a loud, direct manner. These three elements—explicit demands, rigidity, and forcefulness—determine the degree of confrontation of a specific tactic.

National Differences in Confrontational Tactics

The United States

The tactics used to gain public support for suffrage in the United States changed dramatically over time. For most of the movement, suffrage organizations were "virtually educational bodies" (Kraditor 1981: 226). Early activists saw gentle persuasion as the only instrument capable of changing the views of legislators, party leaders, and the public. Suffrage activists grew more confrontational in the wake of the Civil War (1866–1876) and, to a greater extent, during the last decade of the suffrage movement (1910–1920). During these eras, suffrage activists were more insistent. They became more explicit in their demands, they proved less willing to compromise, and they increased their use of public protest.[2] The differences between confrontational and nonconfrontational tactics is best observed by comparing these different eras of U.S. suffrage history along the three dimensions of confrontation.

EXPLICIT DEMANDS

While U.S. suffrage activists were always interested in winning the vote for women, they did not always believe that the best way to do so was to explicitly state their goal at every turn. In order to reach a large audience, the earlier woman suffrage organizations engaged in a number of activities that most observers would consider unrelated to the goal of woman suffrage. During the Civil War, many woman suffrage activists provided services to the army and created support organizations to show that "Woman is equally interested and responsible with man" (Stanton cited in Harper 1969, 1: 227; see also Venet 1991: 152). During peacetime, other activities were seen as a means for subtly inculcating the public with suffrage propaganda. Thus, the proceedings of the 1899 convention of the National American Woman Suffrage Association suggests: "It is advised that the scope of our Leagues be enlarged to work on other club lines for suffrage. The maintenance of a kindergarten . . . might well be considered germane to the work of a Suffrage League. In many localities, the introduction of social features serves to win attendance of men and of young people, and the desired opportunity to inculcate suffrage ideas is thus afforded" (NAWSA 1899: 42). Thus, suffrage activists argued that work on other issues would indirectly increase support for woman suffrage.

In contrast, suffrage demands became explicit during more confrontational periods. In 1866, after reducing their equal rights activity in favor of supporting the war effort and the abolitionist cause, many suffrage activists felt women deserved to be enfranchised. When some abolitionist members of the American Equal Rights Association, ostensibly founded to demand universal suffrage, argued that women should only fight for the vote after voting rights for blacks were assured, suffrage activists felt betrayed and began to be more explicit in their demands. Suffrage activists began to demand women's enfranchisement in referenda, voter registration offices, and public events.

After 1876, suffrage activists returned to the less direct forms of education discussed above, but in the last decade of the suffrage movement direct demands for woman suffrage again became the favored technique. Now suffrage advocacy was a matter of efficiency. The 1917 NAWSA *Yearbook* argued the best means of agitating for women's voting rights were speaking on suffrage before any ready-made audience (such as state fairs, organizations' conventions, and even passersby on the street), pushing suffrage stories in local media, and calling small neighborhood meetings to engage women in intimate discussion of the suffrage cause (Stapler 1917). These later discussions of organizing strategies make no mention of any non-suffrage activities.

RIGIDITY

The aftermath of the Civil War not only created explicit demands for suffrage but also reduced some suffrage activists' willingness to compromise. When Kansas offered both a black voting rights and a woman suffrage amendment to their constitution in 1867, many abolitionists argued that fighting for woman suffrage would hurt the abolitionist cause (Stanton et al. 1881a: 230). However, the founders of the National Woman Suffrage Association refused to accept the suggestion that women should not press their demands. Instead, they insisted "on absolute right. . . . They knew their position was unassailable, for they had learned the lesson taught in the early days of anti-slavery . . . that all compromises with principle are dangerous" (Stanton et al. 1881b: 320).

In the later quarter of the nineteenth century, however, suffrage activists became less rigid and softened their appeals. Local sections focused on municipal and school suffrage as compromise measures they hoped would later lead to full suffrage legislation. On the national level, the suffrage organizations slowly abandoned demands for a federal amendment. Even when requesting that Congress pass such an amendment, they showed a willingness to compromise. In asking for a suffrage plank from the 1900 Republican party convention, Susan B. Anthony, argued:

> The Republican party was organized in response to the demand for human freedom. . . . We appeal to the Republican party to sustain its record by applying this declaration to the lawful women citizens of the United States. You will observe that this petition *does not ask you to endorse the enfranchisement of women*, but simply to recommend that Congress submit this question to the decision of the various state Legislatures. (Anthony and Harper 1902: 440; emphasis added)

Suffrage sentiments shifted again around 1910 as suffrage activists became more inflexible in their appeals. The suffrage activists of the Woman's party best exemplified the new rigidity. Even though the Democratic party was (at least according to the NAWSA) moving toward endorsing suffrage, the Woman's party refused to accept partial change as progress and continued to hold it responsible for women's disenfranchisement. When women were again called upon to engage in war work during World War I, the WP refused to forgo suffrage efforts and even began to utilize war rhetoric as a weapon in their pickets of the White House (Lunardini 1986).

Twenty years after Anthony's moderate petition, new signs of determination and stubbornness could also be seen in the NAWSA. Suffrage activists' quadrennial appeal to the Republican convention showed an unwillingness to accept limited endorsements of women's voting rights and even included a veiled threat to the party: "We are not asking your endorsement of an untried theory but your recognition of a fact. . . . The women of five states have gained the vote since 1912, your last convention, and *have party affiliations yet to make*" (Harper 1922a: 709–10; emphasis added).

FORCEFULNESS

If suffrage activists were more uncompromising and explicit in their requests for suffrage during these two eras, they also chose tactics that forced the public to hear their demands. Between 1866 and 1876, suffrage activists challenged their disenfranchisement using the legal system, mainly by attempting to register and vote. Indeed, most of the litigation on women's right to vote in the United States occurred during this decade.

In 1866, Elizabeth Cady Stanton declared that the Fourteenth and Fifteenth Amendments did not prevent women from holding office and ran as an independent candidate for Congress (Griffith 1984: 119). Between 1871 and 1872, approximately 150 women attempted to cast ballots. The most famous incidents involved Susan B. Anthony and Virginia Minor, who managed to bring her case before the Supreme Court in 1874. The attempts to register were also opportunities for public protest; marching into polling places and registration offices engendered as much publicity as the later legal suits.

Nor were U.S. suffrage tactics limited to legal challenges during this period. Other public acts of protest also occurred. When suffrage activists were told that they would not be included on the program of centennial celebration in Philadelphia in 1876, they chose to interrupt the festivities. After the Declaration of Independence was read, five suffrage activists, including Anthony, presented the Woman's Declaration of Independence in front of foreign dignitaries (Harper 1969, 1: 477–78). However, after 1876, in the wake of other scandals, suffrage activists withdrew from tactics that might be considered disreputable, and returned to the use of educational techniques.

While some suffrage organizations never altered their emphasis on quiet education, many state sections and the national organizations returned to more forceful, confrontational tactics during the last decade of the suffrage battle. Suffrage parades were a significant part of activists' repertoire during these years. Although they had been used in the temperance movement, suffrage activists' adoption of this tactic was instigated largely by British suffrage activists; the first U.S. suffrage parade occurred spontaneously in 1908 after two British suffragists spoke at a meeting of a local Iowa suffrage organization (Evans 1989: 165; Noun 1969). Thereafter, state suffrage organizations increasingly incorporated parades into their campaigns to show the extent of local support for suffrage. Even the relatively staid auxiliaries utilized motor tours and parades to publicize their cause (see, for example, McBride 1993: 210–13). By 1914, the NAWSA also relied on parades to convince the major parties and the Congress to support a national suffrage amendment. NAWSA held parades outside the Democratic and Republican conventions in 1916 and organized a series of nationwide demonstrations when the issue was brought before Congress in 1917. In all, over 9,000 parades and open-air meetings were held in 26 states.[3]

Parades generated considerable publicity for the cause. In 1913, a parade in Washington during Woodrow Wilson's inauguration created a bigger stir than the new president. Five thousand women marched among a hostile crowd while the police provided little protection. Eventually the military was called from Fort Myer to protect the marchers. The ensuing scandal resulted in a Congressional investigation and dismissal of the police chief. Catt and Shuler note that the scandal turned into a great public relations tool: "The dissemination of the news of these events day after day brought discussion on the subject of woman suffrage to every hamlet in the land" (1926: 243). As the parades grew ever larger, their impact multiplied. When 10,000 women marched in the pouring rain at the Republican national convention in Chicago, it publicized the strength of the suffrage movement.

The creation of the Congressional Union, later called the Woman's party (WP), also engendered a rise in protest tactics between 1910 and 1920. Its members split from the NAWSA because they saw its less confrontational strategy as ineffective. Alice Paul, the leader of this new group, had taken part in militant suffrage activities in England and continually tried to adapt the British techniques to the American context (Evans 1989). The WP picketed the White House; they also burned effigies of President Wilson and some of his speeches about democracy in Europe. Although mild in comparison with those of English suffragettes, these actions were highly visible acts of protest. Even though these acts were roundly condemned, they significantly increased publicity around woman suffrage.

Thus, by the end of the suffrage campaign in 1919, the tactics of suffrage activists were much more confrontational than ever before. No longer did American suffrage activists attempt to inculcate suffrage ideas through indirect methods or hope that compromise would be effective. Instead, demands for suffrage were proclaimed loud and clear at every opportunity—in public propaganda, suffrage parades, and protests in front of the White House.

Switzerland

In contrast to efforts in the United States, the activities of the Swiss suffrage movement seem timid. While American suffrage organizations sanctioned a number of national marches, the lone suffrage march on the Swiss capital was not even endorsed by the Schweizerischer Verband für Frauenstimmrecht (SVF). Most of the public awareness about the issue of woman suffrage at the national level was generated during the two referenda on women's voting rights in 1959 and 1971. Otherwise, national activities focused on public meetings, the distribution of press packets or organized letter-to-the-editor campaigns.

One reason for the lack of confrontational tactics is that the national-level organization did not initiate many activities outside of its legislative and referenda work. Most educational work was sponsored by local suffrage organizations. Even in national referenda, much of the public relations work was left to local suffrage organizations or local action committees. At most, the SVF and the Arbeitsgemeinschaft der schweizerischen Frauenverbände für die politischen Rechte der Frau coordinated national propaganda and offered suggestions and information for local suffrage groups. For example, after losing the first national referendum in 1959, the national organization encouraged local sections to memorialize the date as Woman Suffrage Day.

Prior to 1950, the SVF generally avoided uncompromising, confrontational tactics in its sponsored actions. When the centennial celebration of the Swiss constitution in 1948 trumpeted the importance of the ballot for the Swiss democracy, Swiss suffrage activists reacted in a relatively nonconfrontational fashion. The SVF held a public forum to discuss the current state of Swiss women's rights with lectures on citizenship and civil rights for married women, and the meaning of the housewife and social insurance (Ruckstuhl 1986). Meeting participants passed a resolution calling for a revision of the constitution to include equal rights for women. Notably missing from the program was any discussion on women's voting rights. In comparison to American suffrage activists' disruption of the official centennial celebration in Philadelphia, the SVF reacted by raising the issue indirectly and in a manner (public forum) that did not force the public to consider women's enfranchisement.

Even in years when the organization's activities specifically addressed woman suffrage, its eschewed confrontation. The heaviest activity during this early period occurred in 1928 when the SVF participated in a major exhibition on Swiss women and work and ran a petition drive asking the national legislature to consider woman suffrage. Each of these undertakings demanded considerable resources from the suffrage organization.

The exhibition of women's work (Schweizerische Ausstellung für Frauenarbeit [SAFFA]) was organized mainly by women's unions and the Schweizerischer Katholischer Frauenbund to highlight women's contributions to society. As a consequence, little of the 36,000–square meter exhibition space was related to women's political rights. While the SVF was permitted to create an exhibit addressing political rights for women, they were forced to share a 22–square meter room with other exhibits of "social work." Thus, discussions of women's rights were mixed with portraits of famous women educators and social workers. Nonetheless, activists distributed suffrage literature at the exhibition and talked to passing exhibitors. Major publicity for woman suffrage at SAFFA came from the suffrage float in the opening parade, which featured a giant snail with a sign underneath saying "The progress of woman suffrage in Switzerland." While parade participants wore colored sashes as they accompanied the float, there were no other signs demanding votes for women.

The SVF's second major activity in 1928 was an organized campaign to collect signatures for a petition asking the national government to enfranchise women. In conjunction with the petition drive, 355 public meetings were held to raise public support and gather signatures. While the campaign generated considerable media attention, the petition disappeared into obscurity soon after it was delivered to the capital. The government ignored the petition, and press coverage of the suffrage issue quickly died out. Suffrage activists, having handed over the petition, reduced their level of public campaigning while waiting for a response from the government. They waited thirty years.

These two events—SAFFA and the national petition drive—were the highlights of suffrage publicity work during the pre-1950 period. Except for a few cantonal referenda campaigns and some public lectures, suffrage was otherwise absent until the late 1950s when activities increased again. The normal yearly activity of the SVF until the late 1950s—an annual convention, a handful of public meetings where suffrage was infrequently raised, and official letters of petition to the federal government—generated little discussion of women's voting rights among the larger public. The activities of 1928 were only slightly more confrontational. While woman suffrage was mentioned more often than in other years, suffrage activists did not present an unyielding demand for suffrage in their SAFFA work or the suffrage petition. While more public meetings on the topic of women's voting rights were held, most of these did not force the public to confront the issue. Finally, the SVF's decision to collect signatures for a petition rather than an initiative gave government officials the chance to ignore their request.

INITIATIVES IN SWITZERLAND

It is worth a slight digression to discuss national initiative rights in Switzerland. The Schweizerischer Verband für Frauenstimmrecht had an opportunity unavailable in the United States: It could launch an initiative petition to place a national constitutional amendment before the voters (although women were prohibited from signing initiative petitions themselves). This would have authorized a woman suffrage referendum even without the support of the Bundesrat or Swiss Parliament. Thus, an initiative petition drive had the potential to create major opportunities for confronting the public with the woman suffrage issue. Yet, the SVF never availed itself of this opportunity. Several times during the course of the suffrage movement, suffrage leaders considered and rejected using an initiative drive to put a suffrage amendment on the ballot.

In 1928, the SVF chose to run a regular petition drive instead of an initiative because it allowed *women* to support women's enfranchisement and because the requirement that men's signatures to be listed separately by town was considered too onerous (Ruckstuhl 1986). Instead, the SVF collected signatures from men and women on separate petitions, without utilizing the men's signatures for an initiative. Although the petition was presented to the presidents of both houses of Parliament, its delivery was never even noted in Parliamentary records. Ironically, the number of signatures from male voters would have been sufficient to bring a woman suffrage amendment to a national vote.

The possibility of an initiative drive was discussed at least three other times. In 1918, national leaders of the SVF considered an initiative, but delegates at the annual meeting were concerned about how it would be viewed in light of the general strike. Suffrage activists concluded they were spared the necessity of the time and expense of an initiative when two suffrage motions were introduced into the Swiss Parliament (SVF 1934: 19). My interviews with suffrage activists indicate that the initiative was considered a second time in 1952 although no minutes of this meeting are available. One activist claimed to have supported the idea of an initiative drive and was disappointed when the SVF board chose to pursue a different strategy. The issue was also raised during a 1969 meeting of women's organizations to discuss the March on Bern, but it was postponed to a later meeting. Since the Federal Council recommended a second vote on a woman suffrage amendment soon thereafter, the initiative was never discussed again.

In fact, most Swiss woman suffrage activists did not perceive the initiative as a useful means of acquiring woman suffrage, even when suffrage motions were never followed by legislation (officially, the Bundesrat responded to the 1918 motions in 1951). Among the 56 woman suffrage activists I interviewed, very few mentioned the initiative when talking about the tactics available to the organization. It was simply not part of the "repertoire" of tactics that most activists viewed as available to them. One suffrage activist even maintained that "We did not have the possibility of launching an initiative ourselves"(interview of December 15, 1987), implying women lacked the right or ability to run initiative drives. Many others never raised the possibility of initiatives in their interviews. When asked about the possibility, several suggested that the tactic was symbolically wrong because women could not sign the petitions.

SWISS TACTICS AFTER 1950

Three events in the late 1950s heralded a tactical change on the national level: the second SAFFA in 1958, the 1959 referendum on woman suffrage, and an organized attempt to register in 1959 and 1960. At the second SAFFA, held thirty years after the first exhibition, the issue of woman suffrage played an even smaller role than it had in the earlier one.

Officially, the second SAFFA prohibited any advertisement for woman suffrage. As a result, the lack of suffrage was illustrated in a single poster that showed women as unequal to men in a number of political rights. No other exhibition by the SVF was allowed. Indeed, although other women's groups were allowed to use SAFFA grounds to hold conventions, the SVF was prohibited from doing so until the exhibition was over because of its political message (Ruckstuhl 1986: 92). Only the timing of SAFFA and a speech by a pro-suffrage politician created publicity for women's voting rights; by the time the second SAFFA occurred, the Swiss government had already announced that a woman suffrage referendum would be held the following year.

After the government announced that it would put a woman suffrage amendment to a vote, a national action committee was immediately organized to prepare for the referendum campaign. The SVF and other women's groups that belonged to the action committee insisted, however, that the campaign be conducted in as nonconfrontational a way as possible. An action committee policy paper on referendum tactics suggested that: "Women who want to participate in an action-friendly way must remain conscious [of the fact] that action going overboard in extent, material contents or even in tone could hurt the cause" (Document of the Schweizerische Aktionskomitee für das Frauenstimm- und -wahlrecht, dated December 1958, Gosteli Stiftung; translated by author). Indeed, the action committee concluded that, when possible, men should do the publicity work for the campaign. Since women were not voters, they should not take a major role in the campaign. Rather, they "should let the normal legislative evolution take its course and then see what results from it on the first of February [election day]" (Schweizerische Aktionskomitee fuer das Frauenstimm- und -wahlrecht December 1958: 5; translated by author).

The action committee itself focused on creating pamphlets, posters, mass mailings, and a central clearinghouse for specific arguments. The clearinghouse was a card catalog that contained responses to specific objections to woman suffrage and positive arguments that could be employed in particular situations. The major concern of the action committee was press work, placing pro-suffrage messages in newspapers, and answering anti-suffrage articles or opinion pieces in letters to the newspaper or press releases.

Even though this was a national referendum, the national action committee delegated much of the work to local committees. These were responsible for organizing public meetings in their area, supplying propaganda to local newspapers, and providing pro-suffrage speakers to those local political parties or organizations that were holding meetings on the amendment. This created a problem for the nine cantons that lacked local action committees. The national action committee did not organize local committees but expected local women to form their own. In those cantons without a local action committee, no pro-suffrage propaganda was spread except through national newspapers, and no pro-suffrage meetings were organized. It was also difficult for political parties or other groups to locate local spokespeople for the suffrage cause.[4]

Although the 1959 national suffrage referendum was fought using nonconfrontational tactics, the use of forceful tactics began to increase on the local level around this time. Indeed, the major action that made national headlines during this period was an initiative of the French-speaking cantons. Led by Antoinette Quinche, whose lobbying efforts helped make Vaud the first canton to accept woman suffrage, Francophone women went to their local governments demanding to be registered to vote. Over 1,500 women participated in this action, many bravely going alone to their local registration office. When local and cantonal governments refused to enter them into the voter rolls, they sued, claiming that the constitution already granted them political equality. However, the Supreme Court was unsympathetic to their argument and ruled against them (SVF 1959).

The use of direct, forceful tactics increased even further in the 1960s with the emergence of the women's liberation movement (Frauenbefreiungsbewegung or FBB). Younger women from the student movement criticized the staid tactics of the older suffrage women. As this new movement grew, it introduced street theater, demonstrations, and other confrontational tactics to the fight for suffrage. However, on the national level, it resulted in only one major demonstration: the 1969 March on Bern.

The March on Bern was the first and only national woman suffrage demonstration of any size. Both the FBB and the national suffrage organization felt that something should be done to protest the government's decision to exclude the clauses on women's political rights in signing the European Human Rights Convention. FBB women strongly supported a protest march and initially helped to organize the March on Bern along with the local suffrage organizations in Zürich and Basel. Their attitude toward the question of the Human Rights Convention showed an unwillingness to compromise: "Together with the Zürich women of the suffrage movement . . . we will not shy away from any means, in order to prevent the [conditional] signing of the Human Rights convention" (Statement by FBB activist in "Die Protest-Frauen" 1969: 20; translated by author).

On the other hand, the national suffrage organization did not support or approve of the idea of a protest march. In a special meeting of the SVF, a national demonstration was rejected by a majority of delegates as too aggressive, although a few local sections (most notably Zürich and Basel) chose to participate anyway. In a separate meeting, the presidents of the SVF and several other national women's organizations expressed fear that a demonstration would get out of control. Instead, the SVF leaders preferred sending a delegation to the Federal Council, holding a press conference, or organizing letter campaigns. In the end, some suffrage activists stood in the demonstration while others joined in a hastily organized lobbying effort at the Federal Council and a separate public meeting across town.[5]

Soon after these events, the Federal Council prepared another woman suffrage constitutional referendum to be decided in 1971. The tactics of the national woman suffrage organization in the second referendum differed little from those used in 1959. A national action committee coordinated local cantonal committees, prepared press materials, provided speakers for meetings, and created and distributed posters and brochures. Again, activists argued that the majority of propaganda work should be given to men. The only difference between the 1959 and the 1971 referendum campaigns was an increased number of local action committees, indicating both wider support for the enfranchisement of women and more local propaganda than in 1959. However, the character of the suffrage campaign changed very little.

Summing Up National Differences

Swiss and American tactics differed less in the type of confrontation than in the quantity. This discussion of Swiss tactics chronicles *every* national action outside of public lectures and legislative work. Although several— the March on Bern, the attempts to register, and the distribution of literature at SAFFA—were similar to the activities of their American counterparts, such events were rare. American suffrage activists conducted thousands of suffrage parades; Swiss suffrage activists only a dozen, and all but one were orchestrated by local sections. American activists sponsored innumerable suffrage lectures and public information booths. Their Swiss counterparts organized far fewer of these events and many of them were *not* about women's voting rights.

However, there were also important qualitative differences in the way that suffrage activists framed their demands. Swiss activists preferred to raise their demands indirectly and gently. At no point during the 1958/1959 suffrage campaign did they confront male voters with their demands. Instead, they hoped that by making no demands and allowing men to discuss the issue themselves, the majority of male voters would choose to endorse the enfranchisement of women.

Why did the 1971 national referenda finally succeed? Certainly the quiet educational campaigns of the suffrage activists had slowly converted some voters to the suffrage cause. However, a number of other activities also contributed to the general awareness of the suffrage issue. The 1959 referendum followed several decades of almost absolute quiet on the suffrage front. Confrontational actions were relatively new, and, except for the attempt made by French-speaking women to register in 1957, relatively unpublicized. On the other hand, the 1971 campaign followed several years of local suffrage parades, a national demonstration, and a number of other confrontational actions. Between 1950 and 1970, the tactics of the suffrage movement had changed from an occasional and hesitant mention of women's voting rights to more explicit, direct, and forceful actions. Many of these occurred on the local level.

Local Differences in Tactics

Although the preceding section chronicles general trends in the use of confrontational tactics, state and cantonal suffrage organizations often pursued their own strategies. Within each country, some local sections relied exclusively on nonconfrontational tactics while others chose to confront the public with demands for equal voting rights.

Less Confrontational Tactics

State and cantonal movements that utilized less confrontational tactics tended to assume that the issue of woman suffrage elicited automatic negative reactions among the public. For that reason, their activists rarely spoke of voting rights directly, but focused on the positive role women already played and could play in public life. They believed strident, nonconventional tactics were repulsive to the public and therefore counterproductive to the movement's goals of increasing public support. In addition, these groups often focused on partial suffrage, which they thought would be more palatable to the public. Two examples—in canton Bern and the state of Florida—illustrate typical strategies of nonconfrontation.

BERN

The suffrage organization in Bern, an agricultural canton that also contains the nation's capital, was actually unusual for a canton that used less confrontational tactics. While most such suffrage sections were relatively small, its suffrage association was large and very active like sections in other Swiss cantons with major cities (Basel, Zürich, Genève). Unlike these other suffrage associations, however, the Bern section chose to engage in numerous nonconfrontational actions. Its activities exemplify indirect ways of raising the issue, a willingness to compromise and work within the system. Thus, nonconfrontation is not synonymous with inactivity.

The tactics of the Bern suffrage association relied very heavily on the idea that women's voting rights must not be mentioned. Talks sponsored by the Bern suffrage organization focused on topics such as "Our Agriculture Today and Tomorrow" (1967) or "Problems in the Determination of Criminal Sentences" (1966).[6] In addition, education courses, such as the 1955 course on the "The Construction and Function of the State," were held to promote increased knowledge of the political process among women. Suffrage activists believed that this indirect education was very important:

> A lot of work went into political courses, especially in the rural areas. That was very important. . . . When they came to the courses, they found out what the community government actually did, and learned that this was where they could get involved in the schools, for example. What I want to say is that in an *indirect* way, we wanted to show women and the larger community how suffrage worked, and what was behind it since many women were afraid of suffrage. (interview of January 21, 1988)

Similarly, the Bern organization chose not to emphasize full woman suffrage legislation but only bills that gave local governments the option to introduce municipal suffrage. Only after this was achieved in 1968 did cantonal activists advocate full cantonal voting rights. They believed that feelings of local autonomy ran so strong that suffrage was only obtainable by starting at the lowest level. Nonetheless, they were very energetic in pursuing local option bills. After two motions for municipal option suffrage were defeated in the cantonal parliament in 1942, suffrage activists organized a petition drive to convince legislators to reconsider. When the petition did not result in the desired legislation, Bern suffrage activists launched an initiative asking for optional municipal suffrage in 1953. Finally, when a new motion was introduced for full woman suffrage in 1963, the Bern suffrage organization supported the decision of the Governing Council to substitute optional local suffrage legislation instead.

While the Bern suffrage activists were very active, they believed that directly confronting the public with demands was counterproductive. Instead, the best strategy was quiet education, an emphasis on partnership and nonconfrontational activities. "There were many militant women even before the sixties, and they were the ones even today who by their actions . . . work counterproductively. It is a tactical question when you want something, when you want to make progress. Also during the suffrage fight there were women who acted aggressively, and I even knew some. They always had a counterproductive effect" (interview of January 21, 1988).

FLORIDA

The Florida suffrage association also demonstrated a preference for non-confrontational tactics. For example, in the proceedings of the forty-sixth annual convention of the NAWSA (1914: 159), the Florida suffrage organization reported that "Knowing how the men of the smaller towns shrank from the word suffrage, the League adopted the name of Florida Equal Franchise." The Florida section also emphasized activities that avoided the topic of suffrage directly but were designed to attract people to the organization. For example, the Pensacola section sponsored a Better Babies Contest (Taylor 1957a). As in Bern, Florida sections sponsored courses "to study history and the duties of citizenship" (Harper 1922b: 115). These promoted suffrage indirectly by educating women about the important role they could play in politics, and hence implicitly, the necessity of their enfranchisement.

The Florida League also emphasized local forms of suffrage, albeit less persistently than its Swiss counterpart. One Miami section conducted a petition drive requesting the right to vote in municipal elections. Other local areas followed suit, with several localities (including Palm Beach, Daytona, and Daytona Beach) adopting municipal suffrage before 1920. In 1918, the League resolved that it would focus on voting rights in primary elections.

Despite the League's own clear emphasis on avoiding the suffrage label, it was much more willing to openly discuss women's enfranchisement than the Bern organization. Many public meetings involved guest lecturers, usually from outside the state, speaking on suffrage. In addition to municipal and primary suffrage, the Florida group also worked on developing public support for federal and state constitutional suffrage amendments (Harper 1922b: 116). In this sense, the Florida organization was less afraid of the suffrage label and of stating its goal of full suffrage than its Bern counterpart.

Confrontational Tactics

If Bern and Florida represent local movements at one end of a continuum of tactics, both nations also had local groups that were less concerned about shocking or offending the public. Rather, they felt the best means for acquiring suffrage was ensuring that their demands were clearly heard. Confrontational tactics were seen as necessary because they provided clear evidence of a strong demand for suffrage. Using these justifications, confrontational suffrage groups—such as those in Basel-stadt and Georgia—demanded women's enfranchisement in a way that required that the public deal with the issue.

BASEL-STADT

At its founding in 1916, the Basel-stadt suffrage organization petitioned for women's right to vote for church boards and divorce judges (Villard-Traber 1984). In 1920, 1927, and again in 1946, it organized referendum campaigns for full woman suffrage. In fact, Basel-stadt had more referenda on full suffrage during the first half of the twentieth century than any other canton, allowing suffrage activists to publicize the cause of woman suffrage directly and to a larger audience.

In the mid-1950s, Basel suffrage activists also began to use symbolic acts of protest to challenge their disenfranchisement. This use of confrontational tactics started after a fourth attempt to adopt full cantonal suffrage amendment failed in a 1954 referendum. Activists were motivated to greater activity by a previous nonbinding referendum that showed an overwhelming majority of women supported women's enfranchisement. Suffrage activists argued that if women's votes had been counted with the men's, the suffrage amendment would have been ratified. They responded by conducting an initiative drive in 1955 to allow both men and women to vote on the issue. While the initiative acquired the necessary signatures in 1957, the cantonal parliament did not act on the initiative until 1966. Meanwhile, the suffrage organization also supported efforts by political parties to introduce optional community suffrage.

By the 1959 national referendum, women were voting in two of the three local municipalities. Yet, the men of Basel-stadt again rejected women's voting rights in 1959. Pro-suffrage women felt betrayed and 50 women gymnasium teachers (including some suffrage activists) conducted a one-day wildcat strike. One Basel school was forced to close for the day (interview of November 30, 1987). The strike received national publicity, but was largely condemned by the Swiss press and elected officials for "not accepting quietly the decision of the majority according to the rules of democracy" (Ruckstuhl 1986: 97; translated by author). The city government even fined the strikers a day's wages. In support of the strikers, the Basel suffrage association organized a protest meeting, attracting over 500 supporters (Villard-Traber 1984). The rejection of the first national suffrage referendum inspired additional actions in Basel-stadt; in 1960 and 1961, the suffrage group organized torchlight parades to commemorate Woman Suffrage Day and protest the 1959 result.

Thus, Basel suffrage activists pursued more confrontational tactics, particularly in the wake of referendum defeats. Their demands for women's voting rights were direct and uncompromising. Although they supported partial voting legislation introduced by others, their own efforts focused on full enfranchisement. Rather than accept the will of the (male) electorate, they challenged decisions which they thought unjust in a manner that forced public attention.

GEORGIA

The Georgia suffrage organization, while by no means the most confrontational of state suffrage sections in the United States, is particularly interesting since it defies two assumptions: (1) that only eastern and midwestern states utilized confrontational tactics, and (2) that aggressive lobbying and confrontational nonlegislative tactics always occur in tandem. While many groups utilized both types of tactics, the Georgia association did little lobbying but was confrontational in its nonlegislative activities.

The first Georgia association, founded in the early 1890s, included no more than a handful of people and faced bitter opposition from most of the populace. Despite these obstacles, the early suffrage organization clearly and adamantly demanded women's enfranchisement (Taylor 1944, 1958). Unlike many other southern suffrage organizations, the group chose to include the term woman suffrage in its name. Because they were limited in resources, much of their early work was educational. Yet, most of the educational activities involved distributing articles and sponsoring public lectures on woman suffrage (Taylor 1944). Early on, the Georgia Woman Suffrage Association (GWSA) showed an unwillingness to compromise its principles. At its first statewide convention, GWSA activists resolved that "Georgia women be exempt from taxation as long as they were disenfranchised . . . [and] that disfranchised women not be counted in the apportionment of representation in the United States Congress and the Georgia legislature" (Taylor 1958: 341).

The GWSA also used public protests to press for women's voting rights. After Atlanta's mayor refused to consider a bill allowing women to vote in bond issue elections in 1903, women stood at the polls on election day with signs saying "Taxpaying women should be allowed to vote in this bond election" (Harper 1922b: 122). On Susan B. Anthony's birthday in 1909, they started a poster campaign to protest the exclusion of women from a bond issue referendum (Taylor 1958: 345). After 1914, Georgia suffrage organizations also organized outdoor meetings and suffrage parades to push women's demands for the vote. In that year, Georgia women held five outdoor rallies and the first state suffrage parade (although they had created suffrage floats for inclusion in other parades

before). A year later, "Atlanta women staged a Suffrage May Day celebration" where women, wearing yellow suffrage ribbons, spoke on the
steps of the State Capitol (Taylor 1958: 352).

The GWSA was joined by two other organizations advocating the use
of confrontational tactics after 1910. In 1914, the Equal Suffrage party
was created by a group of women who felt that "there had seemed a
necessity in Georgia for an organization which would undertake more
aggressive work in behalf of woman suffrage" (Harper 1922b: 134). It
emphasized the use of suffrage parades and managed to cooperate with
other suffrage groups. In addition, a branch of the Woman's party was
organized in 1917. This was unusual, since the Woman's party generally
found it difficult to make inroads in the South where many suffrage activists believed in states rights and abhorred the WP's militant tactics (Lunardini 1986; Taylor 1958).

The Effectiveness of Confrontational Tactics

While the range of tactics used by local suffrage activists was similar in
both countries, far fewer cantons utilized confrontational tactics than did
American states. No suffrage parade, demonstration, or open-air meeting
was held in 19 of the 25 cantons, during the entire 70-plus years of the
suffrage movement. While 18 American states also lacked suffrage parades or demonstrations, 6 of these states adopted women's voting rights
before 1911, when these tactics became more common. Why were American activists more likely to employ confrontational tactics? Certainly,
many in the Swiss woman suffrage movement argued that these activities
would hurt the cause. However, many American suffrage activists made
the same claims. Is the claim valid? To explore the effect that confrontational tactics had on the success of both movements, we need to examine
differences in local tactics more systematically.

Measuring Confrontational Tactics

We must also decide how to classify confrontational activities. In this
chapter, as in Chapter 6, I limit the analysis to the time periods 1910–
1919 in the U.S. and 1951–1970 in Switzerland because historical records of local suffrage activities are more complete during these years.
Ideally, every action during these periods could be arrayed with subtler
degrees of variation on the three dimensions: explicitness of demands,
rigidity, and forcefulness. In practice, I classify broad classes of events as
confrontational or nonconfrontational rather than attempting to judge
the degree of confrontation in each individual action. For each state and

canton, I recorded the number of public events, legal challenges, and initiatives during the period under study. Public events include only those activities that forced members of the populace to heed the suffrage message, such as demonstrations, parades, symbolic acts of protest, and open-air meetings, but excludes information stands or leafleting in public spaces. (A detailed coding scheme is included in Appendix D.) Legal challenges are also coded as confrontational because they embodied explicit suffrage demands and indicated an unwillingness to compromise. Since there were too few legal challenges to analyze separately, I combine both tactics into a single measure.[7] Initiatives are discussed separately.

For each state and canton, I calculated the annual average number of confrontational tactics. A yearly average is a better indicator than total number of events because some states and cantons enfranchised women early, ending local suffrage activities. A state suffrage organization that held ten confrontational events in the five years before it achieved suffrage is more confrontational than another group that also organized ten actions but spread them out over ten years.

Analysis

I estimated the correlation between the average number of confrontations and four different indicators of success: (1) the average annual number of suffrage bills introduced in the state or cantonal legislature, (2) the average number of referenda held, (3) the average support by male voters in those suffrage referenda that occurred during the time period, and (4) whether women were enfranchised in the state or canton before national suffrage was adopted (coded "one" if suffrage was achieved and "zero" otherwise). I focus on referenda rather than legislative support because suffrage activists' main concern was whether confrontation antagonized the public.

The results, presented in Table 7.1, indicate that in the United States, the frequency of confrontation is significantly related to only one success measure: the introduction of bills. It is positively, although more weakly, correlated with the early adoption of suffrage and the average number of suffrage referenda. The frequency with which U.S. suffrage organizations employed confrontational tactics is unrelated to public support for woman suffrage in the 25 states that held referenda. This runs counter to some suffrage activists' fears that such tactics would suppress public support.

Overall, confrontational tactics appear to have been more strongly associated with success in Switzerland. There, confrontational actions are strongly correlated with the number of referendum opportunities and with the ultimate achievement of suffrage. They are also modestly related to the introduction of suffrage bills in cantonal parliaments and public

TABLE 7.1

Correlation of the Annual Average Number of Confrontations with
Four Measures of Success in the United States and Switzerland

Type of Success	United States 1910–1919 (N)	Switzerland 1950–1970 (N)
Average Number of Bills Introduced	.45[a] (44)	.23 (25)
Average Number of Suffrage Referenda	.12 (44)	.48[a] (25)
Full Suffrage Adopted	.17 (44)	.43[a] (25)
Percent Voters Supporting Suffrage	.01 (25)	.29 (14)

[a] $p < .05$

support in referenda. Thus, although confrontational tactics were more common in the United States, they had less effect on the outcome.

Why were such tactics more successful in the nation where they were used the least? Several possible answers present themselves. First, such tactics could be effective only in small doses and lose their effectiveness at some threshold. Heavy use of confrontation might eventually become counterproductive. If this explanation were correct, only states where suffrage movements used such tactics sparingly should show high levels of success. To explore this theory, I reestimated the correlations between confrontations and success in the United States after excluding states with seven or more confrontational events in the decade. The reestimated correlations are uniformly small, suggesting that this explanation is incorrect.

Alternatively, the explanation may lie in the difference between the significant correlation for introduction of bills and other measures of success in the United States. There may be a reason that explains why the introduction of bills is affected more strongly than the number of referenda, public support, and winning of full suffrage rights. One possible answer is that U.S. legislators may have attempted to pacify women through the introduction of legislation that they had no intention of trying to pass. Once introduced, the sponsors could easily blame others for its failure.

Another possibility is that demonstrations, parades, open-air meetings, and legal challenges increased many legislators' desire to enfranchise women, leading them to introduce legislation. However, legal structures in many states created barriers to getting this legislation passed. Many states required that constitutional amendments be approved by several consecutive legislatures and/or had other barriers such as extra-large majorities or limits on the total number of amendments permitted in a certain period. Carrie Chapman Catt favored woman suffrage by federal amendment for precisely this reason: "The constitutions of many states have provided for amendments by such difficult processes that they either have never been amended or have not been amended when the subject is in the least controversial" (1917: 6–7).

It is especially notable that Swiss suffrage activists utilized few confrontational tactics although their use increased the chances of achieving women's voting rights. Demonstrations, parades, open-air meetings, and legal challenges are positively related to all four measures of success including support of suffrage legislation by male voters. The fears that such tactics would backfire appear to be unfounded. Cantons where activists demonstrated or orchestrated other public acts of protest were in fact *more* likely to achieve woman suffrage.

One possible explanation for the lack of confrontational tactics is that Swiss suffrage activists had another alternative; they could use initiatives to force voters to consider women's voting rights. Initiative petitions did not have the same negative reputation among suffrage activists that confrontational tactics had. Yet, we have already seen that Swiss suffrage activists never attempted to run an initiative petition at the national level. To round out our analysis of confrontational tactics, we need to examine how initiatives were exploited at the local level in both countries.

Local Differences in the Use of Initiatives

It is difficult to compare the use of initiatives in the United States and Switzerland because there were few opportunities to use this tactic in American states. During the U.S. woman suffrage movement (that is, from 1869 to 1920), the right to the initiative for constitutional amendments existed in only 15 states (Ranney 1978: 70–72). Moreover, 4 of the 15 states enfranchised women *before* adopting the initiative. Of the remaining 11 states, 8 adopted the constitutional initiative only during the last decade of the suffrage movement (Banaszak 1991; Price 1975; Ranney 1978). Thus, woman suffrage activists in only 11 states had the right to the initiative available to them and then often only during the last decade of their struggle.

Nonetheless, U.S. suffrage organizations were among the groups that lobbied intensively for the right of the initiative (Cronin 1989: 50–51; Edwards 1990: 231). When it was adopted, woman suffrage activists were eager to exploit them. Initiative petitions for women's voting rights were introduced in 6 of the 11 states. In 4 states—Arizona, Nebraska, Ohio, and Oklahoma—woman suffrage organizations led initiative petition drives for the right to vote in the same year or the year following the enactment of initiative rights. In fact, an amendment for women's enfranchisement was the first to be filed under Ohio's new initiative legislation (Catt and Shuler 1926). In Oregon, woman suffrage activists launched initiative drives 3 times within the space of 6 years.

What of the 5 states where newly won initiative rights were not exploited by suffrage organizations? There, woman suffrage activists did not use the initiative because they were successful through traditional, legislative channels. In 2 states—Arkansas and Michigan—significant voting rights had already been adopted by state legislatures when initiative rights were enacted. In all 5 states, constitutional amendments for full women's voting rights were presented to the voters soon after the right to the initiative was adopted. Arkansas had a woman suffrage referendum in 1918 and Nevada successfully passed a constitutional amendment in a 1914 referendum. Two states had referenda in the same year that initiative rights were introduced: Michigan (1913) and North Dakota (1914). Both states also held additional referenda on women's voting rights before 1920. Massachusetts is an exception in that it held its woman suffrage referendum in 1915, 3 years prior to the introduction of initiative rights. In short, there was little reason for woman suffrage activists to attempt initiatives in these states because their legislatures already had permitted woman suffrage referenda.

The initiative laws in Swiss cantons were much more liberal. All 25 cantons permitted popular initiatives for both constitutional and simple legislative questions (Delley and Auer 1986). Nonetheless, the 21 cantonal referenda introduced by initiative (5 for partial suffrage) occurred in only 13 of the 25 cantons. These include initiatives in three cantons (Glarus, Appenzell Innerrhoden, and Uri) where only one signature is required to bring an issue to a vote. In half the Swiss cantons, initiatives were never attempted.

In the United States, initiative opportunities were exploited in states where traditional channels blocked suffrage legislation. The pattern is very different in Switzerland. Five of the 12 cantons without initiatives had no cantonal woman suffrage referenda prior to 1971. Thus, while the American suffrage activists were moved to utilize initiatives where governments did not respond to their demands, the use of the initiative in Switzerland was unrelated to the willingness of cantonal governments to consider woman suffrage.

More importantly, only 4 of the 21 women's voting rights initiatives between 1920 and 1990 were introduced by woman suffrage organizations. Two of these initiative petitions were run by the Genève woman suffrage organization in 1920 and 1940. The suffrage organization in Basel-stadt also initiated the constitutional amendment that gave them cantonal suffrage in 1966. Finally, the woman suffrage organization in Bern sponsored an initiative in 1956 to bring an optional community suffrage bill to a vote. All other initiatives were introduced by political parties or by other social movement organizations. Thus, Swiss suffrage activists introduced only half as many initiatives as their American counterparts although they had more than twice as many places where they could do so.

Moreover, woman suffrage activists were not always totally supportive of the woman suffrage initiatives introduced by other groups. The Zürich suffrage group was unwilling to support the campaigns to collect signatures on initiative petitions in 1947 and 1954 because they were launched by the Communist party (Partei der Arbeit). In Schaffhausen, suffrage activists complained about the introduction of an initiative: "It was a bit too much, naturally, to have it [a referendum on woman suffrage] again so soon, after only two years. . . . In 1969, we already had to begin to prepare for the national suffrage referendum in 1971. . . . So we said, stop" (interview of March 21, 1988).

Thus, woman suffrage organizations were not always appreciative allies when other groups sponsored suffrage initiatives. Before we can ask why, however, we need to ask whether the right to the initiative made a difference in Switzerland. For if initiatives did not affect the adoption of women's voting rights, Swiss activists had no reason to support or sponsor initiatives.

The Effect of Initiatives on Suffrage Movement Success

To see if initiatives sped the success of suffrage, I would have liked to calculate the correlation between average number of initiatives sponsored by suffrage organizations and the four indicators of success in each country—exactly as had been done for confrontational tactics. Unfortunately, between 1950 and 1970 there were only two initiatives in Switzerland, making statistical analysis impossible. Instead, I compare those cantons that had initiatives sponsored by woman suffrage organizations to the other cantons.[8] The results, reported in Table 7.2, show that the three cantons where woman sponsored initiative drives achieved full voting rights for women an average of six years earlier than other cantons. Even if the two cantons that achieved suffrage in 1989 (Appenzell Ausserrhoden) and 1990 (Appenzell Innerrhoden) are removed from the analysis, there is still a four-year difference between those cantons where suffrage organizations introduced initiative petitions and the other 20 cantons.

Because there were more initiatives in U.S. states, correlations between the number of initiatives and success can be calculated (see Table 7.3).

TABLE 7.2

Use of the Initiative by Woman Suffrage Organizations and
the Passage of Full Women's Voting Rights in the Canton

No Initiative Introduced by Suffrage Organization		Initiative from Women's Organization	
Canton	Year Full Suffrage Passed	Canton	Year Full Suffrage Passed
Aargau	1971	Bern	1971
Baselland	1968	Basel-stadt	1966
Fribourg/Freiburg	1971	Genève	1960
Graubünden	1972		
Neuchâtel	1959		
Niwalden	1972		
Obwalden	1972		
Solothurn	1971		
Thurgau	1971		
Vaud	1959		
Wallis/Valais	1970		
Appenzell Ausserrhoden	1989		
Glarus	1971		
Appenzell Innerrhoden	1990		
Luzern	1970		
St. Gallen	1972		
Schaffhausen	1971		
Schwyz	1972		
Tessin	1969		
Uri	1972		
Zürich	1970		
Zug	1971		
Mean	**1971.5**		**1965.7**
Mean without Appenzell Ausserrhoden and Appenzell Innerrhoden	**1969.7**		

The use of initiatives is modestly but positively correlated with the average number of bills introduced, public support, and eventual adoption of suffrage.[9]

We should not be surprised that the correlations between success and initiatives are modest given the history of initiatives in the United States. The analysis in Table 7.3 only explores the relationship between initiative *use* and the adoption of full suffrage; it understates the effect that the

TABLE 7.3

Correlation of the Annual Average Number of Initiatives with
Three Measures of Success in the United States

Type of Success	United States 1910–1919 (N)
Average Number of Bills Introduced	.24 (44)
Full Suffrage Adopted	.28 (44)
Percent Voters Supporting Suffrage	.27 (25)

introduction of initiative rights had on the early enfranchisement of women. As the previous section suggests, legislators may have been induced to pass suffrage legislation in order to preempt initiative drives by suffragists once that right existed. Given that they could no longer stop suffrage referenda from occurring, there was little reason not to refer a suffrage bill to the voters. Should women actually become enfranchised, legislators could then use their pro-suffrage record to woo women voters. Thus, although there is not a strong relationship between initiative use and the enfranchisement of women, there is a connection between the existence of initiative *rights* and woman suffrage. Of the 37 states lacking initiative rights, 17 failed to adopt full woman suffrage before ratification of the Nineteenth Amendment. In contrast, only 1 of the 11 states with initiative rights still denied women the right to vote in 1920.

Conclusion

The foregoing analyses introduce an interesting puzzle. Swiss suffrage activists employed few confrontational tactics while the evidence suggests that their use could have increased the chances of winning women's voting rights. Suffrage activists' fears that such tactics might backfire were unfounded. Indeed, confrontation appears to have been more successful in Switzerland than in the United States, where it was used with regularity. Moreover, in the United States, most local suffrage movements lacked initiative rights but suffrage activists fought for them. Where they were available, they employed initiatives when they could not obtain women's voting rights by legislative means. Yet, both local and national Swiss suffrage activists failed to take advantage of initiative rights, although these were related to success. Nor did cantonal activists ignore the initiative because their goals were being realized elsewhere. Cantons that had no woman suffrage initiatives were usually those where women's voting rights were also absent from the dockets of cantonal parliaments.

Together with the analyses of Chapter 6, these results paint an interesting contrast between the Swiss and American woman suffrage movements. While the American suffrage movement employed whatever tactics would lead to consideration of suffrage legislation, the Swiss suffrage movement did not. As Chapter 6 notes, they did not lobby national or cantonal legislatures for suffrage legislation. Nor did they utilize initiative rights or confrontational tactics. While most Swiss suffrage activists firmly believed that only public education would lead to the enfranchisement of women, this tenet should have encouraged them to work for more referenda since these provided the greatest opportunities for public education. Yet, suffrage activists did little to create referenda opportunities although there were clearly institutions that would have allowed them to do so.

Although American suffrage activists also believed in the importance of public education, they chose to employ legislative, confrontational, and initiative tactics as well. If the U.S. suffrage movement was in its early years mainly an educational body, by the end it also was a serious lobby in both national and state legislatures. It included many activists who firmly believed that confrontation through pickets, parades, and initiatives (where possible) was the only path to the vote.

Why did Swiss suffrage activists fail to employ these tactics which their American counterparts used so effectively? In Chapter 6, I argue that the structure of political opportunities somewhat restricted the usefulness of lobbying tactics for Swiss suffrage activists, although not enough to account for the difference in tactics. However, there were no such constraints on their use of initiatives or confrontational tactics like demonstrations and public acts of protest. The Swiss government was no more likely to repress protest activities than its American counterpart, and Swiss suffrage activists had a distinct advantage over American activists in the case of initiative rights. To understand this stark difference in tactical choices, we need to examine the information, beliefs, and values of both groups.

8

SOURCES OF THE MOVEMENTS' INFORMATION,

BELIEFS, AND VALUES

THE DISCUSSION in previous chapters has shown that organizational, lobbying, and confrontational tactics are associated with early success in both countries. Yet, it also has left us with a host of unsolved questions regarding the differences between the Swiss and American woman suffrage movements: Why did Swiss activists fail to use the initiative to bring women's voting rights legislation to a vote? Why were American activists more likely than their Swiss counterparts to use highly visible and confrontational tactics, especially when these seem to have been quite effective in Switzerland? Why did American activists develop highly articulated lobbying strategies to win the vote while Swiss activists largely ignored elected officials? To answer these questions, we must begin by examining the origins of tactics in both countries. At a minimum, we need to know how suffrage activists in both countries learned about the tactics they employed.

However, information about strategies and tactics was not the only factor that determined what course of action suffrage activists in both countries pursued. Several key beliefs also played a role in determining the tactics of the two movements. In both countries, the tactics employed by local and national suffrage organizations were influenced by prevailing norms concerning the ideal role of women, local autonomy, and commitment to existing democratic institutions. Thus, beliefs and values also affected strategic choices of suffrage activists. This is particularly true in Switzerland, where status quo beliefs in cantonal autonomy were used to reject several tactics.

Beliefs, values, and tactical repertoires did not spring fully developed from the heads of suffrage activists but evolved in a cultural milieu that included political parties, other social movements, and interest groups. These other political actors affected the perceptions and preferences of the movement's activists—especially where they developed close ties to suffrage organizations through overlapping social networks or organizational coalitions. In the United States, other political movements served as sources of information and reinforced values that made it easier to run initiatives, organize demonstrations, and march in parades. Swiss suffrage activists did not have the strong ties to other social movements, which might have fostered the beliefs and values necessary to engage in confrontational or aggressive tactics. Instead, those political groups connected to the Swiss suffrage movement tended to reinforce perceptions and status quo values that reduced its ability or willingness to conduct some types of suffrage activities.

However, focusing on the external political context tells only half the story. In both countries, local suffrage groups occasionally invented new tactics or tried new forms of organization, expression, or influence. In the United States, these experiments spread to other local sections and eventually to the national organization, which then promulgated them even further. However, in Switzerland information and tactical innovations were not passed on within the movement. Thus, in addition to exploring the external connections between suffrage movement activists and other actors, we must also look within the movement and examine the communication and coordination among activists. While U.S. suffrage activists developed relatively strong ties among local sections in spite of strong feelings of local autonomy, Swiss activists were more divided by language and politics. Those divisions were reinforced by external ties to other political actors.

External Influences on the Development of Woman Suffrage in the United States

The tactics and values that characterized the woman suffrage movement in the United States had numerous sources. In this section, I focus only on those four groups—abolitionists, temperance workers, populists, and progressive activists—that had the greatest effects on the suffrage movement's development.[1] This wide network of movements and political organizations had two effects that contributed to the U.S. suffrage movement's later ability to exploit the opportunities presented by the political system. First, they served as a source of information about new tactics. Many lobbying and confrontational tactics were employed by these other groups long before they became de rigueur in the suffrage movement. Second, these other organizations reinforced values that encouraged woman suffrage activists to participate in politics and challenge the system. For example, women's experiences in the Grange and the WCTU taught them that some goals, like temperance, could not be achieved at the municipal level; instead, they learned to focus on state legislation (Baker 1991: 70–72). Thus, status quo values like local autonomy were countered by their experiences in other movements.

Although I focus on only a select set of influences, there were other groups in the United States that also contributed to the tactics and perceptions of the suffrage movement. These other groups had direct ties to woman suffrage activists but were also linked indirectly through abolitionist, temperance, populists, or progressives. For example, the Chautauqua educational movement included both the original Chautauqua Camp, its study series, and, in a looser sense, numerous lecture series throughout the country; it may have served as one model for American suffrage activists' political study courses and Suffrage Schools. Certainly, woman suffrage activists had direct and indirect ties to the Chautauqua movement; they lectured at regional Chautauquas, and, through their religious affiliations, undoubtedly participated in other aspects of the educational movement. These ties were also strengthened by the connection between Chautauqua and the WCTU; women temperance activists had in fact organized the WCTU at the first Chautauqua in 1874 (Bordin 1981: 34–35; Scott 1991: 95). As in most cases, Chautauqua was not the suffrage activists' only model for the use of lectures and schooling in political campaigns since these tactics were also utilized by the temperance and club movements. Rather than chronicle all the numerous, often reinforcing, influences of the American woman suffrage movement, I have chosen to highlight four groups traditionally tied with the suffrage movement. Focusing on abolitionists, temperance activists, populists, and progressives also accentuates those perceptions and activities that differentiated American women from their Swiss counterparts.

The changes in legislative, electoral, and public tactics of the American women's movement over time can in large part be explained by changes in allies. As the suffrage movement developed new or stronger ties to movements with different emphases and methods, the suffrage movement adopted these new techniques to serve their own goals. Thus, the abolitionist connection to suffrage, forged in the mid–nineteenth century, encouraged certain types of tactics. When that link was broken in the 1870s, however, the tactics promulgated by abolitionists were replaced by new ideas and techniques, particularly those developing within the temperance movement. The creation of populist and progressive organizations also influenced the development of new tactics, particularly in the twentieth century. As women's clubs, Granges, and direct democratic reform movements swept through the states, they brought new ways of looking at the issue of woman suffrage and new techniques for winning the vote.

Abolitionist Influences on the Women's Movement

The ideological development of the suffrage movement began in 1848 with the creation of the women's rights movement. During the early movement, the issue of women's rights was tied to the activities and experiences of women such as Elizabeth Cady Stanton and Lucy Stone who were drawn to women's rights from their experiences in the abolitionist movement (Kraditor 1981). As Chapter 3 notes, many of these women mixed their women's rights efforts with abolitionist work. After the Civil War, abolitionists temporarily joined forces with women's rights activists in the creation of the Equal Rights Association. Until the passage of the Fourteenth and Fifteenth Amendments, the causes of women's and black's rights were intertwined.

Not surprisingly the arguments used by abolitionists to oppose slavery are also found in the early women's rights movement. The most central belief developed in the abolition movement was that an equal rights philosophy originally developed for white men should be extended to African-Americans. Early women's rights activists further broadened this ideology to include women's rights as a component of basic human rights and liberties (Kraditor 1981). Laws against women voting or owning property obstructed women's right to liberty and equality, which white male citizens had already achieved but which should be shared by all. The interactions of women's rights activists with anti-slavery activists encouraged the emphasis on equal rights. More importantly, abolitionists' extension of equal rights beyond the category of white males to blacks suggested that other excluded groups could be included as well.

Many abolitionists were unwilling to negotiate on their demands for equal treatment since they were based on the concept of natural rights. While not all abolitionists were as radical as John Brown, most refused to sanction compromises that permitted states to make their own decisions about slavery. While debates over women's rights were less prevalent in the antebellum United States, when the issue arose, women's rights activists showed the same unwillingness to compromise. They demanded that all laws discriminating against women be repealed. In the case of voting rights, women's rights activists expected women to have the same voting rights and privileges as men. Few women's rights activists of the time advocated limited suffrage, even for tactical reasons, since it would have contradicted activists' natural rights ideology (Baker 1984).

What women's rights activists failed to notice was that abolitionist supporters of women's rights were more willing to compromise on the issue. The Garrison wing of the abolitionist movement, which most of the early women's rights activists joined (Lerner 1979), largely defended women's rights to other abolitionists in the years leading up to the Civil War. Women in the movement thus "saw nothing contradictory in their devotion both to antislavery and to the full freedom of their gender; on the contrary they saw the complementary, interlocking character of the two" (Aptheker 1989: 88). However, there were signs that abolitionists were not as strongly attached to women's rights; Frederick Douglass, for example, opposed the election of women as leaders in abolitionist organizations (Aptheker 1989: 87).

Given their belief in the immutability of natural rights, the reaction of Elisabeth Cady Stanton and Susan B. Anthony to the Fourteenth Amendment becomes more understandable. While the failure of abolitionist men to fight for women's enfranchisement disturbed them, they were particularly appalled at the willingness of abolitionists to include the word "male" in the amendment, especially after women had been asked to put the abolitionist cause first during the Civil War (Deckard 1983; Harper 1969, vol. 1). While the women's rights movement split over this event, Stanton, Anthony, and the other women of the National Woman Suffrage Association reacted by refusing any further compromises on women's rights. Many of their confrontational actions through 1876, described in Chapter 7, reflected both the belief in natural rights and an unwillingness to compromise, values reinforced by the abolitionist movement which no longer supported them.

The tactics that the early women's rights movement adopted also reflected its ties to the abolitionist movement (Baker 1984). The major tactics of the Garrison wing of the abolitionist movement were petitions, mass meetings, and lectures (Aptheker 1989). Petitions played a particularly important role both in publicizing anti-slavery efforts among the public and in trying to affect legislative opinion. For example, the American Anti-Slavery Society ran a year-long campaign in 1837–1838 to collect signatures on a petition asking Congress to end slavery. The leaders of the petition drive included Henry B. Stanton, husband of Elizabeth Cady Stanton, and Theodore D. Weld, who later married Angelike Grimke (Aptheker 1989: 53). Abolitionist women, particularly those in female anti-slavery societies, played a major role in the petition campaigns and on the lecturing circuit (Aptheker 1989; Venet 1991). Indeed, while a woman lecturing before a mixed audience was rare and controversial in the 1830s, by the end of the abolitionist movement, women lecturers had gained a degree of respectability and experience.

Absent from both the early women's rights movement and the Garrison wing of the abolitionists was an emphasis on supporting pro-abolitionist candidates (Lerner 1979: 125). Whatever its source, the later emphasis on electoral-based organizations cannot be attributed to the Garrisonians, who argued that the Constitution itself was a pro-slavery document. Since the entire government was based on an acceptance of slavery, any support for the system (for example, by voting) only strengthened slavery (Fogel 1989; Banks 1981). Thus, electoral strategies such as those conceived by later suffrage activists were excluded from the Garrisonians' activities.

The abandonment of the women's rights issue by male abolitionists after the Civil War had many effects on the suffrage movement. While it divided the women's movement into two groups, it also increased the focus on women's enfranchisement in contrast to other issues. Perhaps the strongest indication that the women's rights activists' ideology of equal rights was influenced by the abolitionist movement and not merely by individuals' convictions is reflected in the changes in values that occurred after the abolitionist influence decreased in 1870. Suffrage activists, even some early women's rights supporters like Susan B. Anthony, began to utilize a different argument for granting women the vote: that public life was a just extension of women's activity in the home (Baker 1984). The rise of these new values and the development of new tactics paralleled the increasing importance of the temperance movement.

Temperance and Woman Suffrage Ideology and Tactics

While the influence of the temperance movement was greatest during the last four decades of the suffrage movement's struggle, women's rights activists had always been linked with the temperance movement, which also dated to the 1840s (Catt and Shuler 1926). Susan B. Anthony was not only an abolitionist but an early activist in the temperance movement (Barry 1988). Despite the long association between the two movements, it was only after the influence of the abolitionist movement waned that the values of the temperance movement began to have a greater impact on the suffrage movement (Banks 1981).

The Women's Christian Temperance Union's (WCTU) support of woman suffrage in the 1880s was based not on a belief in natural rights but rather on the supposed effect that woman suffrage would have. Temperance activists argued that women's enfranchisement would allow them to deal with important social problems such as alcoholism.[2] Many temperance supporters (and opponents as well) noted that it was primarily women who fought for temperance. Activists gave two reasons to explain women's activity on this issue. First, women were seen as the pure and moral sex. It was thus assumed that their political activity would increase the general morality of society. Therefore, temperance activists, who viewed their battle as eliminating one of the major social problems, believed the enfranchisement of women would introduce these moral issues into politics (Baker 1984; Kraditor 1981).

Second, temperance activists argued that women suffered most under the problems of alcoholism; as the main victims, they were unlikely to be protected if they had to rely on the kindness and understanding of male politicians. Thus, to protect their own interests, women also needed voting rights (Banks 1981; Evans 1989; Kraditor 1981). Without the force of government to limit people's access to liquor, wives and mothers had little means of reducing the problems related to alcoholism. Only armed with the ballot could women protect themselves and their families.

The temperance movement was primarily responsible for introducing the legislative tactics that suffrage activists later employed so effectively. Yet, these tactics did not appear until the creation of the WCTU. Its predecessor, the Women's Crusade of 1873–1874, focused on convincing offending businessmen through prayer and pressure to voluntarily give up the liquor trade. To do so, these temperance crusaders utilized confrontational tactics previously unseen in women's organizations; women marched through the streets praying and singing hymns, ending their parade at an establishment selling spirits. Once there, they attempted to convince the owner to sign a pledge not to sell alcoholic beverages. When owners were recalcitrant (as they often were), crusaders pressured them by demonstrating in or in front of their establishment.

While Crusaders made important headlines during 1874 and held over 400 marches, the focus of the temperance movement quickly turned from pledging saloon-keepers to altering state laws on the license and selling of liquor (Blocker 1985b). That change coincided with the creation of the WCTU in 1874. Although the WCTU continued to work on the local level in the early 1880s, temperance workers began to realize that they "could accomplish little without the help of the state, either because of the intransigence of local communities or because of the nature of the problems" (Baker 1991: 80). Thus, beginning in the 1880, WCTU began to develop lobbying tactics in the state legislatures with the goal of passing local option or prohibition legislation. While the WCTU's founders preferred organizations based on congressional districts, after 1890 the WCTU set up a precinct organization that furthered the development of state lobbies (Bordin 1981; Clemens 1993; Scott 1991). In addition, the WCTU and other temperance supporters began to work at the polls for dry candidates and against wet supporters (Baker 1991; McBride 1993).

Woman suffrage activists absorbed many of these tactics and values, particularly during the last three decades of the suffrage battle. In contrast to abolition-era activists, the later generation of suffrage activists argued that society needed women voters because of their high ethical standards and that women needed the ballot in order to protect their families. While the philosophy of equal rights never died out completely, between 1890 and 1920 the main arguments shifted to the differences between men and women and how enfranchising women would protect family life and improve the morality of societal decisions (Kraditor 1981: 65). These beliefs were complemented by populist and progressive values.

In addition, the tactics of women temperance activists provided a model when support for suffrage began to pick up after the turn of the century. For example, woman suffrage activists borrowed the strategy of organizing according to electoral precinct in order to exert greater pressure on state and national legislators. They also utilized many of the

WCTU's lobbying techniques, which were based less on petitions than on applying electoral pressure to candidates and constituent pressure to elected officials. And what of the strategies of the Women's Crusade of 1873? Because the crusaders originally focused on individual saloon-keepers and not the legislative process, the WCTU abandoned these tactics. Marches and parades were not thought to be applicable to the problem of acquiring women's voting rights legislation. Hence, suffrage organizations did not realize the usefulness of these tactics until 1908, when the influence of the British suffrage movement began to be felt in the United States. As American activists returned from Great Britain and British suffragettes visited the United States, these views changed since the British strategy incorporated pickets, marches, and demonstrations. That the United States was such fertile ground for these tactics can in part be attributed to the model that the Crusades had already provided. Suffrage activists could pick up on the marches and even picketing of British suffragettes (but not on the violence) because many U.S. activists had participated in or known about the Crusades of 1873. These tactics were already a part of their repertoire.

Populism, Progressivism, and Suffrage Strategies and Values

Discussing the influence of populists and progressives on the values and tactics of the woman suffrage movement is at once problematic and necessary. It is problematic because the progressives and, to a lesser extent, the populists were characterized by a number of different and often conflicting ideas (Rodgers 1982; Filene 1970). Yet, aspects of these differing ideologies, however muddled, appeared within the suffrage movement. It is therefore difficult to talk about the spread of ideas and tactics without mentioning populist and progressive legacies.

While neither populism nor progressivism can be characterized by a few, all encompassing beliefs, certain ideas are entwined in both groups, particularly in the West where farmers and small-town residents formed the basis of support for both movements (Deckard 1983; Schmidt 1989). The populists and many progressives emphasized the excessive power of large corporations with the populists focusing on the railroad monopoly and anti-monopoly progressives stressing other large trusts or corporations (Rodgers 1982). To solve the problem of monopolies, both movements supported government regulation of big business. Corrupt politics was the other problem that troubled both populists and many progressives. Both groups supported reforms designed to reduce the power of party machines. Many of the democratic reforms developed and endorsed by the populist movements such as the Australian ballot, the initiative, and the referendum found their way into the Progressive party platform and onto the agenda of progressive organizations seeking to rationalize and reorganize government.

However, the progressive era also introduced a new idea, which became important to the woman suffrage movement: social progressivism (see Rodgers 1982). Social progressives sought to reduce a number of societal ills by cleaning up cities, assuring clean food supplies, and improving conditions for those disadvantaged by industrialism. Combined with a belief in rational reform of government, social progressives turned to government bureaucracies and legislation to solve social problems.

All of these values reappeared in some way within the American woman suffrage movement. As Chapter 5 shows, suffrage activists themselves adopted negative attitudes toward corporations and machine politics, often attributing to them the failure of suffrage legislation. Anti-monopolism also blended well with temperance values and beliefs. Liquor interests were viewed by the suffrage activists as a particularly powerful industry, which controlled many votes and was willing to use all means to deny women the vote. The anti–big business and social progressive ideology also complemented the temperance belief that women needed the ballot to fulfill their duties within the home. Changes in the structure of everyday life meant that the health, safety, and welfare of the family were now affected by the food industry and other factors outside of women's control (see, for example, Duncan-Clark 1913: 103–6). All three of these ideologies—temperance, social progressivism, and anti-monopolism—emphasized that women needed the ballot to regain influence in matters directly related to their home (Kraditor 1981). They also emphasized that women needed to protect themselves and their families against external threats to family life: liquor interests, social ills, and monopolies.

Ties between populist and progressive organizations also helped spread or reinforce certain tactics within the suffrage movement. Farmer's Alliances and the Grange had a long tradition of permitting women as members, and from its beginning in 1870, Grange women could also hold office. While the Grange created special, largely ceremonial offices specifically for women, women also held traditionally male offices, particularly the position of Lecturer, at the local level as early as the 1870s. By the 1890s, women moved into similar positions at the state and national level (Marti 1991). The office of Lecturer gave women experiences in mobilization and lecturing. Lecturers planned and conducted the Grange meetings, which often required public speaking. These experiences reinforced women activists' skills in lecturing and their emphasis on public education at the time when these were the major strategies of the suffrage movement.

With the development of the WCTU, Grange organizations (particularly their Women's Committees) began to attempt legislative action

(Marti 1991). Temperance became a major issue to the Grange, resulting in its cooperation with the WCTU on state and local legislation. Thus, Baker (1991: 65) notes that in rural New York, the Grange and women's temperance joined together to petition state legislators for temperance legislation. However, legislative work was never a major activity for the Grange and occurred mainly in conjunction with other organizations.

A more important model for legislative action was the women's club movement, which developed in the 1890s. Women's clubs began as benevolent and literary societies. Yet, when they began to organize into state sections of the General Federation of Women's Clubs (GFWC) after 1890, they also moved into the public sphere, calling for social progressive reforms and pressuring state legislatures and Congress for social legislation (Skocpol 1992). The legislative lobbying of the GFWC began in the early 1890s and increased steadily thereafter. By the time that the national woman suffrage movement was perfecting its legislative techniques (largely after 1915), the GFWC and many state federations of women's clubs had already altered the strategy of lobbying from its old form based on petitions to a new model linked "to the conventions of professionalism and expertise" (Clemens 1993: 784). Suffrage activists thus had both the progressive belief in the need to professionalize and rationalize institutions and the more immediate model of women's clubs to aid them in developing new tactics.

The GFWC also served as a example to the NAWSA of how to spread information and tactics to local sections. In the 1890s, state and national federations of women's clubs encouraged members to share tactics and information (McBride 1993; Skocpol 1992). In Wisconsin, for example, women's clubs activities included instruction in political skills such as conducting campaigns (McBride 1993: 153). The use of convention meetings and study courses within women's clubs reinforced ideas about education that suffrage activists had gleaned from the WCTU, the Grange, and others, but it also provided a practical model for how that education could spread useful tactics throughout the organization.

Finally, because initiatives played such an important role in the American woman suffrage movement and such an insignificant one in the Swiss movement, it is worth noting the ties between American suffrage activists and the progressive direct democratic reformers who promoted the initiative. These ties helped to focus woman suffrage activists' attention on the initiative's usefulness in states considering this reform. Indeed, suffrage activists were well-informed about the uses of the initiative from the very beginning. Soon after Oregon became the first state in the Union to adopt initiatives and before the novelty had spread to other states, the NAWSA held its annual convention there. William S. U'Ren, who had spearheaded the addition of the initiative and referendum to the Oregon constitution, lectured at the convention, speaking "on the need and purpose of these political reforms and answered several questions, especially about the initiative" (Edwards 1990: 230; see also Harper 1922a: 136). While ties between government reformers and woman suffrage activists already existed, this 1905 annual convention spread the news about the initiative widely. In that and future years, the NAWSA passed resolutions supporting the initiative and referendum (Harper 1922a).

In sum, the ties between suffrage activists and the abolitionists, temperance activists, populists, and progressives affected the American woman suffrage movement in two ways. First, suffrage activists' values shifted as they developed ties with new political groups and dissolved ties with others. Second, other organizations served as sources of information about potential tactics and strategies. In some cases, several organizations used the same technique, albeit in slightly different ways, reinforcing its importance to the woman suffrage movement. In other cases, the development of a specific tactic, like the initiative, can be traced to a specific group. These ideas provided suffrage organizations with the perceptions and preferences that helped them to take advantage of political opportunities.

Variation in Suffrage Beliefs and Values Within the United States

As the influence of other political actors waxed and waned, there were broad discernible shifts in the values of the U.S. movement, but these were not strong enough to eliminate geographical differences in ideology. Conflicts over values sometimes caused rifts within the national organization as state sections battled over its strategy. For example, battles over whether the NAWSA should focus on state legislation or pursue a national suffrage amendment were not merely a result of sectional disagreements over the tactic's efficacy but stemmed from differences in the value placed on state autonomy and federal power. Woman suffrage historians (for example, Deckard 1983; Jensen 1973; Kraditor 1981) identify two regional differences within the suffrage movement: West vs. East and North vs. South.

The West

When suffrage activists drew their map of suffrage states in 1912, only states west of the Mississippi had adopted full women's voting rights legislation. Historians have relied on two theories to explain the early willingness of western states to enfranchise women: (1) the unique characteristics of frontier states generated a fundamentally different gender role ideology among their residents, and (2) the popularity of the populist and progressive movements increased support for women's voting rights.

According to the frontier ideology theory, frontier states developed a stronger egalitarianism compared to the East and the South because of the stark living conditions that existed there (Deckard 1983). In taming the wilderness, the work performed by women was as vital to a family's survival as that performed by men. According to this theory, the value of women's work combined with the already existing egalitarianism produced support for women's rights which resulted in the early enfranchisement of women in these states.

However, there is little evidence to support the frontier ideology theory. According to Sinclair (1965), woman suffrage support was relatively weak in those parts of the western states where frontier values would be most likely to appear, namely farms on the frontier where the women worked hard to survive. Rather, the champions of suffrage in the West were middle-class individuals in small to medium size towns where women's work was less essential to the household's survival. If frontier ideology produced the unique western ideology that increased support for women's enfranchisement, one would expect to find more suffrage activism in the rough conditions of the frontier rather than in urban areas.

While the frontier did not generate a belief in gender role equality, it may have given rise to other values that aided the suffrage cause. The greater influence of progressive and populist movements in the West indicates the prevalence of anti-monopolist attitudes and negative views of political machines, which may have strengthened existing women's movements. Moreover, these two movements supported, albeit sometimes weakly, the enfranchisement of women (see Chapter 5) and became a haven for woman suffrage activists. Many western suffrage activists, most notably Abigail Scott Duniway, could be found among their ranks. Other western suffrage activists actively fought for the democratic reforms advocated by the Populist and Progressive parties (Duniway 1971). Thus, the early passage of suffrage legislation in the West probably resulted from alliances between these movements and from the suffrage movement's adoption of populist or progressive values rather than from a unique frontier mentality.

Many western suffrage activists also rejected interference in local affairs by national suffrage association leaders from the East. Duniway, for example, complained heavily about outside interference in her native state of Oregon and in the Idaho suffrage campaign of 1896 (Moynihan 1983). In Oregon, the split between the state and national organization was so severe that the National American Woman Suffrage Association ended up providing financial assistance to the state Women's Club rather than to the state suffrage association (Harper 1922b: 546). Emma De Voe of Washington also felt that NAWSA intervention hurt local movements; she argued that the NAWSA "has been a great hindrance in nearly every state where the National has participated" (cited in Moynihan 1983: 214). While not all western suffrage activists agreed, these feelings of local autonomy inhibited national suffrage activists' attempts to organize and spread tactical information in these states.

The South

The southern woman suffrage movement also exhibited values that differed from the national suffrage movement, largely because of the events surrounding the Civil War. Prior to the 1890s, women in the South were unwilling to create suffrage organizations because the early women's rights movement was despised in the South as a result of its connection to abolition. However, as the northern suffrage movement divorced itself from the abolitionist cause and began to support poll tests or educational requirements for voters, southern women grew more willing to associate with it (Kraditor 1981; Wheeler 1993). The anti-immigrant ideology that had spread through the northern suffrage movement was quite compatible with the anti-black ideology of the South. Moreover, racial arguments began to surface in western (for example, Colorado, see Jensen 1973: 260) and northern states (for example, Iowa, see Noun 1969: 41–43) as well.

As southern suffrage activists joined the movement, they also helped pull the suffrage movement away from its abolitionist roots. In order to avoid divisions within the movement, suffrage leaders connected with abolition often toned down their support of black rights to keep the organization together. At the 1899 NAWSA annual meeting, for example, Susan B. Anthony, an early supporter of abolitionist causes, spoke *against* a resolution asking railroads to provide "suitable accommodations" for black women (Kraditor 1981: 169–72).

When suffrage movements finally emerged in the South, their battle for women's voting rights was influenced by a different political context from northern movements. Many southern whites believed that giving the ballot to women would increase the political power of black women and potentially open the door to major changes in voting rights for blacks. One of the ways southern (white) suffrage activists justified support for women's voting rights was by referring to the racial situation and arguing that woman suffrage could help maintain white supremacy in the South

(Allen 1958; Fuller 1975; Scott 1970; Wheeler 1993). For example, during the 1890 Mississippi constitutional convention, the enfranchisement of those women who owned (or whose husbands owned) $300 worth of property was introduced as a means of strengthening the white vote (Taylor 1968: 2). Moreover, many southern suffrage activists claimed that southern white women were degraded by former black slaves voting (Kraditor 1981: 125). Thus, a Georgia suffrage activist asked the Georgia legislature: "The negro men, our former slaves, have been given the right to vote and why should not we southern women have the same right?" (McLendon, quoted in Taylor 1959: 17).

For many Southern activists, concerns about black voters translated into an unwillingness to campaign for a federal woman suffrage amendment. In their eyes, a federal amendment might further damage the state's rights principle. For that reason, southern suffrage activists like Laura Clay argued that women must be enfranchised by different strategies in the South so that state's rights were not threatened (Kraditor 1981: 187). The National's decision to focus on a federal amendment split the movement into followers of Catt's Winning Plan and the southern movements, which advocated suffrage by state law. Kate Gordon and Laura Clay (among others) resigned from the NAWSA rather than commit themselves to a federal amendment. Both activists then formed a separate southern organization to push for women's voting rights through state legislation. As Kraditor notes, "Misses Clay and Gordon . . . saw a necessary connection between the maintenance of white supremacy in the South and the continued right of Southern legislatures to exercise complete power over local elections. . . . Acceptance of the majority suffragist thesis, Miss Clay and Miss Gordon believed, would shake the very foundations of Southern society" (1981: 217–18).

Thus, the Civil War and its aftermath resulted in strong beliefs in local autonomy in the South. White southern society and the suffrage movement that developed within it argued that suffrage strategies must not diminish southern states' ability to define their own voter eligibility requirements. These beliefs in local autonomy led southern activists to reject certain types of activities (such as lobbying congressmen) and organizations (the Woman's party and, for many, the NAWSA after 1916).

Nonetheless, national suffrage organizations could still play an important role in many local areas. Leaders of the national suffrage organizations, particularly after 1890, largely ignored demands for regional autonomy and pursued their own national policies including the coordination and political education of local suffrage groups. Even those western and southern suffrage activists who advocated local autonomy were willing to learn some of the techniques and tactics the national association advocated and adapt them to their particular situation. Thus, the national suffrage movement developed a movement community that passed on information.

Woman Suffrage Values and Beliefs in Switzerland

The Swiss woman suffrage movement developed in a very different context from the American movement. While the U.S. activists were influenced by several other movements, the Swiss woman suffrage movement lacked similar ties, particularly from 1930 through the 1950s. No *single* movement, party, or religion was tied to Swiss suffrage activists in the way the abolitionists had been tied to the American movement. As a result, the Swiss suffrage movement wrestled with conflicting values, even within local sections.

If Swiss activists lacked strong ties to other political actors, there were some connections between parts of the Swiss woman suffrage movement and other political organizations. However, these groups did not possess values and tactical information that would have encouraged confrontational, legislative, or initiative action among Swiss suffrage activists. The Swiss woman suffrage movement developed at the turn of the century in the context of women's benevolent and moral reform movements, which supported the idea of women's separate sphere and did not pursue legislation to aid their cause.

Catholic and socialist political parties and organizations also colored the values of many of the movement's activists and leaders, and neither group was a completely positive influence. Although supportive of women's enfranchisement, Catholic suffrage activists tended to embrace other conservative values from the Catholic tradition—an acceptance of the status quo and unwillingness to rock the boat—which created a tendency to de-emphasize the suffrage issue. Socialist activists were influenced by their parent organizations' concentration on other aspects of their programs and the assumption that women's rights would follow later. These two influences existed simultaneously and, despite mutual hostility, each had a constant effect on the values of a faction within the suffrage movement.

Only in the 1960s did the arrival of the student movement precipitate changes in the values of some suffrage activists, which led to a more confrontational stance. Even then, the new women's liberation movement remained largely apart from the woman suffrage movement which it regarded as too establishment-oriented.

Early Women's Charitable and
Moral Reform Movements

The character of the Swiss woman suffrage movement, even as late as the 1940s and 1950s, was largely affected by the context in which it arose. While the American movement had the advantage of the influences of abolitionists and the temperance movement, the early women's rights organizations in Switzerland grew mainly out of women's charitable and social reform organizations in the early twentieth century. The particular nature of early Swiss women's organizations therefore played a large role in determining the values and tactics of the suffrage movement.

Like many of the early women's organizations in the United States, Swiss women's organizations in the nineteenth century were largely public extensions of women's "separate sphere." Women were deemed responsible for maintaining home life, raising children, and being paragons of religious and moral values within the home; they believed they were also needed to fill these roles in the public sphere. Thus, Josephine Butler's international campaign against state-controlled prostitution found fertile ground in Switzerland because it "was primarily a moral reform movement, directed against social and spiritual evils and having as its ultimate aim the regeneration of society through expanding the moral sway of women" (Caine 1982: 547). Other Swiss women's organizations concerned themselves with education in home economics for young girls, temperance, care of orphans and the economically destitute, and public health questions (Mesmer 1988). Like the U.S. suffrage movement in later years, Swiss suffrage activists developed values that reflected an appreciation of women's separate sphere. Because many suffrage activists remained active in these charitable organizations and in Catholic women's organizations, these values continued to be reinforced in later years. Suffrage organizations consistently emphasized women's political participation in governmental bodies charged with directing social services and included a wide variety of moral issues on their agenda. In addition, the movement implicitly accepted the idea that women were primarily responsible for the moral and physical care of the home and the family.

Unlike the U.S. temperance movement, however, the activities of charitable and moral reform movements did not lead women to seek a greater role in political life. While these early charitable organizations occasionally supported more rights for women (Woodtli 1983), their activities centered around providing social services. Thus, women's organizations set up schools for young girls, alcohol-free restaurants, and employment offices for working women. Therein lies a major difference in influence from the U.S. temperance and club movements. Swiss women's organizations did interact with local, cantonal, and even the national government, but it was rarely to petition for new laws. Generally, when women's organizations desired a new orphanage for girls, they would petition for donations from the government to provide the service themselves. In response to studies showing widespread malnutrition in the 1880s, for example, women's organizations received funds from the national government to run cooking and nutrition classes (Mesmer 1988: 127). Thus, while women were often petitioning the national government, it was often for financial assistance or for small policy changes that did not require parliamentary action.

Even in the 1940s and 1950s, the emphasis on nonlegislative routes evinced by these organizations was evident in the strategies of the Swiss woman suffrage organization. Of the letters of appeal (*Eingaben*) which the Schweizerischer Verband für Frauenstimmrecht (SVF) introduced between 1934 and 1959, most were to government ministries asking for small policy changes (SVF 1959). Typical were petitions sent to the radio commission or the post and railroad department asking for female representation on particular committees or boards. Only a few letters of petition went to parliamentary committees, the Bundesrat, or the Swiss Parliament. This form of petition and its focus on nonlegislative institutions mirrored the strategies used by Swiss women's charitable or moral reform organizations.

While these women's organizations usually utilized nonlegislative tactics to achieve their goals, they occasionally played a role in legislative reform after 1900 when national umbrella organizations were created. Early in the twentieth century, the national women's charitable organizations sporadically participated in the *Vernehmlassung* process (see Chapter 6) and in parliamentary commissions. However, their position on these committees and in the consultation process was highly dependent on the wishes of male politicians. Mesmer (1988: 167) notes that women's organizations would typically be asked by a Bundesrat politician to participate in the preparation of a bill only when the organization was expected to take a stand consistent with his own.

Moreover, their forays into the legislative process were almost completely limited to organizational petitions and participation on parliamentary committees. Women's organizations appear to have placed no pressure on politicians to initiate or support legislation. Nor is there any indication that women considered using initiatives, although this process was available to them after 1891. In fact, I found only one reference to women's organizations in connection with initiatives. In 1906, the Bund Schweizerischer Frauenorganisationen "placed itself . . . at the service of the Initiative committee for the prohibition of absinthe" (Mesmer 1988: 239; translated by author). Thus, women's charitable and moral reform organizations could not provide models of legislative or initiative strategies to the Swiss suffrage movement.

Finally, women's moral reform and charitable organizations provided a poor model for how to spread information and tactics within a federalized movement. These organizations often found themselves divided by religion, language, or locale. There was little communication between national organizations and their local groups outside of a few printed brochures and letters (Mesmer 1988: 187). Indeed, women's reform organizations in one area were often ignorant of the activities of its counterparts in other areas even when national organizations existed. For example, Mesmer notes that even Marie Goegg, the president of Association internationale des femmes, did not know that the Zürich women were working on the same issues as her organization in Genève: "Inside of Switzerland the language borders apparently represented a much stronger information barrier than in international cooperation" (1988: 92; translated by author). Thus, while women's charitable and moral reform organizations formed an important part of the context of Swiss suffrage movements in the early years, they did not provide a model that encouraged women's rights ideology or the tactics needed to acquire woman suffrage legislation.

Socialist Influences

All over Europe, socialist parties were the first to officially support women's rights and to encourage women to organize (Lovenduski 1986). This was no less true in Switzerland where the Social Democratic party (SP) and socialist organizations supported women's enfranchisement throughout the twentieth century. One of the demands of the 1918 general strike was that women receive the vote. Social Democratic members of the Swiss national parliament also initiated half of the postulates and motions that called for the women's voting rights.[3] In both national and cantonal referenda, the SP always endorsed woman suffrage amendments.

Despite these endorsements, however, early socialist ideology actually de-emphasized the importance of women's rights and encouraged divisions within the women's rights movement. Early socialists like Bebel ([1883] 1950) and Engels ([1883] 1973) argued that the emancipation of women could only be obtained through a socialist revolution. Toward that end, socialist women were expected to focus their energies on the socialist movement and not on women's rights. At the 1910 International Women's Conference in Copenhagen, socialist women's organizations were forbidden from joining neutral or middle-class organizations. Swiss socialist and working women's clubs were thus forced to leave the Bund Schweizerischer Frauenorganisationen which was one of the largest organizations working for women's rights at that time (Mesmer 1988; Woodtli 1983).

Even in later years, the SP's actual influence on the suffrage movement remained small despite its consistent advocacy of women's enfranchisement. Although socialist women later returned to women's rights organizations, the majority of women in the suffrage movement were not socialist but belonged to Catholic or Free Democratic parties. While suffrage activists appreciated the socialists' assistance, both socialist and nonsocialist women in the SVF told me in interviews that woman suffrage was not a major focus of socialist activism. The Social Democratic party gave higher priority to other aspects of its platform.

The result was an ambiguous relationship between the Social Democrats and the woman suffrage organizations. On the one hand, the suffrage activists applauded the support from the socialists, particularly during the years when the other major parties opposed enfranchising women. For the most part though, the leaders of the suffrage movement did not approve of the SP. The reaction of the suffrage organization to the demands of the 1918 general strike is a good example of its mixed relationship to the socialists. In a telegram to the Bundesrat, the leadership of the Schweizerischer Verband für Frauenstimmrecht (SVF) expressed sympathy for the government and condemned the activities of the socialist strikers; at the same time, they reminded the Bundesrat that the strikers' demands included woman suffrage, which was a goal worthy of governmental response (Ruckstuhl 1986).

The Social Democrats had little influence on the middle-class, Catholic, and conservative suffrage activists. Nevertheless, some socialist values penetrated the movement through the suffrage activists with Social Democratic connections. The SP, for example, was an active user of the initiative; 29 of the 89 initiatives introduced between 1892 and 1968 stemmed from the SP or related trade unions (Werder 1978: 26). Before 1930, socialists also utilized confrontational tactics such as the 1918 general strike. Thus, if Social Democrats had an effect on woman suffrage activists, it would have been in the direction of more confrontational tactics and initiatives. Indeed, in a number of cantons, and more rarely on the national level, socialist women influenced the course of the suffrage movement. Compared to more conservative activists, socialist activists were usually more willing to engage in initiatives or actions that openly opposed governmental decisions. As we shall see below, this made a difference in particular regions of Switzerland. However, after 1943, the SP also became a coalition partner in the Bundesrat, and its emphasis on oppositional values and confrontational tactics declined. Moreover, as a political party, the SP did not emphasize lobbying tactics as a means of achieving its goals. As such, it provided no examples of legislative tactics that suffrage activists could borrow.

As a whole, then, the SP had little influence on the suffrage movement and where it did, it was not always positive. Social Democrats encouraged splits within the suffrage movement based on party affiliations. In this way they reinforced differences between suffrage activists rather than providing an example of solidarity within the movement. In the early years, it encouraged socialist women to view their cause as different from those of middle-class women and to ignore the suffrage issue in favor of other goals. Moreover, since socialist women made up such a small proportion of woman suffrage activists, the SP's actual influence was small.

The Influence of Catholic Organizations

Because a large proportion of suffrage activists were active in Catholic organizations, ties to these groups were an important influence on the suffrage organization. Unfortunately, the beliefs and values inculcated by these organizations only served to exacerbate the existing splits within the suffrage movement. In the nineteenth century, Catholic women joined national and local women's charitable and moral reform organizations with little concern for religion, since they shared the belief in women's primary role in these areas (Mesmer 1988). In response to the creation of socialist working women's associations, however, the church encouraged Catholic women to form separate organizations, such as the Schweizerischer Katholischer Frauenbund (SKF), under the guidance of the church (Mesmer 1988; Woodtli 1983). Following the urging of the Catholic hierarchy, Catholic organizations abandoned the Bund Schweizerischer Frauenorganisationen in 1910 (Woodtli 1983: 122). Thus, just as socialist women were encouraged to believe that they could not work with middle-class women, Catholic women were being inculcated with the belief that socialist and even Protestant middle-class women's organizations were not an appropriate forum for their activism.

The major Catholic women's organization, the SKF, was founded as an arm of a wider Catholic movement in 1912 and therefore was largely dependent on male-dominated organizations and the church. Indeed, these groups created the SKF because they recognized the necessity of having organizational outlets for their wives and sisters in countering the influence of other national women's organizations. The independence of the SKF was quite limited even in the 1950s. The initial statutes of the SKF called for the president and general secretary of the men's Catholic organization, plus a spiritual advisor appointed by the bishop, to sit on its Board of Directors (Mesmer 1988: 276). Even in later years, one Catholic suffrage activist whom I interviewed noted that the spiritual advisor occasionally tried to impose his opinions on the group.[4]

The SKF's activities otherwise mirrored those of other women's charitable and moral reform organizations. Its political agenda largely consisted of providing services and representing Catholic women in parliamentary commissions or the *Vernehmlassung* process on such "women's issues" as social services, marriage laws, or education. Like other women's charitable and moral reform groups, it did not engage in lobbying or confrontational tactics. Its other political activity, to the extent it engaged in politics at all, was focused almost exclusively on letters of appeal. Thus, the political experiences of the SKF were not good models for the legislative politics necessary to speed women's enfranchisement.

Nonetheless, Catholic organizations had a major impact on the woman suffrage movement through the ties of national leaders and because of the lack of woman suffrage sections in eastern Switzerland. A number of SVF leaders were active in the Swiss women's Catholic organization, the SKF. In fact, the distinction between the SKF and the SVF sometimes blurred. For example, Lotti Ruckstuhl, one-time president of the SVF, discusses the activities of the SKF in her book on the Swiss woman suffrage movement. Another president of the SVF, and an SKF member, Dr. Gertrude Heinzelmann, used the suffrage newspaper to publicize her activities promoting women's status within the Catholic Church (interview of December 15, 1987).

The church had a particularly strong influence in those cantons with the largest Catholic populations. In about half of the ten Catholic cantons, the women's organization most visible in suffrage politics was not an affiliate of the SVF but a Catholic organization: either the Staatsbürgerlicher Verband Katholischer Schweizerinnen (commonly known as STAKA) or the SKF.[5] The emphasis of the Catholic Church and affiliated organizations on the traditional roles for women led Catholic suffrage activists to de-emphasize the *right* to vote for women. When church-affiliated women's organizations involved themselves in the suffrage issue, they focused almost exclusively on educating and interesting women in politics. For example, the STAKA section in canton Schwyz sponsored talks about consumer politics, protecting the water supply, education, juvenile law, and governmental committees dealing with the handicapped ("Der STAKA Sektion Kanton Schwyz," September 16, 1969). Thus, even where Catholic women pushed for suffrage, they often carried values promoting traditional roles into the suffrage movement.[6]

The end result was that the values and information inculcated by Catholic organizations did not aid the Swiss woman suffrage movement in their struggle for the vote. Catholic organizations, like their socialist counterparts, encouraged splits within the suffrage movement by encouraging Catholic women to organize separately. Thus, suffrage activists believed that they were separated by religion as well as political beliefs. Catholic organizations also mirrored other women's charitable and moral reform organizations in their lack of a legislative agenda. As a result, they could not serve as a source of information about legislative, confrontational, or initiative tactics to woman suffrage activists. By and large, the SKF did not even focus on achieving any sort of legal changes. When it became involved in parliamentary commissions, it was often at the behest of the church or male leaders of Catholic political organizations.

The Rise of Sixties' Movements

While the student movement and the new women's liberation movement of the late 1960s and early 1970s only appeared in the last years of the Swiss suffrage movement, they had a small but important impact on the tactics of some suffrage activists. The impact of the women's liberation movement was limited by the fact that few ties existed between the two women's movements, and even those were problematic. FBB women were uninterested in joining the existing suffrage movement (or allying with them) because they felt the suffrage organization was much too complacent about their disenfranchisement. Nonetheless, Swiss suffrage activists in Zürich and Basel created a dialogue with these women and even worked with them on a few projects.

The interaction between activists in the woman suffrage and women's liberation movements changed the orientation of the suffrage movement slightly during its last years. The FBB were fundamentally opposed to compromise, preferring confrontational tactics. Prior to the student movement, suffrage activists generally emphasized only normal political channels. While earlier a national march protesting the activities of the government would have appalled most suffrage activists, the student movement and the women's liberation movement enhanced convictions that protest against the government was acceptable and even necessary. A number of suffrage activists began in the late 1960s to advocate and participate in slightly more confrontational actions. In my interviews, several suffrage activists, who otherwise argued against being too confrontational, proudly stated in interviews that they participated in the March on Bern despite concerns that the demonstration was too radical.

Combined Influence of Groups on Ideology

Each of these four groups—women's charitable and moral reform associations, socialist political organizations, Catholic institutions, and the women's liberation movement of the late 1960s—affected the values of the Swiss suffrage activists, albeit in some cases only slightly. The largest effect these groups had was to de-emphasize a legislative approach to winning the vote. Women's Catholic, charitable, and moral reform associations as well as socialist organizations motivated suffrage activists to emphasize issues other than women's voting rights. Moreover, none of these four groups utilized lobbying or pressure tactics to achieve legislation. Thus, woman suffrage organizations had few sources of information about such techniques although they were utilized by other Swiss groups. Although both socialist organizations and, later, the FBB did provide examples of confrontational or initiative tactics, these groups were connected with only a small proportion of suffrage activists and hence did not have a widespread effect on the suffrage movement.

Indeed, none of these four political actors had an overwhelming effect on the ideology of the Swiss woman suffrage movement in the way that the abolitionists, temperance activists, populists, or progressives affected the woman suffrage activists in the United States. Some suffrage activists were motivated by values obtained through their socialist connections; others adopted values from Catholic organizations; and yet others were influenced by their work in the moral reform movement. Thus, it is impossible to talk about *the* ideology of the Swiss woman suffrage movement since no single set of values outweighed the others. Instead, at every point in time, the national movement was characterized by a number of different, coexisting values and beliefs all loosely bound by the themes of women's rights and interests. These divisions, combined with socialist and Catholic organizations' emphasis on the religious and political differences among women, exacerbated splits within the suffrage organization. Because the SVF also lacked models for reducing these differences (for example, by disseminating information and tactics), the suffrage movement failed to develop a coherent community with shared values or beliefs.

Regional Variation in Swiss Woman Suffrage Values

The political and religious divisions within the Swiss suffrage movement would have been less serious if local associations had believed that the problems and activities of other local suffrage sections were applicable to their own situation. However, regional differences within the movement and strong beliefs in local autonomy further divided the Swiss suffrage movement.

Many regional differences can be explained by the strength of the socialist or religious groups. Suffrage movements in Catholic cantons were less insistent about the importance of women's enfranchisement and tended to argue that women's political involvement would aid their traditional roles. They often avoided the topic of woman suffrage and preferred public education to the initiative or tactics that emphasized explicitly demands for women's voting rights. On the other hand, cantons with strong socialist organizations tended to have suffrage organizations that were more willing to confront the government and discuss the rights of women. Socialist activists focused on equal rights arguments rather than women's special characteristics or duties. They also felt that it was important to push for suffrage openly and with as much vigor as possible and were willing to demonstrate, petition, and conduct initiatives in order to press for women's voting rights.

Although most of the regional differences can be explained by the strength of Catholic and socialist organizations, suffrage activists often argued that two particular regions were unique. First, many claimed in interviews that French-speaking areas emphasized equality and the necessity of suffrage more than other cantons. Second, they often stated that Appenzell Innerrhoden and Appenzell Ausserrhoden had traditional democratic institutions that encouraged distinctively negative attitudes about woman suffrage and particularly strong feelings of cantonal autonomy.

The French Cantons

The Swiss often speak of the Röstigraben, or the border between German-speaking and French-speaking Switzerland, as separating two distinct cultures. In the case of woman suffrage, many of the German-speaking suffrage activists argued that French culture enhanced support for women's voting rights in Francophone cantons. The French revolution was often mentioned as a major influence. "The entire argument was different in French-speaking Switzerland during the campaign for suffrage. There one spoke about justice, equality, human rights. Like the French, they speak in great ideas. . . . These phrases come from the French Revolution, from the French mentality" (interview of November 26, 1987). Although the French government and people were unwilling to apply the principles of the French Revolution to the issue of woman suffrage (Hause and Kenney 1984), German-speaking suffrage activists maintained that these arguments influenced suffrage activists in French-speaking Switzerland.[7]

While an emphasis on equal rights was more prevalent in French cantons, most of the French cantons were also overwhelmingly Protestant and had strong socialist traditions. In particular, Neuchâtel and Genève had been strongholds of the socialist movement since the beginning of the twentieth century. As a result, it is difficult to determine whether values in these cantons stemmed from French culture or from the socialist influence. The only counterexample to the French culture theory is the canton Wallis/Valais. Here the Catholic church is particularly strong, there is no socialist tradition, and 60 percent of the population speak French. Despite the heavy French influence, the Wallis/Valais suffrage movement closely resembled those in central German-speaking Switzerland. The impetus for woman suffrage legislation in Wallis/Valais came principally from men (interview of June 22, 1988; Kantonale Kommission zum Studium der Rechtlichen und Tatsächlichen Lage der Frau 1988), and the tiny suffrage organization focused on civic education emphasizing women's traditional roles and downplaying the suffrage issue (Ruckstuhl 1986).

Regardless of whether these differences stemmed from cultural factors or from the political composition of most French-speaking cantons, suffrage activists, convinced of their uniqueness, believed what occurred on one side of the Röstigraben was not usually applicable to the other. For example, when German-language anti-suffrage propaganda after 1959 noted the low turnout rate of women in the elections of Francophone cantons, suffrage activists countered that those numbers would not reflect women's turnout in German-speaking Switzerland because of the difference in culture and political institutions (see, for example, Ruckstuhl 1986: 165). Thus, beliefs about cultural differences between cantons resulted in another division among Swiss suffrage activists.

The Two Appenzells

Swiss suffrage activists also characterized the two half cantons—Appenzell Innerrhoden and Appenzell Ausserrhoden—as having unique values, although most of their statements do not bear up under close examination. For example, many activists blamed the lack of support for woman suffrage on the rural character of the canton or the existence of the *Landesgemeinde*, a yearly meeting of citizens in the canton where enfranchised citizens publicly vote on governmental business. However, other rural and *Landesgemeinde* cantons did not manifest the same lack of support, making it unlikely that these factors explain the uniqueness of the two Appenzells. Nor was religion a factor, as Appenzell Innerrhoden is overwhelmingly Catholic while Ausserrhoden is predominantly Protestant. In fact, Appenzell split into two half-cantons over religious differences. Therefore, Catholicism cannot explain their negative attitudes toward enfranchising women.

One possible explanation for the Appenzells' rejection of woman suffrage is the value placed on local autonomy. The two Appenzells are isolated; they lie in the mountains surrounded by another canton, yet separated from it by their dialect and traditions. This isolation enhances the strong feeling of local autonomy within the Appenzells. Many suffrage activists argued that Appenzell citizens are suspicious of outsiders and resent being forced to accept certain ideas by the national government. One Appenzell Innerrhoden activist illustrated how these feelings affected attitudes toward women's enfranchisement: "Another colleague of mine

. . . said he was actually for it [woman suffrage] but when he was at the Landesgemeinde and saw the ring of people, people from outside Appenzell, who screamed out so loud that the members had to ask for silence, it had irritated him so much that he also voted against it. It was a kind of defiance—'I won't let myself be forced or persuaded'" (interview of November 22, 1990). A number of other suffrage activists also noted this tendency for Appenzell men to feel that their autonomy was being threatened by outside interference.

Outside pressure to adopt woman suffrage came from two different sources after 1971. First, national party organizations encouraged local parties to press for cantonal women's voting rights after 1971. However, national parties refused to do anything that could be construed as coercing the cantons. For example, an attempt by Appenzell women to get the national government to introduce legislation forcing cantons to enfranchise women failed precisely because many national politicians did not want to compel the canton. Instead, local party sections were urged by the national party organizations to support woman suffrage.

Despite the lack of coercion, even the pro-suffrage activities of local party organizations were unfavorably perceived by many Appenzell residents. Political parties themselves are almost considered outside influences in these two cantons. Both cantons are completely dominated by a single political party—in Ausserrhoden, the Free Democratic Party (FDP), in Innerrhoden, the Christian Democratic People's party (CVP). These party institutions exist to elect representatives to the Swiss Parliament, but have little impact on local issues. Although other parties are virtually nonexistent, the FDP in Appenzell Ausserrhoden and the CVP in Appenzell Innerrhoden have few members. When these political parties encouraged the passage of woman suffrage legislation, their advice was ignored or viewed as outsider interference.

The second source of outside pressure was the media. Each time woman suffrage came up for a vote in an Appenzell *Landesgemeinde* during the 1980s, TV and print journalists (from Switzerland and beyond) descended upon the small canton in droves. Their stories emphasized how backward and unique Appenzell was compared to the rest of Europe; this magnified the feelings of isolation and local autonomy within Appenzell.

Interestingly, many Appenzell suffrage activists were not as concerned about outside interference as activists in other cantons. Indeed, many argued that the federal government should force Appenzell to enfranchise women. No other local suffrage movement developed strategies that involved asking the federal government to reduce local autonomy. While the suffrage activists I interviewed elsewhere typically did not mention any sort of national aid, several Appenzell activists stated that contact with and aid from women outside the canton was important. The positive feelings toward outside influence were not a response to the increased activity of outside groups. In fact, the national suffrage association was careful not to participate too much in the Appenzell debate, and some Appenzell activists mentioned that they would have preferred *more* outside "interference." Thus, if beliefs in local autonomy were stronger in the two Appenzells, they were weaker among Appenzell suffrage activists.

Hence, Swiss suffrage activists faced the same problem as their American counterparts: regional differences in suffrage beliefs and values. In Switzerland, local differences increased beliefs in the necessity of local autonomy. Since suffrage activists believed the success or failure of women's voting rights legislation was related to different factors in different regions, tactics successful in one canton were not necessarily applicable in others. Thus, regional differences reinforced the political and religious divisions within the Swiss suffrage movement.

Comparing Swiss and American Suffrage Organizations: A Summary

Although the values of the Swiss and American woman suffrage movements were affected by other political actors, the consequences were quite different. First, the ties between political actors and the Swiss suffrage movement were weaker than those between the American suffrage movement and the abolitionist, temperance, populist, and progressive movements. In the United States, changes in suffrage activists' networks resulted in shifts in their tactics, their rationale for woman suffrage, and their appraisals of the government and business. In Switzerland, simultaneous weak ties to several different political actors meant no single political actor had a decisive influence on the values of the suffrage movement.

Second, the overall effect of these other political actors was much more positive in the United States than in Switzerland. The values transmitted through coalitions in the United States encouraged activists to seek voting rights for women. The equal rights values provided by abolitionists and the belief that women need to encourage legislative changes in order to implement moral reform led women to aggressively seek political rights. In Switzerland, many of the values transmitted by political actors deemphasized woman suffrage. Even the early socialists, who advocated political rights for women, argued that socialist reforms would bring equality for women and, therefore, women's rights did not need special emphasis. Moreover, while the values of different movements complemented each other in the United States, socialists and Catholics in Switzerland were more often opponents than allies. Catholics favored traditional roles for women while socialists did not. The socialists advocated systemic change while the Catholics did not. As a result, the Swiss national suffrage movement was often splintered by differences in values, while the U.S. movement developed coalition-level values that challenged the status quo.

American suffrage activists also received information about appropriate tactics through their ties to other groups; their Swiss counterparts did not. Abolitionists, temperance organizations, populists, and progressive groups were all actively seeking legislative changes. Especially in later years, temperance, populist, and progressive organizations provided functional examples of lobbying, initiatives, and electoral tactics. However, the Catholic, charitable, and moral reform women's organizations associated with most Swiss suffrage activists were largely uninterested in new legislation. As a result, they could not provide models for pressuring governmental institutions; those techniques they did know were inappropriate for the changes that suffrage activists desired.

Finally, both the American and Swiss woman suffrage movements faced regional differences in values that reinforced beliefs that local suffrage organizations should be free from national interference. Both southern states and Appenzell cantons exhibited resistance to national interference in local affairs. Beliefs that western states in the U.S. and Francophone cantons in Switzerland were culturally distinct from the rest of the country reinforced local differences and, therefore, indirectly the belief that individual states and cantons should decide their own strategies.

In the United States, national organizations counteracted this tendency by disseminating tactical information and sending resources and organizers into different states. However, Swiss suffrage organizations never developed values that countered the status-quo norm of regional autonomy. Indeed, the character of the Swiss woman suffrage movement—a loose aggregation of local sections split between middle-class, socialist, and Catholic women each with fundamentally different philosophies—only validated existing beliefs in local autonomy. The diverse ties of activists compounded the federalist divisions within the suffrage movement. Since no agreement on the values or principles behind the fight for suffrage existed, each local movement followed its own course.

Because there was only loose coordination at the national level, tactical innovations by one section were not passed on to other cantonal organizations. This explains why Swiss suffrage activists in some cantons were unaware of the use of initiative tactics elsewhere. In fact, many of the local suffrage activists I interviewed knew little of the history and activities of woman suffrage movements in other cantons. Unlike in the United States, the national organization could not counteract divisions within the movement by coordinating activities, encouraging the spread of knowledge about techniques, or advocating the use of certain tactics. Even during national suffrage referenda, cantonal suffrage organizations were largely left to their own devices. In the end, the networks of Swiss suffrage activists hindered success whereas those of the American movement aided their cause.

9

WHY MOVEMENTS SUCCEED OR FAIL

B Y THE TIME Swiss women were enfranchised on the national level in 1971, two generations of American women had voted all of their adult lives and Wyoming women had been casting ballots for over a century. It took another twenty years for the last Swiss canton to adopt woman suffrage and then it did so only by order of the Federal Court. In order to understand the differences in the timing of woman suffrage between Switzerland and the United States and within each country, I examined the effects of several factors: the mobilization of members into suffrage organizations, the financial resources of the suffrage movement, the alliances formed with other political actors, the characteristics of the political system, and the perceptions and preferences of activists reflected in the specific tactics they employed. These factors are related to the three different perspectives that have arisen as important explanations of movement success and failure: resource mobilization theories, political opportunity structure theories, and theories focusing on collective beliefs and values (often stated in the language of "frames," "culture," or "discourse"). While all three perspectives were important in understanding the Swiss and American woman suffrage movements, the latter goes the furthest in helping us to understand why the United States enfranchised women so much earlier than Switzerland.

Resource Mobilization and Political Opportunity Structure

The success of the Swiss and American woman suffrage movements was affected by both resources and political opportunity structures. The woman suffrage movement in the United States controlled more money than its Swiss counterpart. It also benefitted from connections to the abolitionist, temperance, populist, and progressive movements which served as a source of support, resources, and recruitment. While many aspects of the political opportunity structure—the federal structure, the role of interest groups in political parties, and the weak and decentralized parties—were similar in both countries, there were also some differences that disadvantaged the Swiss woman suffrage movement. The Swiss movement had to operate in a system where decisions were made by a carefully constructed consensus and where opposition parties never launched an electoral challenge that might have prodded governing parties into action. The closed legislative process made it difficult for suffrage activists to participate in, or even track, women's voting rights legislation. Finally, Swiss suffrage activists lacked strong allies in its struggle for the vote.

However, even after exploring the role of resources and political opportunities, some puzzles remain unanswered. For one, the Schweizerischer Verband für Frauenstimmrecht mobilized a much larger proportion of the population than the National American Woman Suffrage Association. Swiss suffrage activists also had more opportunities to launch initiative campaigns than their American counterparts.

Moreover, even where clear differences in resources and political opportunity structure existed, these often appear less important to the final outcome than suffrage movements' strategic decisions. The statistical evidence linking movement membership to success was, at best, weak. In the United States, only the final adoption of suffrage legislation was related to the suffrage organizational membership on the state level. In contrast, the size of cantonal suffrage organizations was unrelated to the number of cantonal women's voting rights bills, the pro-suffrage vote in cantonal legislatures or referenda, or the speed of women's enfranchisement. Although the U.S. movement was better funded, Swiss suffrage activists saved a higher percentage of their annual budgets and often chose not to spend money already budgeted to cantonal referenda campaigns. Thus, much depended on how money was spent, rather than on total budget size.

Similarly, there were some available avenues of influence that Swiss activists did not utilize. Suffrage activists rarely attempted to recruit members or organize those local areas that lacked their own suffrage associations. They seldom engaged in confrontational tactics, such as parades or demonstrations, although these techniques helped to win the vote in several cantons. They did not employ lobbying techniques, although both American suffragists and other Swiss interest groups used these tactics effectively. Nor did they utilize initiatives to bring suffrage amendments to a vote, although they had more opportunities to do so than their American counterparts.

Resource mobilization and political opportunity structure theories cannot explain the failure of the Swiss suffrage movement because they assume that movements with insufficient resources or political opportunities are either doomed to failure or (knowing that the conditions are unfavorable for success) will not make fruitless attempts at achieving their goals. However, the Swiss woman suffrage movement conforms to neither of these scenarios. Swiss suffrage activists did not attempt certain tactics and fail as the first scenario suggests. Indeed, if there is one finding that is echoed throughout this book, it is that Swiss suffrage movements failed to try a number of potentially useful tactics.

Nor were Swiss suffrage activists choosing not to act because of full or accurate information about political opportunities or certain types of tactics. Many suffrage activists argued that confrontational tactics would be counterproductive because they would alienate potential suffrage supporters. They also believed that attempts by the SVF to organize local suffrage sections would be open to accusations of outside interference, thereby hurting the suffrage cause. Yet the evidence indicates that these perceptions did not necessarily reflect the true opportunity structure: Confrontational tactics in Switzerland were associated with success, not failure. Moreover, the interviews and historical record suggest that Swiss suffrage activists *failed* to perceive some of the opportunities open to them. Thus, their decisions were not always based on a dearth in resources or an adverse political opportunity structure but a paucity of information.

The Role of Perceptions and Values

Suffrage activists' values and perceptions largely determined whether and how the movement acted. Swiss activists' perceptions of available tactics were frequently biased, incomplete or inaccurate, and their values also caused them to reject strategies that might have been effective. On the other hand, women in the U.S. suffrage movement assessed their political opportunities more accurately and utilized them effectively. Norms of professionalism, legislative activism, and reform led the American movement to adopt successful techniques.

The result was two very different woman suffrage movements. While in their early years, both movements shared an emphasis on education, only the U.S. movement developed into a full-blown reform movement that understood how initiatives, lobbying, referenda, and organizing could be utilized to create winning political strategies. When one of these avenues was blocked, American activists switched to other applicable tactics in their repertoire. Their push for the vote led to the consideration of countless suffrage bills, numerous legislative votes, and a fair number of state referenda. The U.S. movement took full advantage of its own federal structure to spread the knowledge and information about tactics to local areas. Innovations of state sections were picked up and spread throughout the movement by an activist national organization despite regional divisions within the movement, thereby resulting in growing homogeneity of suffrage movement tactics.

The Swiss suffrage movement developed extensive educational tactics but rarely engaged in political activities beyond referenda campaigns. When women's voting rights amendments were referred to the voters, the Swiss movement reacted with intensified educational efforts and helped to organize extensive propaganda campaigns. However, suffrage activists at both the national and cantonal level did not encourage the introduction of suffrage legislation, either in parliaments or through initiatives. As a result, there were long periods when no parliament (national or cantonal) was considering woman suffrage legislation and no suffrage referenda were on the horizon. However, local movements also varied considerably in Switzerland. A few exceptional local organizations pressured politicians to adopt women's voting rights, utilized the initiative when they could not work through legislatures, or protested the unresponsiveness of governments and the electorate with marches, strikes, and other symbolic acts. Yet these tactics never spread—partially because the national suffrage organization did little to encourage them but mainly because Swiss suffrage activists were themselves divided by language, religion, politics, and region. These divisions further inhibited the flow of information between activists and reinforced the belief that the tactics of one segment of the movement were not applicable elsewhere.

In the end, the United States and Switzerland differed from one another not in the kind of strategies they used but in the degree to which certain strategies were adopted. Similar tactics and strategies appeared in Switzerland and the United States, but the most effective ones were much more common and important to the American movement.

The Source of Information and Values

If perceptions and values determined the way the Swiss and American suffrage movements responded to their resource capabilities and political opportunities, these were themselves a product of the social contexts of the two movements. Strong social ties both among movement activists and between them and other groups were especially important in determining which values developed. These values then served to filter and interpret the available information. Social interaction also transmitted specific information about actions and strategies, which affected the movements' tactical repertoires.

The U.S. suffrage movement benefitted from interactions with other movements that utilized the types of actions that proved successful. Not only did the natural rights argument of the abolitionists serve as a normative basis for the early women's rights movements, their organizing strategies provided concrete techniques for overcoming the status-quo norm of local autonomy prevalent in many regions of the United States. The temperance movement's "Home Protection Ballot" provided new methods for seeking legislative reform and a new philosophy that attracted previously alienated groups (for example, southern women) to the cause. Ties to the populist and progressive movements reinforced these values and tactics and contributed to local suffrage movements' focus on initiatives.

In contrast, the Swiss suffrage movement lacked close political allies which could have provided values or information encouraging successful action. While other women's organizations had ties to the Swiss suffrage movement, most of these—reform and charitable associations, socialist groups, women's centers, and Catholic organizations—de-emphasized women's rights and political roles. Since these groups were mainly interested in providing services rather than seeking legislative changes, they did not develop techniques for pressuring Swiss legislators or for launching initiatives. Their traditional values also steered them away from confrontational activities. Only women's party organizations and the new women's liberation movement were strong advocates of women's enfranchisement. However, both appeared only in the late 1960s, toward the end of the suffrage movement, and their effect on the values and perceptions of the Swiss woman suffrage movement was limited.

Of the major political parties, only the Social Democrats continually supported women's voting rights before 1959; yet it rarely pushed the suffrage issue, even encouraging socialist women to withdraw from suffrage organizations in the early years. Although the Social Democrats countenanced more confrontational values and imparted an alternative view of women as participants in political life, these values touched only a minority of suffrage activists. Most had ties to the center and religious parties which emphasized women's traditional roles and discouraged their participation in politics until youth organizations and, later, women with suffrage forced changes in the 1960s. The values of these parties only reinforced suffrage activists' status quo values of local autonomy and nonconfrontation. Indeed, party and religious connections increased the divisions within the Swiss suffrage movement, as each subgroup developed strong ties with a different political actor. As a result, the Swiss suffrage activists shared few common values beyond the goal of suffrage itself. Without the creation of a suffrage "community," information about and innovation in tactics did not spread throughout the movement.

In the United States, two factors aided in the development of a single suffrage community. First, the early women's rights activists shared many of the same values. While the movement split during the post–Civil War period over the Fourteenth Amendment and tactical issues, the divisions diminished as these events receded into history. The shared values and beliefs endured long enough to help suffrage activists reunite in 1892. Second, suffrage activists worked to maintain common values within the movement and overcome beliefs in local autonomy. Innovations were consciously disseminated throughout the United States and diverse groups were incorporated into the national movement. In both the United States and Switzerland, federalism translated into strong beliefs that the national government and national organizations should not interfere in states and cantons. However, coalition and group values in the American woman suffrage movement counteracted this belief, while it went unchallenged in Switzerland.

Implications for the Study of Woman
Suffrage Movements

The approaches taken in this book and the conclusions drawn in it, have several implications for the study of woman suffrage movements, both in the United States and in other countries. First, the political context of each woman suffrage movement can have significant and complex effects on its activities and success. The most important aspect of that political context is the network of allies formed by other organizations. These groups influence not only the composition of the pro- and anti-suffrage coalitions but also can affect, in subtle ways, the values and information available to woman suffrage movements. No matter how supportive an ally is, its overall effect on the timing of woman suffrage is not always positive. Allies may bring with them strong opponents or contribute values and information that hurt the suffrage cause.

Indeed, my findings mirror those of other scholars of comparative women's movements who have found that socialist alliances with women's rights groups must be considered in a critical light (see, for example, Hellman 1987; Lovenduski 1986). Even as socialists all over Europe advocated the enfranchisement of women, their support may have had negative consequences. In countries where the socialists were strong enough to engender a negative reaction but not powerful enough to institute woman suffrage on their own, the alliance may have hurt more than it helped. Socialists may also have contributed to the widespread splits in the women's movements on the Continent. In countries like Germany, the divisions between socialist and middle-class women were exceedingly deep and are still discernible today.

Yet, it is not only the official allies that had profound effects on the woman suffrage movement, as the history of the Swiss suffrage movement shows. Swiss activists had ties to groups which were decidedly resistant to women's voting rights and which profoundly affected activists' values and perceptions. By creating women's organizations that were closely tied to church hierarchy, the Catholic Church provided poor organizational models for activists seeking to reform the political system. The church also encouraged specific values that were nonconfrontational and focused on women's traditional roles as caregiver, mother, and religious keystone. Thus, in overwhelmingly Catholic countries, we find that suffrage movements have a character that reflects these values (see, for example, Lovenduski 1986: 53–55, on Belgium, Italy, and Spain).

All of this reinforces the importance of examining values and beliefs in order to understand the activities and success of women's movements. Many scholars have already chronicled the different views of women's roles and place in the public sphere (see, for example, Cott 1987; Kraditor 1981). However, it is not simply values or beliefs related to women or women's roles that are critical in understanding the characters, actions, and success of women's movements. Other values, like attaching import to local autonomy or being open to confrontational politics, can affect the movement as well.

Moreover, although authors have noted the divisions within woman suffrage movements, few have attempted to examine how these influence movement activities or the timing of women's enfranchisement. I have presented two cases where divisions were present within the movement from the beginning—one where those divisions had few concrete effects on the outcomes and one where they had a profound effect, hindering its ability to achieve women's voting rights. In the United States, the organization of NAWSA worked to the advantage of the woman suffrage movement, spreading information (and implicit therein, certain values). Yet, I would not argue that centralized, hierarchical organization is a necessity to construct and maintain common values. Other tactics that encourage the spread of common beliefs and values might work better in other settings. However, for a federal system with stark regional variation and local influence over women's voting rights, the national activities of the U.S. suffrage organizations helped to overcome the feelings of regional difference that threatened to divide the movement. Swiss suffrage activists never overcame these feelings.

An additional implication bears on debates among historians concerning the use of parades, pickets, and symbolic protest in the United States, especially after 1910. Scholars of the U.S. woman suffrage movement have disagreed on which tactics—the militant activities of the Woman's party or the less controversial methods of the National American Woman Suffrage Association—were more useful (see, for example, Catt and Shuler 1926; Deckard 1983; Ryan 1992). By exploring differences in local movement tactics, I have provided one more piece of evidence to the supporters of confrontation. State movements that engaged in parades, pickets, and open-air meetings were more likely to succeed.

Implications for Social Movement Theories

This book also illustrates how social movements may miss political opportunities or not use resources to their greatest advantage. This is not to imply that movement activists are irrational or stupid. Rather, missing an opportunity may be the result of a fully rational and intelligent decision. Movement activists may make decisions without fully knowing all options or discounting certain viable options because of their values.

Understanding the success and failure of social movements requires a careful examination of *both* their political context and their values and beliefs. The perceptions of movement activists constitute an important and understudied concept for social movement research. In the cases of the Swiss and American suffrage movements, they played a major role in determining success, along with political opportunities and resources. Previous scholars have assumed that movements see all political opportunities. This assumption need not be unrealistic if one believes that misperceptions have only random effects on success, and therefore can be safely ignored. Yet, this study shows that the effect of perceptions is decidedly not random. Since beliefs and values are affected by an individual's social ties, they differ systematically for members of key groups at specific times. Indeed, given that perceptions and values derive from an individual's ties to broader society, other political groups (whether allies or not), and the more intimate bonds with fellow activists, it seems unlikely that movements will ever perceive all available opportunities or resources.

For social movements opposing the status quo, the development of values and perceptions that encourage confrontation, reform, or challenge of the political system is vital. Such ideas are not likely to be a part of societal (status quo) beliefs and values disseminated by system-supporting groups. Rather, status quo dogma will have a view of how politics can and should be done that ignores or downplays exactly those tactics and values most helpful to a movement. Thus, unless a social movement has a source of values and beliefs (from coalitions with other groups or within the movement itself) that counter those of the status quo, the movement faces an uphill battle in achieving its goals. This suggests that social ties to other challenging or reformist political actors and/or strong social interaction within the movement are key determinants of success.

Political alliances have long been considered important by resource mobilization and political opportunity structure theorists, but for reasons other than those I have emphasized. Not only do allies provide crucial resources for social movements and make the system more open to movement demands, they may immutably alter the perceptions and values of social movement activists. Since the beliefs and values transmitted through these social ties can have a negative effect, even when the political group is supportive of a movement, it is insufficient to merely document the alliances formed around a particular social movement. Rather, understanding the actual effect of other political actors on a social movement requires examining the social ties between groups and the values and information transmitted between them. Thus, analyses of political opportunity structures need to focus more specifically on the ideological impact of other political actors and not merely on the power relationships so central in most analyses of the political context.

In addition, I also underscore the importance of collective identity and common values in achieving desired outcomes. Without a movement "community" and intense social interaction among activists, a social movement will remain divided, impeding the flow of information and reducing its capacity for effective innovation and action. While several authors have noted the importance of collective identity or solidarity in the formation and sustenance of a movement, only a few (see, for example, McAdam 1988) have explored how that community transmits tactics and values that ultimately affect its activities and success. The discussion of the Swiss and American suffrage movements underscores the importance of collective identity while at the same time suggesting that its effects have a wider range of consequences than most scholars have suggested.

Finally, the necessary connection between values and beliefs on the one hand, and the success of social movements on the other is their tactical decision making. It is in the decisions of a social movement to take a distinct course of action, to expend its resources in a particular way, or to take advantage of a specific opportunity that values and beliefs increase or decrease the chances of success. Thus, to understand the outcomes of social movements, even to explore the role of resources and political opportunities, requires a focus on social movements' decisions and activities. However, movement decisions and tactical considerations have generally not been a focus of social movement research. The missed opportunities of the Swiss suffrage movement and the success of its American counterpart demonstrate that perceptions and their effect on tactical decisions are a vital link in determining the outcomes of social movements.

APPENDIXES

A

INTERVIEW METHODS

IN SWITZERLAND, the few secondary accounts and the original historical record available from activists and archives (Gosteli Stiftung in Worblaufen and the Schweizerisches Sozialarchiv in Zürich) concentrate on referendum campaigns and legislation to the exclusion of the organizations, their tactics, and their mobilization of constituents. The interviews provided more data on how mobilization, the group's activities, and success or failure tie together. They also presented specifics about the tactics of the group and its alliances with other groups which are unobtainable elsewhere. Hence, interviews with suffrage activists furnished essential information about the woman suffrage movement.

I conducted in-depth interviews with 62 people (61 women and 1 man) from 25 of the 26 cantons. The newest canton, Jura, was excluded because it first adopted woman suffrage when it was still a region of the canton Bern. The interviews ranged in length from 45 minutes to 4 hours, with an average interview lasting 90 minutes. With one exception, all the interviews were recorded on tape. The activists appeared comfortable with the use of tape recorders in interviews probably because many of them had held or run for public office or dealt with journalists in the past.

Finding Informants

Since the interviews' main purpose was to obtain detailed information about the cantonal suffrage campaigns, random sampling of suffrage organization members made little sense. With random sampling, I could not assure interviews in all 25 cantons, nor could I be certain that the most knowledgeable individuals would be participating in the study. In each canton, I tried to locate individuals who were well informed about the local suffrage campaign and the activities of suffrage organizations. Three means were utilized to locate the best informants. First, informants were chosen most often by asking other informants and activists for names, that is, by reputation. Second, if a person was prominent in the historical records of a particular canton, I attempted to locate that person. Only a few informants were found this way, as most of the people in the historical record not named by other activists were deceased. Finally, in a few cantons in the eastern and central part of Switzerland, where no suffrage organizations existed and where contacts to other Swiss suffrage activists were rare, I asked the women's centers of these cantons for appropriate contacts. I then tried to confirm these names using the other sources.

I decided at the outset to interview at least two individuals from each canton. While I exceeded this number in many cantons, in two cantons—Aargau and Uri—I only managed to locate one informant. Since Uri lacked both a section of the Schweizerischer Verband für Frauenstimmrecht (SVF) and of Staatsbürgerlicher Verband katholischer Schweizerinnen (STAKA), I was not surprised by the difficulty in finding an activist to discuss the canton's history of woman suffrage. Unfortunately, the deaths of several suffrage activists and one refusal to participate made it impossible to find another respondent in Aargau.

All potential respondents were first contacted by letter, in which I explained who I was, described the project, and asked permission to interview them. Almost all of the women who received this letter contacted me to arrange an interview. In only a few cases, did I have to make an additional contact. The refusal rate was very low; only three women refused to be interviewed for this project. However, three other activists who initially agreed to talk to me could not be interviewed because of death or serious illness. In addition, many other activists could not be contacted since they had already passed away by 1987. This was particularly a problem in the French-speaking cantons, where cantonal suffrage had passed earlier and the women activists were therefore older than in other parts of Switzerland.

While the respondents interviewed were all actively involved in some way in the woman suffrage movement, not all were members of the SVF since not all cantons had a section of the suffrage organization. Where the suffrage group existed, I usually interviewed presidents or former presidents of the SVF section or people who had been members of the governing board for a long period. In cantons where no suffrage organization existed, I interviewed women who had been actively involved in the fight to enfranchise women. By and large, these individuals were members of other organizations with similar goals—the cantonal women's centers, women's organizations of political parties, and, in the eastern part of Switzerland, STAKA. Four respondents, however, were not members of such organizations. Two of these were well-known feminists on the national level who also participated in cantonal activities. One respondent (the only man interviewed) had proposed women's voting rights legislation in both the national and cantonal parliaments and was editor of the canton's major newspaper. The fourth activist had tried and failed to organize a suffrage association in a canton without any active movement organizations.

Group Interviews

Most of the sessions were conducted with a single individual, usually in her home or office. However, 8 group interviews were conducted, and 20 of my respondents were interviewed in groups. With the exception of 1 interview that included 7 people, only 2 or 3 activists were questioned at a time. I did not originally intend to conduct group interviews. Whenever activists suggested joint meetings, I attempted to convince the individuals to meet with me one person at a time. In these 8 cases, however, the women could not be dissuaded.

The activists who requested group sessions gave three reasons for wishing to meet jointly. First, as my letter of introduction asked for names of other individuals who should be interviewed, some activists arranged group meetings for my convenience. Since the number of suffrage activists in some cantons was quite small, I would often also send letters to close friends who, when they realized that both were to be interviewed, simply made plans to do the interview together before I contacted them. By that time, it was usually impossible to forgo a joint meeting. No amount of polite protest convinced these women that in fact it was more convenient to interview individually.

Second, many of the individuals who did group interviews expressed joy or satisfaction at the possibility of seeing old friends. Some of these women had not seen their comrades since women's voting rights legislation had been adopted, and the process of recounting old battles seemed to make the interview process a very pleasant experience for them. Third, a few women expressed reluctance to be interviewed alone, since they claimed that they did not know or could not remember enough about past events. While I reassured every woman that whatever they remembered would certainly be sufficient for my purposes, several women who expressed this fear requested that they be interviewed with so-and-so, who would certainly remember more than they. The women who emphasized the third reason were not any less informed on average than other respondents.

Language

With three exceptions, all interviews were conducted in German. Since most of the people whom I interviewed were graduates of the Swiss university system, they also spoke German even if it was not their native language. The largest difficulties were presented by respondents in the French-speaking cantons, where several activists did not wish to be interviewed in German. In one case, this problem was solved by conducting the session in English, but in the other two, I had to utilize a translator to conduct the interviews. The translators were not professionals, but women active in the movement who were fluent in both French and German. Hence, the translations were not always completely accurate. Since both the original French and the translations were recorded on tape, I was able to procure their complete answers to my initial questions and to compare the translators' answers to the original. However, the flow of conversation was impeded and follow-up questions were occasionally difficult to ask.

The Content of the Interview

Because the main purpose of the interviews was to supply detailed historical accounts of the suffrage process, the interviews were open-ended and informal. This allowed the activists the freedom to center on issues they felt were important, and permitted the interviewer to follow trains of conversation that arose during the course of the session. This method helped to foster rapport between interviewer and respondent, and many activists were more candid about the organization and its activities than I had anticipated. Nonetheless, all respondents were asked the same list of questions and whenever the conversation allowed, the questions were asked in the same order.

The interviews aimed at understanding both the individual's and the organization's activities. Respondents were asked how they came to join the organization, what positions they held and what activities they participated in within the group, and their opinions on the factors leading to the success of the movement. They were also questioned about how the organization was formed (if this occurred within their period of involvement), how the organization recruited new members, what tactics were used, what alliances the organization forged with other groups, and what effects initial successes or failures had on the organization.

B

MEASURING SUFFRAGE ORGANIZATION

MEMBERSHIP IN THE UNITED STATES

AND SWITZERLAND

A Note on Finding the Membership Figures
for Suffrage Organizations

THE STUDY of social movement organizations is often limited by a lack of information regarding the number of participants and activists. This study is no exception. In both the United States and Switzerland membership figures are only available for the largest suffrage organization, and even then only for some years.

In the United States, data on the size of membership in woman suffrage organizations are consistently available on the state level only for the biggest suffrage organization, the National American Woman Suffrage Association (NAWSA) and then only for the years 1893–1920. Other suffrage organizations such as the Woman's party and the predecessors to the NAWSA—the National Woman Suffrage Association and the American Woman Suffrage Association—did not keep yearly membership figures. As a result, I can only examine the effects of membership in the later years of the movement. Moreover, the numbers underestimate the actual number of movement participants since the Woman's party members and those Women's Christian Temperance Union (WCTU) members who were active in the Franchise Department are excluded from these data. However, since the leaders of the Woman's party themselves emphasized commitment over membership (Irwin 1921: 323), the Woman's party was probably small compared to that of the NAWSA. In addition, while the WCTU was a mass organization, its primary purpose was not suffrage, and therefore many members were not engaged in the suffrage cause. As a result, the number of suffrage activists within the WCTU is also probably small, and some of these will also belong to woman suffrage organizations. Thus, NAWSA membership, while not perfect, is probably a good indicator of suffrage activism and membership in each state and over time.

State membership data are available because the National American Woman Suffrage Association required state sections to pay a per-member fee to the national association. Thus, the number of members in every state can be derived from the yearly treasurer's report, which was published from 1892 to 1920. The predecessors to the NAWSA demanded dues directly from individuals or required that state auxiliaries pay a set fee, making it impossible to determine their organizational membership in this manner.

However, the membership numbers in state NAWSA sections may not be completely accurate. As Kraditor (1981: 6–7) notes, because state affiliates were often extremely lax in sending in their money, the numbers may underestimate the actual membership in suffrage organizations. The result of this laxness is twofold. First, state organizations might disappear for one year and then reappear because they had not paid their dues by the time the national convention was held. For example, Missouri had 62 members in 1894 and 64 members in 1896, but in 1895 appeared to have no members. In this case, it appears more likely that the state organization simply failed to (or delayed) paying their dues and therefore its membership did not appear in the treasurer's report.

A second problem is that groups may have chosen to misreport their true membership since the state affiliates were required to pay a per-person fee to the national organization. For example, between 1897 and 1906 Connecticut reported their state membership as exactly 100 people every year. It seems highly dubious that the local membership could be that stable for a decade. A much more likely hypothesis is that the Connecticut suffrage club decided that dues amounting to 100 members was the appropriate amount of money to pay to the national association regardless of their true membership. The false reporting of membership figures was a topic at several national conventions (NAWSA 1896, 1897), as national officers exhorted their state organizations to cease false reporting.

Given that the NAWSA had and recognized this problem, the question then becomes: What is the decision rule by which state organizations chose how much they will contribute to the national association? Two considerations apparently went into the decision about whether to report membership correctly. On the one hand, state organizations probably desired to keep as much of their dues in the state organization as possible. This tendency would lead a local affiliate to underreport their membership. On the other hand, local suffrage organizations also received something from their payment of dues to the national association; representation in the annual convention was determined by the number of members an organization had. Local organizations received an additional delegate for every additional 50 members over a minimum number (which varied between 150 to 300 over the years). Since many decisions were made at these annual meetings, there was also an impetus to overreport the membership in an organization if the overreporting resulted in additional delegates to the convention. Larger organizations received more of a voice in determining the course of national decisions. For that reason, groups might be interested in rounding up as well as down if it resulted in an additional delegate. Thus, at the 1897 NAWSA convention, the treasurer reported: "It is undoubtedly true that other states do not pay in the whole of this auxiliary fee, and that still others pay a larger fee than they have membership" (NAWSA 1897: 25–26). Since local groups could find it in their interest to round up as well as down, I will assume that the error in reported membership is unbiased, and generally approximates the state group's true membership.

Membership data for Swiss suffrage organizations are also somewhat problematic. Again, membership information could only be found for the largest suffrage organization, the Schweizerischer Verband für Frauenstimmrecht (SVF). Membership figures by canton for STAKA, the Catholic suffrage organization, were not available. Unlike in the United States, however, the SVF was concentrated in some cantons and STAKA in others. For example, the SVF never developed local affiliates in either Schwyz or Obwalden, while STAKA organizations were active in these areas. Thus, there is a bias against registering membership in certain cantons. However, since in most of these cantons STAKA developed only in the late 1960s, its absence in membership figures does not affect membership figures for most of the time period (1926–1976).

Local sections of other women's organizations were also active in the suffrage issue in some cantons but not in others. For example, while the women's groups of the Free Democratic party and Social Democratic party participated in the suffrage debate in the canton Zug, the women's groups of these parties did not exist or were not active in most cantons. In a few cantons, women's centers or the Schweizerischer Katholischer Frauenbund were also major supporters of suffrage. This activity, though, was usually conducted by a small group of activists within these larger groups, and therefore the membership of these groups cannot be simply taken as indication of suffrage support. In addition, like STAKA, these organizations began their suffrage activity quite late, and so for the bulk of the period under study, the membership figures in the SVF are the best indicator of suffrage organization membership.

A second challenge is that although the national suffrage organization calculated delegates on the basis of the local affiliate's membership, the Swiss organization was more lax in keeping accurate records of dues paid than the American organization. As in the United States, the number of votes allowed a section at the annual convention also reflects the number of members that a section had. However, the Swiss records from annual conventions only provide accurate membership data at irregular intervals over the years (see years listed in Table 3.1). For example, Swiss records have the exact number of members in each section for seven years during the 1950s, but no membership figures were recorded during the 1940s.[1]

Two other approximate indicators of the size of local suffrage organizations exist, however, none was consistently collected over the years. One measure is the number of votes allowed a section at the annual convention since this was based on the number of members a local section had. The protocol of suffrage organizations only provides this information between 1926 and 1939. Between 1951 and 1976, the SVF generally alternated between reporting the allowed number of votes or the exact number of members for each section. However, during the 1940s, the only indicator of the size of a suffrage organization regularly reported is the number of delegates attending the annual convention from the section. This is less accurate than the other measures, as the number of delegates attending is a function of the number of votes and the ability of the delegates to attend the convention.

Calculating a Swiss Mobilization Index

In order to create an indicator of suffrage organization membership for the cantons in as many years as possible, I combine these three types of data—exact membership, the number of delegates the cantonal section(s) is allowed, and the number of delegates attending the annual convention—into a single Swiss membership index. This index, which represents the strength of the suffrage organization in each canton, was calculated in three steps.

1. All three measures of suffrage organization strength were transformed into per 1,000 population measures by dividing by the total population of the canton in that year and multiplying by 1,000. The Swiss census provided cantonal population figures in 1920, 1930, 1941, 1950, 1960, 1970, and 1980. Population in other years was calculated by a linear interpolation between two census years.

2. All three measures were then transformed into Z-scores (i.e., given a mean of 0 and a standard deviation of 1) by subtracting the mean over all cantons and years and then dividing by the standard deviation.

3. For each year and canton, there were nonmissing values on either one or two or all three of these three measures. If only one measure had nonmissing data, its Z-score became the value of the mobilization index. If two or three measures had nonmissing data, the Z-scores of these measures were averaged. Table B.1 indicates the years in which each measure is available:

TABLE B.1
The Availability of Swiss Suffrage Organization
Membership Indicators by Year

Year	Exact Membership	Delegates Allowed	Delegates Present
1920	—	—	—
1921	—	—	—
1922	—	—	—
1923	—	—	—
1924	—	—	—
1925	—	—	—
1926	—	X	X
1927	—	X	X
1928	—	X	X
1929	—	X	X
1930	—	X	X
1931	—	X	X
1932	—	X	X
1933	—	X	X
1934	X	X	X
1935	—	—	X
1936	—	—	X
1937	X	X	X
1938	—	—	X
1939	—	—	X
1940	—	X	X
1941	—	X	X
1942	—	—	X
1943	—	—	X
1944	—	—	X
1945	—	—	X
1946	—	—	X
1947	—	—	X
1948	—	—	X
1949	—	—	X
1950	—	—	X
1951	X	—	—
1952	X	—	—
1953	—	—	X
1954	X	—	—
1955	X	—	—

TABLE B.1 (*cont.*)

Year	Exact Membership	Delegates Allowed	Delegates Present
1956	—	—	—
1957	—	X	—
1958	X	X	X
1959	X	—	—
1960	—	X	X
1961	—	X	X
1962	—	X	X
1963	—	X	X
1964	X	X	X
1965	X	X	—
1966	X	X	—
1967	—	X	X
1968	—	X	X
1969	X	X	X
1970	—	X	—
1971	—	X	—
1972	—	X	—
1973	—	—	—
1974	—	X	—
1975	X	X	—
1976	X	X	—
1977	—	—	—
1978	—	—	—
1979	—	—	—
1980	—	—	—

Interitem Correlations of Individual Indicators and Index Reliability

Finally, the interitem correlation matrix and Cronbach's alpha indicate high internal reliability. None of the correlations between the three individual indicators is lower than r=.86. Cronbach's alpha was equal to .96. Table B.2 presents two interitem correlation matrices; one using pairwise deletion of cases and the other (using listwise deletion) on a small subset of cases where all three indicators were available. While the correlations do drop somewhat all remain high (r ≥ .86) and Cronbach's alpha is unchanged.

TABLE B.2

Correlation Matrices of Individual Indicators and Swiss
Mobilization Index by Pairwise and Listwise Deletion

Pairwise Deletion (Number of Cases):

	MEMBERPC[a]	ALLOWPC[b]	PRESENTPC[c]
ALLOWPC[b]	0.912		
	(221)		
PRESENTPC[c]	0.860	0.910	
	(122)	(518)	
MEMINDEX[d]	0.979	0.980	0.983
	(346)	(749)	(867)

Average interitem correlation: r = .894   Cronbach's alpha = .96
(not including MEMINDEX[d])

Listwise Deletion (N=122):

	MEMBERPC[a]	ALLOWPC[b]	PRESENTPC[c]
ALLOWPC[b]	0.895		
PRESENTPC[c]	0.860	0.900	
MEMINDEX[d]	0.958	0.970	0.955

Average interitem correlation: r = .885   Cronbach's alpha = .96
(not including MEMINDEX[d])

[a] The mnemonic "MEMBERPC" stands for the exact membership in cantonal suffrage organizations per 1,000 population in the canton.

[b] The mnemonic "ALLOWPC" stands for the number of delegates cantonal suffrage organizations are permitted at the annual meeting per 1,000 cantonal population.

[c] The mnemonic "PRESENTPC" stands for the number of delegates from cantonal suffrage organizations present at the annual meeting per 1,000 population in the canton.

[d] The mnemonic "MEMINDEX" stands for the mobilization index created from the other three measures.

C

DATA SOURCES FOR LEGISLATIVE HISTORIES

AND VARIABLE CODING IN POOLED-TIME

SERIES ANALYSIS

THROUGHOUT this book, I discuss and analyze the legislative histories of woman suffrage in 48 American states and 25 Swiss cantons. This appendix describes the historical sources used to create these legislative histories, and the coding of specific variables in the statistical analyses of Chapter 4. Information about measures of woman suffrage organizations' membership is provided separately in Appendix B.

Data Sources for Histories of Woman
Suffrage Legislation

In the United States, it is impossible to sift through the mass of primary materials on woman suffrage located in dozens of libraries across the country. Therefore, I limited my data collection to a few major archives and the wealth of secondary sources on state woman suffrage movements. Of the secondary works on woman suffrage, I utilized the classic historical texts, particularly the six-volume *History of Woman Suffrage* (Stanton et al. 1881a, 1881b, 1886; Anthony and Harper 1902; Harper 1922a, 1922b) and a number of articles, books, and theses on state suffrage campaigns (Allen 1958; Caldwell 1943; Catt 1940; Catt and Shuler 1926; Edwards 1990; Fox 1918; Gallaher 1918; Jensen 1973; Kenneally 1968; Krone 1946; Larson 1970, 1972; Nichols 1983; Noun 1969; Pillsbury 1926; Reed 1958; Scott 1920; Stapler 1917; Taylor 1944, 1956, 1957a, 1957b, 1958, 1959, 1961, 1968, 1987; Trout 1920; Wilhite 1968; Youmans 1921). In looking at primary materials, I concentrated on documents located in the Library of Congress from national suffrage organizations, such as the National American Woman Suffrage Association (NAWSA) and its predecessors, the National Woman Suffrage Association (NWSA) and the American Woman Suffrage Association (AWSA). These documents provided data on legislative activities, the tactics of state branches and affiliates, and the interaction between the national association and local sections.

There is considerably less secondary material available in Switzerland. Only two books—Woodtli (1983) and Ruckstuhl (1986)—deal at length with woman suffrage. However, in recent years, a few privately published pamphlets (L'Association Vaudoise pour les Droits de la Femme 1979; Joho n.d.; Villard-Traber 1984) and student theses (Blattner 1979; Mock n.d.; Vonwyl 1988; Wettstein 1990, 1991) have chronicled the suffrage movements in a few cantons.

Because of the lack of secondary sources, most of the information about cantonal suffrage movements came from primary sources. Many of these materials are still in the possession of individuals and have yet to be donated to libraries. I gained access to many of these private documents through my interviews with Swiss suffrage activists. During the interview, activists were asked if they had kept any records or materials related to woman suffrage. Those that still had such files (over 15 in all) were willing to let me examine them.

In addition, two major library collections on Swiss woman suffrage exist: the Schweizerisches Sozialarchiv in Zürich and the Gosteli Stiftung in Worblaufen. Both house some of the files from the Schweizerischer Verband für Frauenstimmrecht (SVF), the records of some of the local SVF sections, and archives of newspaper articles on cantonal suffrage.

Coding Suffrage Success

For the statistical analyses in Chapter 4, three dependent variables are extracted from the detailed legislative histories provided by the above mentioned sources. First, in each canton-year and state-year, I measured whether legislation for full women's voting rights (as defined in Chapter 4) was introduced into the legislature. This was coded 1 if legislation was introduced, 0 otherwise. The introduction of legislation was fairly easy to track in Switzerland since so few bills were considered. However, it was more difficult in the United States because hundreds of bills were introduced; so many, that often a particular bill received little or no attention.

While these data are by no means perfect, I believe whatever bias exists is likely to make estimation more conservative. That is, in states with little suffrage legislation, the historical sources were more specific and mentioned all suffrage bills in detail. On the other hand, where many pieces of suffrage legislation were introduced, there is a higher probability that a particular piece of legislation was not mentioned. This tendency to underreport in states with many bills should make it more difficult to show a connection between organization or tactics and the introduction of legislation.

These data are also used to create other indicators of the introduction of suffrage legislation in Chapters 6 and 7. There, I create aggregate measures of suffrage legislation introductions in a state or canton during a specific period. In Chapter 6 the measure is the sum of the number of introductions in the same canton or state over the specified time period, and in Chapter 7, I use the average number of introductions in a canton or state.

In order to measure the degree of legislative support for women's enfranchisement, I recorded all final legislative votes (usually the third reading) on woman suffrage bills or amendments. Chapter 4 describes in detail how these votes were translated into percentages. I also utilize this measure of legislative support in Chapter 6.

Public support for women's voting rights is determined by the percentage of voters that voted for the enfranchisement of women in referenda. In Chapter 7, where I need to measure support in referenda between 1910 and 1919 in the U.S. and 1951 and 1971 in Switzerland, I aggregate multiple referenda in a single canton by taking the average vote in all referenda during this period.

Regional Dummy Variables

Included in the analyses of Chapter 4 are dummy variables representing certain regions in the United States and Switzerland. In the United States, I utilize the same regional categories used in the U.S. census (see, for example, Table 2 in United States, Bureau of the Census 1920: 108). In Switzerland, I create regional categories based on language spoken, region, and degree of urbanization. A list of the regional variables and the specific states or cantons associated with them follows.

Switzerland:

Omitted Category (Italian-speaking Canton)	Ticino
Appenzell AR and IR	Appenzell Innerrhoden, Appenzell Ausserrhoden
Eastern Mountain Cantons	Glarus, Graubünden, Niwalden, Obwalden, Schwyz, Uri
French-speaking Cantons	Genève, Neuchâtel, Vaud
German Urban Cantons	Bern, Basel-stadt, Luzern, St. Gallen, Zürich
German/French Cantons	Fribourg/Freiburg, Wallis/Valais
Other German Cantons	Aargau, Basel-land, Schaffhausen, Solothurn, Thurgau, Zug

United States:

Omitted Category (East South Central States)	Kentucky, Tennessee, Alabama, Mississippi

Mountain Region	Montana, Idaho, Wyoming, Colorado, New Mexico, Arizona, Utah, Nevada
West South Central	Arkansas, Louisiana, Oklahoma, Texas
Pacific Region	Washington, Oregon, California
New England	Maine, New Hampshire, Vermont, Massachusetts, Rhode Island, Connecticut
South Atlantic	Delaware, Maryland, Virginia, West Virginia, North Carolina, South Carolina, Georgia, Florida
East North Central	Ohio, Indiana, Illinois, Michigan, Wisconsin
West North Central	Minnesota, Iowa, Missouri, North Dakota, South Dakota, Nebraska, Kansas
Mid-Atlantic	New York, New Jersey, Pennsylvania

D

CODING CONFRONTATIONAL AND LOBBYING

TACTICS IN THE UNITED STATES

AND SWITZERLAND

C HAPTERS 6 and 7 analyze the role of tactics in suffrage movement success. To do so, I constructed measures of the use of confrontational and lobbying tactics by woman suffrage movements. These measures were coded from the same sources that provided the legislative histories (see Appendix C). This appendix discusses some of the problems associated with creating measures of tactics and describes how the indicators of the suffrage organizations' confrontational and lobbying tactics were fashioned.

Confrontational Tactics

Confrontational tactics were coded for specific time periods: 1910–1919 in the United States and 1951–1970 in Switzerland. The decision to limit the indicators to these time periods was made for two reasons. First, Swiss and American suffrage organizations only began to utilize confrontational tactics toward the very end of the movement; in Switzerland, these tactics did not appear until the 1950s. A few confrontational tactics were used in the late 1870s in the United States, but the bulk of all protests, demonstrations, and picketing occurred in the last decade of the suffrage struggle. Thus, very few confrontational events are lost by focusing only on the last decade in the United States.

Originally, I planned on coding confrontational activities for a ten-year period in both countries. In coding the Swiss tactics, however, it became clear that very few confrontational events took place at all. In any particular year, there might be at most one or two such events in the entire country. In order to be able to contrast confrontational cantons with less confrontational cantons, I doubled the time period under study and examined tactics in two decades, thereby increasing the total number of events.

Second, the quality of reports about organizational activities varied considerably. In the United States, reports on state organizational activities were not as extensive prior to 1900. In Switzerland, many of the reports on organizational tactics came from archived documents and personal descriptions of activities in interviews. Both of these materials focused on the period after 1950; a little information was available for the 1920s, but there was almost no data on the World War II period (1930–1949). Thus, attempts at coding confrontational tactics during this period would have been more prone to omission and errors.

Two different measures of confrontational tactics are included in Chapter 7; in both cases, I calculated the measures by simply counting the number of a certain type of event that had occurred in each state and canton during the specified time period. First, I counted the number of woman suffrage initiatives that were conducted by woman suffrage organizations during the time periods. Because so few American states permitted initiatives and so few Swiss cantons took advantage of initiative rights, I am certain that these data are quite accurate.

The second measure indicates the number of other confrontational events sponsored by the suffrage organizations, including suffrage litigation and extra-governmental confrontations. Litigation that attempted to alter laws by challenging them directly (for example, suing for voting rights) were counted as confrontational events. While this description covers all the legal challenges by suffrage organizations, the number of suits was so small that they could not be coded as a separate category. Only 2 legal challenges occurred in the United States during the ten-year time period and only 4 suits were brought in Switzerland between 1951 and 1970. All of the Swiss cases were heard before the court, but in one of the U.S. legal challenges, an attempt to register to vote in Florida in 1912, the purpose was to gain publicity for the suffrage cause and the suit was dropped after the city attorney issued a legal opinion (Taylor 1957a).

Extra-governmental tactics involve confrontational events not specifically designed to influence institutions of government (in contrast to petitions to the Federal Council or legislative lobbying). Two coding rules were used to determine if an activity qualified as an extra-governmental confrontation. First, I chose to classify specific types of events according to how confrontational they were. Events that forced bystanders and passersby to listen to a suffrage message were considered confrontational. Thus, information stands and people handing out leaflets, although they reached many people, can be successfully ignored by passersby. Speeches that are held in public spaces, parades, or groups picketing streets or walkways, however, are impossible to overlook. Thus, suffrage parades, automobile campaigns, open-air meetings and speeches, symbolic protests, and picketing all constitute confrontational events.

The Basel teacher strike was also included as a confrontational event. While this event did not occur in a public space, which would have subjected bystanders to the suffrage message, the strike was the subject of so much publicity that most Basel residents could not avoid the issue. More important, the strike fits the other two dimensions of confrontation discussed in Chapter 7. It expressed explicit demands for suffrage and an unwillingness to compromise even in the face of electoral defeat. Indeed, the strikers were criticized as having undemocratic attitudes as evinced in their decision to strike against a referenda result.

Second, a confrontational activity must be organized by the suffrage organization itself; that is, where the suffrage organization took advantage of existing events by adding their demands to the fray, the event was not coded as confrontational. For example, California suffrage activists joined in the 1910 Labor Day parade, where they had a float promoting the vote for women. In addition, suffrage activists in many states held events at state fairs to urge women's enfranchisement. However, in both cases, suffrage activists were merely including their statement with those of other organizations. Since in such cases, the public received a number of messages from different groups, it was not compelled to listen to the pro-suffrage activists. Thus, only those confrontational events where the suffrage organization was a major sponsor were included.

Finally, in the United States, it was difficult to count the exact number of events because sources were often vague about how many suffrage parades or open-air meetings had happened in a particular state. Where many events occurred, reports on suffrage activities often mentioned them in plural without specifying the actual number. For example, historical accounts of the suffrage movement in Louisiana indicate that some open-air rallies occurred in 1913, but the exact number of rallies is not given. When an unspecified number of confrontational events was indicated in the historical record, these were coded as only two events. As a result the actual number of confrontations is probably underestimated in the United States. However, since this tendency not to specify the number of events was evident in states that held a lot of activities, this bias is likely to depress rather than inflate any connections between the confrontational variables and other measures of success. I encountered no such problem with reports of events in Switzerland. There, so few events transpired that each elicited many comments among suffrage activists and the press.

Lobbying Tactics

Lobbying tactics, discussed in Chapter 6, are coded slightly differently from confrontational tactics because they were hard to divide into discrete events as I do with confrontational tactics. For one thing, lobbying techniques like personal visits to legislatures do not occur in a distinct time period but over longer periods of time. Moreover, activities overlap and are therefore not likely to be described separately. For example, many accounts of suffrage campaigns mention informal pressure on legislators; this may involve personal visits by suffrage activists, letter-writing campaigns, as well as informal arm-twisting by a legislator's friends and acquaintances. Different historical accounts may describe this informal pressure as one, two, or three separate events depending on the language used. This ambiguous definition of a "lobbying event" makes it difficult to code.

Instead, I decided to determine whether the suffrage organization lobbied during each legislative session. I then counted the number of sessions during which lobbying transpired. In the United States, I created a trichotomous measure where lobbying was recorded in zero, one, or two or more legislative sessions. Suffrage activists were coded as having lobbied during a legislative session if the historical accounts mentioned one of the following: (a) setting up suffrage headquarters in the state capitol, (b) polling legislators, (c) attempting to influence legislators' opinions or votes, (d) endeavoring to marshall votes within the legislature, or (e) striving to elect pro-suffrage legislators or defeat anti-suffrage legislators. Participation in committee hearings and petitions delivered to entire legislative bodies were not considered a lobbying effort.

In Switzerland, two measures of lobbying tactics were utilized. First, a dichotomous measure was created indicating whether any of the techniques described in the previous paragraph were *ever* utilized by cantonal suffrage activists. One indication of the lack of lobbying in Switzerland is that even using this criteria, only five cantonal legislatures were coded as having lobbied between 1920 and 1971.

A second measure of lobbying was created in Switzerland to examine whether petitions and letters to cantonal legislatures influenced the success of suffrage. In this case, I counted the number of legislative sessions (because cantonal parliaments meet annually, a legislative session is the equivalent of a year) in which letters and petitions asking for women's voting rights were sent to the cantonal parliament. As in the U.S. case, I transformed this information into a trichotomous variable: suffrage organizations were coded as sending petitions or letters on the suffrage issue during zero, one, or two or more years.

Finally, the reader should note that in counting the number of lobbying events, I utilized larger time periods than in Chapter 7. As in the case of confrontational tactics, I focused on those periods when lobbying tactics were used. In the United States, this means that I coded lobbying tactics between 1900 and 1919. In Switzerland, lobbying of any kind was very rare and it was not concentrated in any particular period. In order to pick up any episodes of lobbying at all, it was necessary to examine the entire period prior to the adoption of the national suffrage amendment in 1971.

NOTES

CHAPTER ONE

1. From a letter to A. Leusch, president of the Schweizerischer Verband für Frauenstimmrecht found among uncataloged materials from the Schweizerischer Verband für Frauenstimmrecht donated to the Sozialarchiv Zürich.

2. Those states were Michigan in 1874, Nebraska in 1871 and 1882, Oregon in 1884, Rhode Island in 1887, South Dakota in 1890; and Washington in 1889 and 1884.

3. Anna Howard Shaw was president of the NAWSA from 1904 to 1915. Although Carrie Chapman Catt was Susan B. Anthony's original choice as a successor, she served as NAWSA president for only four years before her and her husband's ill health forced her to resign (Van Voris 1987).

4. Hereafter, I refer simply to the Woman's party when talking about Alice Paul's organizations after 1910. This is meant to include the Congressional Union as well.

5. The Swiss Parliament is divided into two houses that are elected in the same way as the U.S. Congress: In the Nationalrat representation is proportional to population, and in the Ständerat each canton elects two representatives.

6. In four cases, the party of the legislator making the motion could not be identified.

7. Full suffrage legislation passed in Zürich, Neuchâtel, and Basel-stadt, where the total vote for the SP and PdA equaled or exceeded 35 percent. Where these parties received less than 35 percent in all but one case (St. Gallen) the legislation enfranchising women, when it came to a vote, was defeated.

8. In Switzerland, all constitutional amendments must have the approval of a majority of the voters and a majority of the cantons.

9. For information about how the interviews with Swiss suffrage activists were conducted, see Appendix A.

10. At the last minute, the FBB decided not to be an official organizer of the March on Bern. However, some FBB women did participate.

11. Optional city suffrage consisted of legislation permitting communities to pass local women's suffrage if they so desired.

CHAPTER TWO

1. Calculated by author based on data from Eidgenössisches Statistisches Amt (1985: 15–21).

2. In fact, an examination of data in 1910 shows no statistically significant difference between states with suffrage and those without. States with suffrage had 40 percent of their population in towns over 2,500; states with no suffrage had 37 percent.

3. This difference in means is statistically significant in a t-test.

4. In 1841, three women received A.B. degrees from Oberlin College (Deckard 1983; Newcomer 1959). Swiss authors (Mesmer 1988; Woodtli 1983), who clearly do not rate American colleges in the same category as Swiss universities, note that in 1867 the Universität Zürich became the first university to confer a diploma on a woman.

5. Some Swiss cantons began to require basic education for both sexes as early as the 1830s.

6. The lack of women teachers in Switzerland resulted from the opposition of existing male teachers who feared a loss of status and pay as a result of the entry of women into their profession and from attempts in the overwhelmingly Catholic cantons to fight the expansion of lay educators (Mesmer 1988).

7. It is difficult to find dependable statistics on women's access to education during this period. Nonetheless, using several secondary sources, I examined the correlation between the year women were allowed to get university degrees and the year women were enfranchised in eight countries—France, Britain, Switzerland, Germany, Sweden, Italy, Norway, and the U.S. The correlation was negative ($r=-.48$, $N=8$), suggesting that where women could enter universities, they were likely to get the vote *later* and not earlier.

8. On the other hand, the availability of basic education for women was not related to women's voting rights in the United States.

9. Both of these differences are statistically significant in t-tests for the difference in means. Data on women's education taken from Statistisches Jahrbuch der Schweiz (Eidgenössisches Statistisches Amt 1962: 460–61, and 1970: 458–59).

10. See, for example, the 1988 special issue of *Government and Politics* on "Can the Confederation Helvetica Be Imitated?"

11. Indeed, Germany had a stronger tradition for women's rights.

12. Davies (1974), Gurr (1968, 1970), Smelser (1963), and other "classical" theorists (McAdam 1982), were primarily concerned with explaining why individuals *participate* in social movements.

13. Resource mobilization theorists have never discussed the connection between individual and group rationality. This is problematic since Arrow (1951), among others, has shown that a group of rational individuals may make irrational decisions under certain conditions. As Jenkins (1983) notes, social movement theorists have generally ignored the problem of how and whether social movements as a whole are rational. While I do not address this problem directly, I delineate, in later chapters, some of the obstacles that prevent social movements from making optimal decisions.

14. It is common to see the words "and so on" or "etc." in definitions of resources, a linguistic indication that the term is without precise boundaries.

15. Kitschelt (1986) also argues that the benefits that derive from that outcome may differ according to the effectiveness of governments to implement a policy once it is introduced. In this case, movements benefit more from a centralized state apparatus if they are successful.

16. For example, Kriesi (1995) argues that radical right movements are less influenced by competition between leftist parties within a country than new left movements.

17. While I have not explicitly discussed the different dimensions of political

opportunity structure or the differences between authors in their views of these dimensions, the different variations are in some way included in Kriesi's (1995) dimensions of political opportunity structure. Readers should note that I utilize these three dimensions to organize the discussion below of the political opportunity structure of the American and Swiss suffrage movements.

18. McAdam (1982: 48–51) comes the closest to exploring the possibility that groups may not always respond to existing political opportunities in discussing the role of "cognitive liberation." He argues that movement participants must believe (1) that conditions are unjust and (2) that the group has the ability to alter these conditions before they can take advantage of existing political opportunities. He also acknowledges that information about political opportunities filters through "subtle cues communicated by other groups" (McAdam 1982: 49). Yet, outside of this caveat and his discussion of cognitive liberation, he also assumes that movements' perceptions will mirror the objective political opportunities.

19. While all of these authors are implicitly dealing with collective values and beliefs, their differing terminology reflects subtle differences in focus. The word "frame" implies cognitive structures that define individuals' perspectives and are actively constructed by movements themselves. "Discourse," on the other hand, captures the dynamic aspects of communication, but loses the structural and restraining aspect of frames. "Culture" connotes the shared systemic symbols, yet does not specify the mechanics of change or transmission (as do discourse and frames). Despite the slightly different focuses, the underlying argument of these theories is that collective beliefs and values affect the mobilization of a movement, its strategic choices, and even the outcomes of movement activities. In addition, the authors all see collective values and beliefs as structured or affected by the political context. In the discussion that follows, I employ the more general term "collective beliefs and values," although my argument speaks, I believe, to the literatures on frames, discourses, and culture.

20. One might think that faced with biased information sources individuals or movements would seek out the most complete and unbiased information or draw information from a wide variety of sources. However, rational choice theorists have shown that choosing to take information from biased sources is a fully rational act since it reduces information costs and may enhance the ability of the individual to make rational decisions in an uncertain world (Calvert 1985; Downs 1957; Grofman and Norrander 1990; Grofman and Withers 1993; Popkin 1993).

21. I have chosen to use a different division from that of Snow and Benford (1992), who distinguish between master frames and collective action frames. I provide the additional layer of status quo beliefs and values because I believe the collective beliefs and values extolled by the state fundamentally differ from other types. The term coalition beliefs and values differs from the master frame terminology by emphasizing the necessity of interaction between groups. Finally, I choose the term group beliefs and values rather than collective action frame because the latter term implicitly connects the beliefs and values to the action rather than the group. The divisions used here are similar, but not equivalent, to those used by Klandermans (1992) and Tarrow (1992).

22. The prefixes micro- and macro- have long been attached to other concepts

to indicate specificity to the individual and to society, respectively. Recently the meso-level has been introduced in order to discuss contexts involving the interaction of groups (Gerhards and Rucht 1992).

23. A common philosophy need not be a result of interaction. Indeed, even something as specific as the value of certain social movement tactics may be included in status quo beliefs and values. For example, Tarrow (1994) notes the adoption of civil disobedience by anti-abortion groups in recent years. This tactic did not result from interactions between pro-life groups and the civil rights and new left groups which traditionally utilized this tactic. Rather the tactic itself became a part of conventional politics largely through its dissemination by the mass media.

24. Their common values were certainly a result of experiencing the same macro-level social changes (Kriesi 1988). However, some studies of new social movement organizations (Gerhards and Rucht 1992; Melucci 1989) have noted an extensive interaction (both personal, and through media such as books and newsletters) among these movements, which helped to reinforce and spread these shared values and beliefs.

25. This distinction corresponds to McAdam and Rucht's (1993) relational and nonrelational channels. A third possible means of collecting information is by direct observation. In politics, however, few pieces of information can be directly observed. Even in that rare instance when an event or fact can be observed, the information is often later interpreted, selected, or redefined through social interaction (Klandermans 1992).

26. Snow et al. (1986) also consider how movement beliefs and values can be linked to those of individuals and other groups in their discussion of "frame alignment." Their concepts of "frame bridging," "frame alignment," and "frame extension" correspond to my discussion of supplementing collective values and beliefs. Their concept of "frame transformation" parallels my discussion of the creation of contradictory values.

Besides supplementing or contradicting, a new set of values and beliefs may also reinforce already established philosophies. Because reinforcement requires no change in values and beliefs, it is less useful in understanding the rise and success of social movements.

27. In the long term, status quo beliefs and values may even be altered by serious challenges from other sets of values. If challenging beliefs and values are disseminated through strong social ties, maintained over long periods of time, and incorporated in a wide variety of groups, they may in time replace existing beliefs and values and become part of the status quo. This, in part, explains the adoption of civil disobedience values by anti-abortion groups. Since the 1960s, civil disobedience has spread to multiple groups, becoming a central value in many cases. Mass media have also transmitted the normative (and tactical) worth of civil disobedience to the point where it is considered an acceptable and even respected form of collective action.

28. Such strong bonds are a result of shared characteristics and intense social networks (see Tilly's discussion of "catnet" [1978: 62–64]).

29. Because the values and beliefs of the status quo reflect the political, economic, and social system, they are also malleable—albeit mainly at glacial speeds.

The development of new social classes and thereby new issues (Inglehardt 1977), crises of states (Skocpol 1979), or the introduction of new political actors within the polity may all alter status quo values and beliefs if these changes are substantial enough or sustained over long periods of time. This means that current interactions among political actors may also affect status quo values and beliefs in the long term. However, status quo values and beliefs are very resistant to change. Usually only those changes that are constantly reinforced for years result in new status quo values and beliefs. In rare cases, the force of profound and crucial events can completely revolutionize the status quo.

30. The canton Jura did not become a separate canton until 1979. Prior to that time, this geographical area was a part of the canton Bern and women in Jura were enfranchised along with other Bernese women. Hence, Jura is not included as a separate canton in the analysis that follows.

CHAPTER THREE

1. For more information about these data see Appendix B.

2. On the local level, a few suffrage societies did develop during these years, but no national organization grew to connect them. Moreover, in many areas, formal organizations were forgone in favor of a committee appointed each year to arrange the next convention.

3. There were occasional references to the organization of action committees for referenda. Action committees were the groups that ran referendum campaigns for suffrage. They were temporary organizations that disbanded as soon as the campaign ended and included only important politicians representing the different interest groups and political parties. As such, these organizations are more relevant to alliance building (Chapter 7) than to organizational development.

4. Following Steiner (1974) and Steiner and Dorff (1980), I use the term Free Democratic Party throughout the book to refer to the Freisinnig-Democratische Partei.

5. Some readers may note that I discuss only the NAWSA and its predecessors. The other major suffrage organization, the Woman's party (previously the Congressional Union) did not emphasize the creation of suffrage organizations. Irwin (1921) notes that the Woman's party usually sent only one inexperienced woman into each state. Much of the organizing efforts described by Irwin focused on lobbying a particular person or party and not on creating sustained organizations or recruiting new converts. Nor are any membership data available for state affiliates of the Woman's party.

6. Some readers might note that both are German-speaking cantons, and question whether examining French- or Italian-speaking cantons might elicit different results. However, similarity in organizational strategies and forms of organization did not correspond to language. Both German and non–German-speaking cantons had cantonal organizations, single-leader dominated organizations, and so forth. These cantons were chosen as examples because they are good illustrations of the different types of organization and because extensive archival documentation was available.

7. *Die Staatsbürgerin* began publication in 1945. Earlier, the Zürich suffrage

association had published another journal, *Die Frauenbestrebungen*, between 1903 and 1921.

8. Horgen's history is described in *Die Staatsbürgerin* (November 1968). Information about the Bulle and Wallis/Valais sections came from interviews (interviews with activists on June 9, 1988, and June 22, 1988).

9. Elazar (1987) and Duchacek (1987) have labeled these sorts of beliefs cultural federalism.

CHAPTER FOUR

1. The budget information for the National American Woman Suffrage Association comes from the report of the treasurer in the proceedings of the yearly national conventions. In Switzerland, the budgets of the Schweizerischer Verband für Frauenstimmrecht were only available between 1946 and 1950, in the fiscal year 1956/1957, and in the years 1962–1966 from the Schweizerisches Sozialarchiv, Zürich. A search of other archives for more complete information on the budget of the SVF proved unsuccessful.

2. Inflation increased by over 82 percent between 1937 and 1958 alone. These cost of living statistics, and others cited in this section, were calculated from the Cost of Living index provided in *International Financial Statistics* (International Monetary Fund 1955, 1960, 1965, 1970).

3. After 1949, SVF budgets do not even include a separate line for individual donations, except for membership dues (*Mitgliederbeiträge*). While it is possible that additional individual contributions were included under this heading, they could not have amounted to much. The income under this item remains relatively stable and appears commensurate with absolute membership.

4. Emilie Gourd also donated a considerable amount of money to the SVF; in fact, a fund for special actions bore her name. However, I was unable to uncover the exact amount of the donation or the year in which the donation was made.

5. These came from opposition parties and the largest Swiss trade union, the Schweizerischer Gewerkschaftsbund.

6. One exception was the 1908 Oregon referendum. In that year, the NAWSA budget shows no contributions to state campaigns. However, animosity between Oregon suffrage activists, particularly Abigail Scott Duniway, and the national leadership explains this aberration. Duniway felt donations from the national organization, which usually came in the form of field-workers, would attract eastern suffragists with prohibitionist connections, thereby hurting the referenda campaign. As a result, she asked the NAWSA national leadership for monetary contributions that would be completely controlled by the Oregon association. The national association refused to comply (Moynihan 1983).

7. Budgets prior to 1948/1949 do not break down the expenses of the organization, so it is impossible to say whether volunteers were reimbursed during those years.

8. It is also possible that a particular region at a particular time has a significant effect on the success variables. Several interactions of this type were included in analyses not reported here. These interaction variables were not significant

except in the analysis of the adoption of woman suffrage. However, these interaction models are not reported since the addition of the interactions does not alter the significance of the main variable of interest—membership.

9. Ruckstuhl (1986: 206) attributes this strategy to Professor Carl Hilty.

10. Suffrage activists also apparently believed primary suffrage in these states resulted in significant voting rights for women: their maps of suffrage success (for example, in Harper 1922b: 627) portrayed the two southern states with primary suffrage—Texas and Arkansas—as having fully enfranchised women.

11. Indeed, several researchers (Schumaker 1975; Gamson 1975; Klein 1984) employ similar concepts to gauge the success of social movements.

12. Although Switzerland currently has 26 cantons, throughout this book the canton Jura is not included in analyses as a separate canton. Jura was a part of Bern canton until it received its independence in 1974; full woman suffrage was achieved while Jura was still a part of the canton of Bern.

13. The sources of these data are described in Appendix C. Analysis of a dichotomous dependent variable using Ordinary Least Squares introduces some problems of efficiency and breaks some of the assumptions of Ordinary Least Squares estimation (Hanushek and Jackson 1977). In the interest of parsimony, I utilize the same technique in all sections of this chapter. However, estimating the same model with logistic regression produced similar significance levels and estimates.

14. As a result, one U.S. state—Wyoming—is completely excluded from this analysis because it included full women's voting rights in its first state constitution in 1890, three years before data on suffrage organization membership are available.

15. Because cantons may only introduce their first suffrage motion once, it does not make sense to include cantons in the data set once that event occurs. Hence, after the canton introduces its first motion, it is excluded from the analysis.

16. In the end, the choice of measure makes no difference since the means and standard deviations are virtually the same (they differ by only .2 percent) and the two measures are very highly correlated (r=.99).

17. The mean and standard deviation of the dependent variable do not change greatly if estimated votes are removed. When the analyses were conducted on the smaller number of nonestimated datapoints, the direction of the coefficients remains the same, although some year and region variables lose significance.

18. If more than one legislative body considered legislation in the same state-year or canton-year, this was only counted as a single vote.

19. Some readers may be surprised to note that the average support in both countries exceeded 50 percent. While in Switzerland this means that most suffrage legislation was passed, the same is not true in the United States. Bills often died in committee or were tabled before coming to a vote (only 296 out of 418 bills actually survived until a final ballot). Moreover, bills that passed one house often failed in the other; generally, it was the smaller, legislative body (the state senates) that rejected suffrage legislation.

20. This figure includes votes on full woman suffrage in the *Landesgemeinden* of Appenzell Innerrhoden, Appenzell Ausserrhoden, Glarus, and Nidwalden.

However, it does not include the two national referenda in 1959 and 1971. In addition to the full suffrage referenda counted above, there were also 26 referenda on partial woman suffrage legislation in Switzerland. Four other suffrage referenda concerned what could be called procedural questions. Two asked citizens to support the principle of introducing woman suffrage in stages (without actually including any suffrage legislation). The other two simply stated that women could be enfranchised via simple legislative acts rather than only by amendments to the cantonal constitutions.

21. When these states were coded "one" in 1920, under the supposition that the Nineteenth Amendment enfranchised women in all states, the regression analyses produced nearly identical results.

CHAPTER FIVE

1. One short-lived independent women's temperance group was the Women's State Temperance Society, created by Anthony in 1852. During its first year, it seems to have led a very independent existence. Thereafter, it allowed men to join and quickly became a mixed organization (see Harper 1898, 1: 62–96).

2. Since WCTU policy was implemented by state and local sections, opposition had a concrete effect on WCTU in those areas. Only two southern temperance organizations—the Arkansas and West Virginia WCTU—endorsed women's voting rights (Anthony and Harper 1902; Catt and Shuler 1926).

3. Wyoming, which had already adopted suffrage before the 1892 election, is excluded from this analysis. Other missing states are territories that had not become states by 1892. In 1896, Wyoming and Colorado had already enfranchised women; Arizona, New Mexico, and Oklahoma are also excluded from this analysis because they were still territories.

4. Many historians have argued that it is impossible to speak of a progressive movement since progressivism encompassed many disparate ideologies (see, for example, Filene 1970; Rodgers 1982). Acknowledging the different and sometimes conflicting ideas that made up the movement known by this label, I continue to use "progressive" to describe the various groups and ideologies that have traditionally fallen under this classification. In part, I do so because this is the way which the various groups viewed themselves. Moreover, while the progressives may have constituted more than a single movement, they certainly coordinated efforts and worked together. In that sense, they were also more than a set of separate movements. If anything, progressive movements mirrored the new social movements of the 1960s and 1970s; even while pursuing separate goals they shared several general beliefs and formed loose coalitions around specific issues. Thus, it seems appropriate to speak of progressive movements as one speaks of new social movements today.

5. The six states excluded from the analysis—California, Colorado, Idaho, Utah, Washington and Wyoming—all enfranchised women prior to 1912.

6. For one study of progressive Democrats see Crawford and Musslewhite (1991).

7. The organizations associated with the BSF changed over time. In 1910, a

number of socialist and Catholic organizations withdrew from the BSF. Even the Swiss suffrage organization (SVF) was not a member until 1949. Changes in the by-laws of the BSF and a decrease in class conflict brought many of these organizations back to BSF in the 1950s, although the Schweizerischer Katholischer Frauenbund (SKF) never rejoined.

8. The name of the organization translates as Working Community of Swiss Women's Organizations for the Political Rights of Women. For convenience, I refer to this organization as the Arbeitsgemeinschaft.

9. I use the term Governing Council throughout the book to refer to the cantonal executive councils, which go by different names in various cantons. The most common names for these Governing Councils are Regierungsrat (in German-speaking Switzerland) and Conseil d'Etat (in the French-speaking parts), although a few cantons (such as Appenzell Innerrhoden and Jura) use other labels.

10. In the 25 cantonal suffrage histories I studied, I found evidence of only one disagreement between a party and its women's auxiliary. In the 1960 Luzern suffrage referendum, the FDP recommended the defeat of a woman suffrage referendum which its women's group supported.

11. I classified cantons as having a coalition between its suffrage organization and other women's organizations only if there was historical evidence (from interviews or archives) that the other women's groups did more than merely endorse suffrage referenda or serve in a titular capacity on action committees.

12. Including French-speaking cantons does not change the conclusion that the participation of other women's organizations was not always beneficial. In fact, when Francophone cantons are added, cantons where suffrage organizations worked alone adopt cantonal suffrage amendments much earlier than those where the SVF worked with other women's organizations.

13. The status of the SP as an oppositional party could be questioned because they also hold seats in the Bundesrat and in many cantonal Governing Councils. Nonetheless, despite its position of power, the SP often tries to emphasize its oppositional role in elections.

14. The five cantons where the PdA received more than 5 percent of the vote were Basel-stadt, Genève, Neuchâtel, Schaffhausen, and Vaud. Since these were split between Francophone and German-speaking cantons, the differences in timing cannot be attributed to cultural differences.

15. Local cantonal parties sometimes chose a different name from the national party with which they affiliated. Thus, the names may be different when cantonal parties are discussed. When a cantonal party's name differs from its national party's, I place the national affiliation in parentheses. In addition, I utilize the current name of the Schweizerische Volkspartei (SVP) although it was called the Bauern-, Gewerbe- und Bürgerpartei until 1971.

16. Translated by author from a document of the Schweizerische Aktionskomitee für das Frauenstimm- und -wahlrecht in the Gosteli Stiftung labeled "Aufklärungskampagne für den 1. Februar 1959."

17. Women's anti-suffrage organizations also played a significant role in the United States (Marshall 1985). However, American woman suffrage activists did not attribute anti-suffrage success to these women's organizations.

CHAPTER SIX

1. While I concentrate on woman suffrage organizations in this section, between 1880 and 1900, the Women's Christian Temperance Union lobbied state legislatures for voting rights legislation (Women's Christian Temperance Union ca. 1900).

2. Local suffrage movements did not alter their lobbying tactics at the same speed. Some of the smaller suffrage organizations, particularly in the South, were slower to adopt the new lobbying techniques and continued to use petitions indiscriminately even after 1910. Others altered their tactics prior to 1910.

3. Information about suffrage organizations' lobbying tactics used in this chapter was coded from the same sources as the state and cantonal legislative histories of woman suffrage mentioned in Appendix C. Interviews with Swiss suffrage activists also served as a source of information about tactics. For a detailed description of the coding of these measures, see Appendix D.

4. Other measures of association yield comparable results.

5. Including these cases does not alter the significance or direction of the correlations between lobbying tactics and the adoption of suffrage or the introduction of suffrage legislation. However, for the percentage of legislators supporting women's voting rights, the correlation becomes small and insignificant ($r=.15$, $p=.34$) when these two states are included. In examining the shift in the slope when each of these two states is omitted (a common diagnostic measure), Montana and Washington were both more than two standard deviations less than the mean. They also accounted for unacceptably high levels of heteroscedasticity.

6. Nothing in the letter indicates that they felt the advice was too patronizing. Instead, the activists clearly felt it necessary to relay these details to other leaders of the movement.

7. In another canton, one activist reported to me that she was asked privately to write the suffrage legislation introduced into the cantonal parliament. However, her role in the legislation was expressly kept secret (interview of April 15, 1988).

CHAPTER SEVEN

1. Tarrow includes an unwillingness to compromise, which he labels "movement determination" in his definition of disruption (1994: 108). His two other characteristics—obstruction and broadening the conflict–do not apply to the sorts of tactics that suffrage activists utilized.

2. Identical changes are evident in the activities of the Franchise Department of the Women's Christian Temperance Union as well (see Women's Christian Temperance Union ca. 1900).

3. The number of parades and open-air meetings is calculated by the author from the histories of state campaigns in Harper (1922b). The actual number of activities is probably drastically underestimated since often states reported having an unspecified number of parades or outdoor meetings in a particular year. When the number was unspecified, only two parades or open-air meetings were counted.

4. Cantonal returns of the 1959 referendum show that the average vote in

cantons without a local action committee was 18 percent compared to 34 percent for the rest of Switzerland. However, this difference cannot be attributed directly to the lack of a supporting organization in the canton. It is possible that no local action committee formed because there was no support for suffrage in the first place.

5. Ultimately, the FBB women also withdrew their sponsorship of the March, leaving it in the hands of a few local suffrage organizations.

6. The information on specific events held in Bern is drawn from the files of the Gosteli Stiftung.

7. The results reported below do not change if legal challenges are excluded from the analysis.

8. The analysis does not include woman suffrage initiatives sponsored by other organizations because most of these occurred only in the 1960s and 1970s, as support for woman suffrage was already rising. Thus, initiatives run by other organizations are associated with *delays* in success (see Banaszak 1991).

9. In addition, there is a strong, significant relationship between the average number of suffrage referenda and the use of initiative petitions (r=.48). Since initiatives automatically result in referenda when they are successful, this relationship is not particularly interesting.

CHAPTER EIGHT

1. Some readers will note that I do not discuss the influence of the anti-suffrage movement on woman suffrage activists. Although woman suffrage activists were forced to counter anti-suffrage arguments, the "antis" had little impact on the values or tactics of the suffrage movement. The anti-suffrage movement developed only after the suffrage movement was already firmly established and had succeeded in several western states (Marshall 1985). By the time this movement rose to defend women's separate role as wife and mother, suffrage activists were already arguing that women needed the vote to protect that separate sphere (Marshall 1985; Kraditor 1981). Moreover, both movements developed within the same political context which resulted in the adoption of similar values, albeit to obtain the opposite goals. For example, anti-black and anti-immigrant sentiment affected both movements; while suffrage activists argued that enfranchising women would lessen the influence of undesirable voters (such as blacks or illiterate immigrants), the anti-suffrage movement argued that doubling the electorate would increase their numbers (Kraditor 1981).

2. Kraditor (1981) labels this value the "expediency argument" because suffrage was viewed merely as a means to other social change.

3. Calculated by the author from data in Ruckstuhl (1986).

4. This activist argued that the bishop opposed the enfranchisement of women and tried, unsuccessfully, to keep the SKF from supporting woman suffrage.

5. Catholic cantons are defined as those where over 80 percent of the population are Catholic according to the Swiss census.

6. In several cantons, individual priests or churches actively discouraged women in their parish from getting involved in the suffrage issue.

7. Interestingly, no Swiss argued that German-speaking Swiss had similar cul-

tural ties to Germany. In fact, the German-speaking suffrage activists I interviewed occasionally mentioned an aversion to Germany left over from World War II. Because of the war, they argued, German-speaking Swiss did not turn to Germany in the way that French-speaking Swiss turned to France. Others attributed it to Swiss dialects, which separated German-speaking Swiss from the German culture.

APPENDIX B

1. There are two possible reasons for the lack of data in the 1940s. First, the years surrounding World War II were stressful for Switzerland. In spite of neutrality, Switzerland was mobilized during the war so that, as in other countries during this time, political and social organizations often were neglected. A second reason, suggested to me by one long-time activist, was that some presidents were simply better than others at keeping records of that sort, and that the president during this period was probably not concerned with keeping the numbers for posterity.

REFERENCES

Abbott, Andrew. 1992. "What Do Cases Do? Some Notes on Activity in Sociological Analysis," in *What Is a Case? Exploring the Foundations of Social
Inquiry*, edited by Charles C. Ragin and Howard Becker. Cambridge: Cambridge University Press.

Allen, Lee N. 1958. "The Woman Suffrage Movement in Alabama, 1910–1920."
Alabama Review 11:83–99.

Anthony, Susan B., and Ida Husted Harper, eds. 1902. *History of Woman Suffrage*. Vol. 4, *1883–1900*. Salem, N.H.: Ayer.

Aptheker, Herbert. 1989. *Abolitionism: A Revolutionary Movement*. Boston:
Twayne.

Argersinger, Peter. 1974. *Populism and Politics: William Alfred Peffer and the
People's Party*. Lexington: University of Kentucky Press.

Arrow, Kenneth J. 1951. *Social Choice and Individual Values*. New York: Wiley.

L'Association Vaudoise pour les Droits de la Femme. 1979. "1959–1979:
Vingtème Anniversaire du Suffrage Féminin." Pamphlet.

Astin, Alexander, Helen Astin, Alan Bayer, and Ann Bisconti. 1975. *The Power
of Protest*. San Fransisco: Jossey Bass.

Baker, Paula. 1984. "The Domestication of Politics: Women and American Political Society, 1780–1920." *American Historical Review* 89: 620–47.

———. 1991. *The Moral Frameworks of Public Life: Gender, Politics, and the
State in Rural New York, 1870–1930*. Oxford: Oxford University Press.

Banaszak, Lee Ann. 1991. "The Influence of Direct Democratic Institutions on
the Swiss and American Women's Suffrage Movements." *Schweizerisches
Jahrbuch für Politische Wissenschaft* 31: 187–207.

Banks, Arthur S. 1971. *Cross-Polity Time-Series Data*. Cambridge: MIT Press.

Banks, Olive. 1981. *Faces of Feminism: A Study of Feminism as a Social Movement*. New York: St. Martin's Press.

Barry, Kathleen. 1988. *Susan B. Anthony: A Biography of a Singular Feminist*.
New York: New York University Press.

Bebel, August. [1883] 1950. *Die Frau und der Sozialismus*. Stuttgart: Dietz.

Blattner, Thérèse. 1979. "Peuple et Autorités Vaudoises Face au Suffrage Fe-
minin, 1907–1959: Evolution d'une opinion publique." Lizentiat Arbeit (Thesis), Université de Lausanne.

Blocker, Jack S., Jr. 1985a. "Separate Paths: Suffragists and the Women's Temperance Crusade." *Signs* 10: 460–76.

———. 1985b. *"Give to the Winds Thy Fears": The Women's Temperance Crusade, 1873–1874*. Westport: Greenwood Press.

———. 1989. *American Temperance Movements: Cycles of Reform*. Boston:
Twayne.

Blum, Roger. 1978. "Rolle, Schwierigkeiten, und Reform der kantonalen
Parlamente." *Schweizerisches Jahrbuch für politische Wissenschaft* 18: 11–
32.

Bollen, Kenneth A. 1979. "Political Democracy and the Timing of Development." *American Sociological Review* 44: 572–87.

Bordin, Ruth. 1981. *Woman and Temperance: The Quest for Power and Liberty, 1873–1900*. Philadelphia: Temple University Press.

Brown, Gertrude Foster. 1940a. "A Decisive Victory Won," in *Victory: How Women Won It*, edited by Carrie Chapman Catt. New York: H. W. Wilson.

———. 1940b. "The Opposition Breaks," in *Victory: How Women Won It*, edited by Carrie Chapman Catt. New York: H. W. Wilson.

Buechler, Steven M. 1986. *The Transformation of the Woman Suffrage Movement: The Case of Illinois, 1850—1920*. New Brunswick, N.J.: Rutgers University Press.

Buhle, Mari Jo, and Paul Buhle, eds. 1978. *The Concise History of Woman Suffrage*. Urbana: University of Illinois Press.

Bund Schweizerischer Frauenvereine. 1950. *Bund Schweizerischer Frauenvereine, 1900–1950*. Gosteli Stiftung, Worblaufen, Switzerland.

Caine, Barbara. 1982. "Feminism, Suffrage, and the Nineteenth Century English Women's Movement." *Women's Studies International Forum* 5: 537–50.

Caldwell, Martha. 1943. "The Woman Suffrage Campaign of 1912." *Kansas Historical Quarterly* 12: 300–318.

Calvert, Randall L. 1985. "The Value of Biased Information: A Rational Choice Model of Political Advice." *Journal of Politics* 47: 530–55.

"Can the Confederation Helvetica Be Imitated?" 1988. *Government and Politics* 23 (Special Issue).

Catt, Carrie Chapman. 1917. *Woman Suffrage by Federal Constitutional Amendment*. New York: National Woman Suffrage Publishing Company.

———, ed. 1940. *Victory: How Women Won It*. New York: National American Woman Suffrage Association.

Catt, Carrie Chapman, and Nettie Rogers Shuler. 1926. *Woman Suffrage and Politics: The Inner Story of the Suffrage Movement*. Seattle: University of Washington Press.

Clanton, O. Gene. 1969. *Kansas Populism: Ideas and Men*. Lawrence: University Press of Kansas.

Clemens, Elisabeth S. 1993. "Organizational Repertoires and Institutional Change: Women's Groups and the Transformation of U.S. Politics, 1890–1920." *American Journal of Sociology* 98: 755–98.

Cott, Nancy. 1977. *The Bonds of Womanhood: "Woman's Sphere" in New England, 1780–1835*. New Haven: Yale University Press.

———. 1987. *The Grounding of Modern Feminism*. New Haven: Yale University Press.

Crawford, Suzanne, and Lynn Musslewhite. 1991. "Progressive Reform and Oklahoma Democrats: Kate Barnard versus Bill Murray." *Historian* 53: 473–88.

Cronin, Thomas E. 1989. *Direct Democracy: The Politics of Initiative, Referendum, and Recall*. Cambridge: Harvard University Press.

Curtis, James, Edward Grabb, and Douglas Baer. 1992. "Voluntary Association Membership in Fifteen Countries." *American Sociological Review* 57: 139–52.

Cutright, Phillips. 1963. "National Political Development." *American Sociological Review* 28: 253–64.

Cutright, Phillips, and James Wiley. 1969. "Modernization and Political Representation: 1927–1966." *Studies in Comparative International Development* 5: 23–44.

Daalder, Hans. 1974. "The Consociational Democracy Theme." *World Politics* 26: 604–21.

Davies, James C. 1974. "The J-Curve and Power Struggle Theories of Collective Violence." *American Sociological Review* 39: 607–13.

Davis, Angela. 1981. *Women, Race, and Class*. New York: Vintage Books.

Deckard, Barbara Sinclair. 1983. *The Women's Movement: Political, Socioeconomic, and Psychological Issues*. New York: Harper and Row.

Delley, Jean-Daniel, and Andreas Auer. 1986. "Structures politiques des cantons," in *Handbuch Politisches System der Schweiz*. Vol. 3, *Föderalismus*, edited by Raimund Germann and Ernest Weibel. Bern: Paul Haupt.

"Die Protest-Frauen." 1969. *Züri-Leu*, February 6, p. 20.

Downs, Anthony. 1957. *An Economic Theory of Democracy*. New York: Harper and Row.

Duchacek, Ivo D. 1987. *Comparative Federalism: The Territorial Dimension of Politics*. Lanham, Md.: University Press of America.

Duncan-Clark, Samuel John. 1913. *The Progressive Movement*. Boston: Small, Maynard, and Company.

Duniway, Abigail Scott. [1914] 1971. *Path Breaking: An Autobiographical History of the Equal Suffrage Movement in Pacific Coast States*. Reprint, New York: Schochen Books.

Earhart, Mary. 1944. *Frances Willard: From Prayers to Politics*. Chicago: University of Chicago Press.

Edwards, G. Thomas. 1990. *Sowing Good Seeds: The Northwest Suffrage Campaigns of Susan B. Anthony*. Portland: Oregon Historical Society Press.

Eidgenössische Kommission für Frauenfragen. 1984. *Die Stellung der Frau in der Schweiz. Part 4, Frauenpolitik*. Bern: Eidgenössische Kommission für Frauengragen.

Eidgenössisches Statistisches Amt. 1951. *Statistisches Jahrbuch der Schweiz*. Bern: Eidgenössisches Statistisches Amt.

Eidgenössisches Statistisches Amt. 1962. *Statistisches Jahrbuch der Schweiz*. Bern: Eidgenössisches Statistisches Amt.

Eidgenössisches Statistisches Amt. 1970. *Statistisches Jahrbuch der Schweiz*. Bern: Eidgenössisches Statistisches Amt.

Eidgenössisches Statistisches Amt. 1977. *Statistische Quellenwerke der Schweiz. Vol. 596, Nationalratswahlen 1975*. Bern: Eidgenössisches Statistisches Amt.

Eidgenössisches Statistisches Amt. 1985. *Statistisches Jahrbuch der Schweiz*. Bern: Eidgenössisches Statistisches Amt.

Eisinger, Peter. 1973. "The Condition of Protest Behavior in American Cities." *American Political Science Review* 67: 11–28.

Elazar, Daniel J. 1987. *Exploring Federalism*. Tuscaloosa: University of Alabama Press.

Engeler, Urs Paul. 1986. "Personalverbindungen zwischen Altparteien und neuer Politik." *Schweizerisches Jahrbuch für Politische Wissenschaft* 26: 225–42.

Engels, Friedrich. [1883] 1973. "The Origins of the Family," in *The Feminist Papers*, edited by Alice Rossi. New York: Bantam.

Evans, Richard J. 1976. *The Feminist Movement in Germany, 1894–1933.* Beverly Hills, Calif.: Sage.

Evans, Sara M. 1989. *Born for Liberty: A History of Women in America.* New York: Free Press.

Faganini, Hans Peter. 1978. "Die Rolle der Parteien auf kantonaler Ebene." *Schweizerisches Jahrbuch für Politische Wissenschaft* 18: 75–94.

Fahrni, Dieter. 1983. *An Outline History of Switzerland.* Zurich: Pro Helvetia.

Farago, Peter. 1986. "Vergleichende Darstellung Verbandlicher Strukturen in vier Industriebranchen," in *Wirtschaftsverbände in der Schweiz*, edited by Peter Farago and Hanspeter Kriesi. Grüsch: Verlag Rüegger.

Faulkner, Harold Underwood. 1960. *American Economic History.* New York: Harper and Row.

Ferree, Myra Marx, and Frederick D. Miller. 1985. "Mobilization and Meaning: Toward an Integration of Social Psychological and Resource Perspectives on Social Movements." *Sociological Inquiry* 55: 38–61.

Filene, Peter G. 1970. "An Obituary for 'The Progressive Movement.'" *American Quarterly* 22: 20–34.

Flexner, Eleanor. 1975. *Century of Struggle: The Woman's Rights Movement in the United States.* 2d ed. Cambridge: Harvard University Press.

Fogel, Robert William. 1989. *Without Consent or Contract.* New York: W. W. Norton.

Ford, Linda G. 1991. *Iron-Jawed Angels: The Suffrage Militancy of the National Woman's Party, 1912–1920.* Lanham, Md.: University Press of America.

Fowler, Robert Booth. 1986. *Carrie Catt: Feminist Politician.* Boston: Northeastern University Press.

Fox, Karolena. 1918. "History of the Equal Suffrage Movement in Michigan." *Michigan History Magazine* 2: 90–109.

Freeman, Jo. 1975. *The Politics of Women's Liberation.* New York: McKay.

————. 1987. "Whom You Know versus Whom You Represent: Feminist Influence in the Democratic and Republican Parties" in *The Women's Movements of the United States and Western Europe*, edited by Mary Fainsod Katzenstein and Carol McClurg Mueller. Philadelphia: Temple University Press.

————, ed. 1983. *Social Movements of the Sixties and Seventies.* New York: Longman.

Frenkel, Max. 1978. "Swiss Federalism in the Twentieth Century," in *Modern Switzerland*, edited by J. Murray Luck. Palo Alto, Calif.: Sposs.

Friedman, Debra, and Doug McAdam. 1992. "Collective Identity and Activism: Networks, Choices, and the Life of a Social Movement," in *Frontiers in Social Movement Theory*, edited by Aldon D. Morris and Carol McClurg Mueller. New Haven: Yale University Press.

Fuller, Paul. 1975. *Laura Clay and the Woman's Rights Movement.* Lexington: University of Kentucky Press.

Gallaher, Ruth. 1918. *Legal and Political Status of Women in Iowa.* Iowa City: Iowa State Historical Society.

Gamson, William A. 1975. *The Strategy of Social Protest.* Homewood, Ill.: Dorsey Press.

———. 1992. "The Social Psychology of Collective Action," in *Frontiers in Social Movement Theory,* edited by Aldon D. Morris and Carol McClurg Mueller. New Haven: Yale University Press.

Gerhards, Jürgen, and Dieter Rucht. 1992. "Mesomobilization: Organizing and Framing in Two Protest Campaigns in West Germany." *American Journal of Sociology* 98: 555–95.

Granovetter, Mark. 1973. "The Strength of Weak Ties." *American Journal of Sociology* 78: 1360–80.

Griffith, Elisabeth. 1984. *In Her Own Right: The Life of Elizabeth Cady Stanton.* New York: Oxford University Press.

Grimes, Alan. 1967. *The Puritan Ethic and Woman Suffrage.* New York: Oxford University Press.

Grofman, Bernard, and Barbara Norrander. 1990. "Efficient Use of Reference Group Cues in a Single Dimension." *Public Choice* 64: 213–17.

Grofman, Bernard, and Julie Withers. 1993. "Information-Pooling Models of Electoral Politics," in *Information, Participation, and Choice: An Economic Theory of Democracy in Perspective,* edited by Bernard Grofman. Ann Arbor: University of Michigan Press.

Gruner, Eric. 1977. *Die Parteien in der Schweiz.* 2d ed. Bern: Francke Verlag.

Gruner, Eric, and Karl Frei. 1966. *Die Schweizerische Bundesversammlung, 1848–1920. Vol. 2, Soziologie und Statistik.* Bern: Francke Verlag.

Gurr, Ted Robert. 1968. "A Causal Model of Civil Strife: A Comparative Analysis Using New Indices." *American Political Science Review* 62: 1104–24.

———. 1970. *Why Men Rebel.* Princeton: Princeton University Press.

Hanushek, Eric, and John E. Jackson. 1977. *Statistical Methods for Social Scientists.* Orlando: Academic Press.

Harper, Ida Husted. [1898] 1969. *Life and Work of Susan B. Anthony.* 3 vols. New York: Arno Press and the New York Times.

Harper, Ida Husted, ed. 1922a. *History of Woman Suffrage. Vol. 5, 1900–1920.* Salem, N.H.: Ayer.

———. 1922b. *History of Woman Suffrage. Vol. 6 1900–1920.* Salem, N.H.: Ayer.

Hause, Steven, with Anne Kenney. 1984. *Women's Suffrage and Social Politics in the French Third Republic.* Princeton: Princeton University Press.

Heidenheimer, Arnold. 1994. "Locality and Gender in Swiss, German, and Japanese Education Policy: Comparing Sub-National Variations." Paper presented at the annual meeting of the Midwest Political Science Association, Chicago, April 14–16.

Hellman, Judith. 1987. "Women's Struggle in a Workers' City: Feminist Movements in Turin," *The Women's Movements of the United States and Western Europe,* edited by Mary Fainsod Katzenstein and Carol McClurg Mueller. Philadelphia: Temple University Press.

Hertig, Hanspeter. 1978. "Party Cohesion in the Swiss Parliament." *Legislative Studies Quarterly* 3: 63–81.

Höpflinger, François. 1984. "Verbände," in *Handbuch Politisches System der Schweiz* Vol. 2, *Strukturen und Prozesse*, edited by Ulrich Klöti, 2: 163–88. Bern: Haupt.

Huckfeldt, Robert, and John Sprague. 1987. "Networks in Context: The Social Flow of Political Information." *American Political Science Review* 81: 1197–1216.

Inglehardt, Ronald. 1977. *The Silent Revolution: Changing Values and Political Styles among Western Publics.* Princeton: Princeton University Press.

———. 1990. *Culture Shift in Advanced Industrial Countries.* Princeton: Princeton University Press.

International Monetary Fund. 1955. *International Financial Statistics*, vol. 8. Washington, D.C.: IMF.

———. 1960. *International Financial Statistics*, vol. 13. Washington, D.C.: IMF.

———. 1965. *International Financial Statistics*, vol. 18. Washington, D.C.: IMF.

———. 1970. *International Financial Statistics*, vol. 23. Washington, D.C.: IMF.

Irwin, Inez Haynes. 1921. *The Story of the Woman's Party.* New York: Harcourt, Brace, and Company.

Jenkins, J. Craig. 1983. "Resource Mobilization Theory and the Study of Social Movements." *Annual Review of Sociology* 9: 527–53.

Jenkins, J. Craig, and Charles Perrow. 1977. "Insurgency of the Powerless: Farm Worker Movements (1946–1972)." *American Sociological Review* 42: 249–68.

Jensen, Billy Barnes. 1973. "Colorado Woman Suffrage Campaigns of the 1870's." *Journal of the West* 12: 254–71.

Jenson, Jane. 1987. "Changing Discourse, Changing Agendas: Political Rights and Reproductive Policies in France," in *The Women's Movements of the United States and Western Europe,* edited by Mary Fainsod Katzenstein and Carol McClurg Mueller. Philadelphia: Temple University Press.

Johnson, D., and K. Porter eds. 1973. *National Party Platforms, 1840–1972.* Urbana: University of Illinois Press.

Joho, Dora. n.d. *Das Frauenstimmrecht im Aargau.* Pamphlet.

Judge, George G., W. E. Griffiths, R. Carter Hill, Helmut Lütkepohl, Tsoung-Chao Lee. 1985. *The Theory and Practice of Econometrics.* 2d ed. New York: John Wiley and Sons.

Kantonale Kommission zum Studium der Rechtlichen und Tatsächlichen Lage der Frau. 1988. *Frau und Politik im Wallis.* Publication of the Canton Wallis.

Kenneally, James J. 1968. "Woman Suffrage and the Massachusetts Referendum of 1895." *Historian* 30: 617–33.

Kerr, Henry. 1978. "The Structure of Opposition in the Swiss Parliament." *Legislative Studies Quarterly* 3: 51–62.

Key, V. O. 1977. *Southern Politics in State and Nation*. 3d ed. Knoxville: University of Tennessee Press.

Kitschelt, Herbert P. 1986. "Political Opportunity Structures and Political Protest: Anti-Nuclear Movements in Four Democracies." *British Journal of Political Science* 16: 57–85.

Klandermans, Bert. 1984. "Mobilization and Participation: Social Psychological Expansions of Resource Mobilization Theory." *American Sociological Review* 49: 583–600.

———. 1992. "The Social Construction of Protest and Multiorganizational Fields," in *Frontiers in Social Movement Theory*, edited by Aldon D. Morris and Carol McClurg Mueller. New Haven: Yale University Press.

Klein, Ethel. 1984. *Gender Politics: From Consciousness to Mass Politics*. Cambridge: Harvard University Press.

Knapp, Blaise. 1986. "Etapes du fédéralisme suisse," in *Handbuch Politisches System der Schweiz*. Vol. 3, *Föderalismus*, edited by Raimund E. Germann and Ernest Weibel. Bern: Haupt.

Kraditor, Aileen S. 1969. *Means and Ends in American Abolitionism*. New York: Pantheon.

———. 1981. *The Ideas of the Woman Suffrage Movement: 1890–1920*. 2d ed. New York: W. W. Norton.

Kriesi, Hanspeter. 1985. *Bewegung in der Schweizer Politik: Fallstudien zu politischen Mobilisierungsprozessen in der Schweiz*. Frankfurt: Campus Verlag.

———. 1988. "The Interdependence of Structure and Action: Some Reflections on the State of the Art." *International Social Movement Research* 1: 349–68.

———. 1990. "Political Power and Decision Making in Switzerland," in *Switzerland in Perspective*, edited by Janet Eve Hilowitz. New York: Greenwood Press.

———. 1995. "The Political Opportunity Structure of New Social Movements: Its Impact on Their Mobilization," in *The Politics of Social Protest*, edited by J. Craig Jenkins and Bert Klandermans. Minneapolis: University of Minnesota Press.

Krone, Henrietta Louise. 1946. "Dauntless Women: The Story of the Woman Suffrage Movement in Pennsylvania." Ph.D. diss., University of Pennsylvania.

Larson, T. A. 1970. "Woman Suffrage in Western America." *Utah Historical Quarterly* 38: 7–19.

———. 1972. "Dolls, Vassals, and Drudges: Pioneer Women in the West." *Western Historical Quarterly* 3: 5–16.

Lazarsfeld, Paul, Bernard Berelson, and Hazel Gaudet. 1968. *The People's Choice*. 3d. ed. New York: Columbia University Press.

Legislative Drafting Research Fund. 1915. *Index Digest of State Constitutions*. New York: New York State Constitutional Convention Committee.

Lembruch, Gerhard. 1974. "A Non-Competitive Pattern of Conflict Management in Liberal Democracies: The Case of Switzerland, Austria, and Lebanon," in *Consociational Democracy: Political Accomodation in Segmented Societies*, edited by Kenneth McRae. Toronto: McClelland and Stewart.

Lerner, Gerda. 1979. *The Majority Finds Its Past: Placing Women in History.* Oxford: Oxford University Press.

Levy, Rene. 1984. *The Social Structure of Switzerland.* Zürich: Pro Helvetia.

Linder, Wolf. 1987. *Politische Entscheidung und Gesetzesvollzug in der Schweiz.* Bern: Haupt.

———. 1994. *Swiss Democracy: Possible Solutions to Conflict in Multicultural Societies.* New York: St. Martin's Press.

Lipset, Seymour Martin. 1959. "Some Social Requisites of Democracy: Economic Development and Political Legitimacy." *American Political Science Review* 53: 69–105.

Lorwin, Val R. 1971. "Segmented Pluralism: Ideological Cleavages and Political Cohesion in the Smaller European Democracies." *Comparative Politics* 3: 141–75.

Lovenduski, Joni. 1986. *Women and European Politics: Contemporary Feminism and Public Policy.* Amherst: University of Massachusetts Press.

Lunardini, Christine. 1986. *From Equal Suffrage to Equal Rights: Alice Paul and the National Woman's Party, 1910–1928.* New York: New York University Press.

Magleby, David B. 1984. *Direct Legislation: Voting on Ballot Propositions in the United States.* Baltimore: John Hopkins University Press.

Marshall, Susan. 1985. "Ladies against Women: Mobilization Dilemmas of Antifeminist Movements." *Social Problems* 32: 348–62.

Marti, Donald B. 1991. *Women of the Grange: Mutuality and Sisterhood in Rural America, 1866–1920.* New York: Greenwood Press.

McAdam, Douglas. 1982. *Political Process and the Development of Black Insurgency, 1930–1970.* Chicago: University of Chicago.

———. 1988. *Freedom Summer.* Oxford: Oxford University Press.

McAdam, Douglas, and Dieter Rucht. 1993. "The Cross-National Diffusion of Movement Ideas." *Annals of the American Academy of Political and Social Sciences* 528: 56–74.

McBride, Genevieve G. 1993. *On Wisconsin Women: Working for Their Rights from Settlement to Suffrage.* Madison: University of Wisconsin Press.

McCarthy, John, and Mayer Zald. 1977. "Resource Mobilization and Social Movements: A Partial Theory." *American Journal of Sociology* 82: 1212–41.

McDonagh, Eileen. 1989. "Issues and Constituencies in the Progressive Era: House Roll Call Voting on the Nineteenth Amendment, 1913–1919." *Journal of Politics* 51: 119–36.

———. 1990. "Women's Right to Vote in a Gendered American State: 'Winning Plan' Politics and Maternalist Reform in the Progressive Era." Paper presented at the conference on Women, Politics, and Change in Twentieth-Century America, New School for Social Research, New York, April 27.

McDonagh, Eileen, and H. Douglas Price. 1985. "Woman Suffrage in the Progressive Era: Patterns of Opposition and Support in Referenda Voting, 1910–1918." *American Political Science Review* 79: 415–35.

Melucci, Alberto. 1989. *Nomads of the Present: Social Movements and Individ-*

ual Needs in Contemporary Society, edited by John Keane and Paul Mier. London: Hutchinson Radius.

Mesmer, Beatrix. 1988. *Ausgeklammert—Eingeklammert: Frauen und Frauenorganisationen in der Schweiz des 19. Jahrhunderts.* Basel: Helbing and Lichtenhahn.

Mitau, G. Theodore. 1966. *State and Local Government: Politics and Processes.* New York: Charles Scribner's Sons.

Moaddel, Mansoor. 1992. "Ideology as Episodic Discourse: The Case of the Iranian Revolution." *American Sociological Review* 57: 353–79.

Mock, Vreni. n.d. *Das Frauenstimmrecht in Appenzell Innerrhoden.* Unpublished Paper.

Morris, Aldon D. 1993. "Birmingham Confrontation Reconsidered: An Analysis of the Dynamics and Tactics of Mobilization." *American Sociological Review* 58: 621–36.

Mowry, George E. 1951. *The California Progressives.* Chicago: Quadrangle Books.

Moynihan, Ruth Barnes. 1983. *Rebel for Rights: Abigail Scott Duniway.* New Haven: Yale University Press.

Nanchen, Gabrielle. 1985. "Die traditionellen Frauenorganisationen," in *Die Stellung der Frau in der Schweiz.* Part 4, *Frauenpolitik.* Bern: Eidgenössische Kommission für Frauenfragen.

National American Woman Suffrage Association. 1896. *Proceedings of the Twenty-eighth Annual Convention.* Philadelphia: National American Woman Suffrage Association.

———. 1897. *Proceedings of the Twenty-ninth Annual Convention.* Philadelphia: National American Woman Suffrage Association.

———. 1899. *Proceedings of the Thirty-first Annual Convention.* Philadelphia: National American Woman Suffrage Association.

———. 1904. *Proceedings of the Thirty-sixth Annual Convention.* Warren, Ohio: National American Woman Suffrage Association.

———. 1914. *Proceedings of the Forty-sixth Annual Convention.* New York: National American Woman Suffrage Association.

Neidhardt, Friedhelm, and Dieter Rucht. 1992. "Towards a 'Movement Society'? On the Possibilities of Institutionalizing Social Movements." Paper presented at the First European Conference on Social Movements, WZB Berlin, October 29–31.

Neubauer, Deane E. 1967. "Some Conditions of Democracy." *American Political Science Review* 61: 1002–1009.

Newcomer, Mabel. 1959. *A Century of Higher Education for American Women.* New York: Harper and Brothers.

Nichols, Carole. 1983. *Votes and More for Women: Suffrage and After in Connecticut.* New York: Hansworth Press.

Noun, Louise R. 1969. *Strong-Minded Women: The Emergence of the Woman Suffrage Movement in Iowa.* Ames: Iowa State University Press.

Oberschall, Anthony. 1973. *Social Conflicts and Social Movements.* Englewood Cliffs, N.J.: Prentice Hall.

Olson, Mancur. 1971. *The Logic of Collective Action*. Cambridge: Harvard University Press.

Park, Maud Wood. 1940. "Campaigning State by State," in *Victory: How Women Won It*, edited by Carrie Chapman Catt. New York: H. W. Wilson.

Paulson, Ross Evans. 1973. *Women's Suffrage and Prohibition: A Comparative Study of Equality and Social Control*. Glenview, Ill.: Scott, Foresman.

Pillsbury, Hobart. 1926. "History of Woman Suffrage in New Hampshire." *The Granite Monthly* 58: 260–68.

Piven, Frances Fox, and Richard A. Cloward. 1979. *Poor People's Movements: Why They Succeed, How They Fail*. New York: Vintage Books.

Popkin, Samuel L. 1988. "Political Entrepreneurs and Peasant Movements in Vietnam," in *Rationality and Revolution*, edited by Michael Taylor. Cambridge: Cambridge University Press.

Price, Charles M. 1975. "The Initiative: A Comparative State Analysis and Reassessment of a Western Phenomenon." *Western Political Quarterly* 28: 243–62.

Przeworski, Adam, and Henry Teune. 1970. *The Logic of Comparative Social Inquiry*. New York: John Wiley and Sons.

Ranney, Austin. 1978. "The United States of America," *Referendums: A Comparative Study of Practice and Theory*, edited by David Butler and Austin Ranney. Washington, D.C.: American Enterprise Institute.

Reed, Dorinda. 1958. *The Woman Suffrage Movement in South Dakota*. Government Research Bureau Report #41. Vermillion: State University of South Dakota.

Rice, C. Duncan. 1975. *The Rise and Fall of Black Slavery*. Baton Rouge: Louisiana State University Press.

Riklin, Alois, and Alois Ochsner. 1984. "Parlament," in *Handbuch Politisches System der Schweiz*. Vol. 2, *Strukturen und Prozesse*, edited by Ulrich Klöti. Bern: Haupt.

Rodgers, Daniel T. 1982. "In Search of Progressivism." *Reviews of American History* 10: 113–31.

Rosenthal, Naomi, Meryl Fingrutd, Michele Ethier, Roberta Karant, and David McDonald. 1985. "Social Movements and Network Analysis: A Case Study of Nineteenth-Century Women's Reform in New York State." *American Journal of Sociology* 90: 1022–54.

Ruckstuhl, Lotti. 1986. *Frauen sprengen Fesseln, Hindernislauf zum Frauenstimmrecht in der Schweiz*. Bonstetten: Interfeminas Verlag.

Ruggie, Mary. 1987. "Workers' Movements and Women's Interests: The Impact of Labor-State Relations in Britain and Sweden," in *The Women's Movements of the United States and Western Europe*, edited by Mary Fainsod Katzenstein and Carol McClurg Mueller. Philadelphia: Temple University Press.

Ryan, Barbara. 1992. *Feminism and the Women's Movement: Dynamics of Change in Social Movement Ideology and Activism*. New York: Routledge.

Sayrs, Lois. 1989. *Pooled Time Series Analysis*. Newbury Park, Calif.: Sage.

Schaffer, Fritz. 1972. *Abriß der Schweizer Geschichte*. Frauenfeld: Verlag Huber.

Schattschneider, E. E. 1960. *The Semi-Sovereign People*. New York: Holt, Rinehart, and Winston.

Schmidt, David. 1989. *Citizen Lawmakers: The Ballot Initiative Revolution*. Philadelphia: Temple University Press.

Schneider, Dorothy, and Carl Schneider. 1993. *American Women in the Progressive Era, 1900–1920*. New York: Facts on File.

Schumaker, Paul. 1975. "Policy Responsiveness to Protest-Group Demands." *Journal of Politics* 37: 488–521.

Schweizerischer Verband für Frauenstimmrecht. 1934. *Schweizerischer Verband für Frauenstimmrecht: 1909–1934*. Gosteli Stiftung Archives, Worblaufen, Switzerland.

———. 1948. *Aktionsprogramm: Anregung zu aktiven Propagandamethoden*. Gosteli Stiftung Archives, Worblaufen, Switzerland.

———. 1959. *Schweizerischer Verband für Frauenstimmrecht: 1934–1959*. Gosteli Stiftung Archives, Worblaufen, Switzerland.

Scott, Anne Firor. 1970. *The Southern Lady: From Pedestal to Politics, 1830–1930*. Chicago: University of Chicago Press.

———. 1991. *Natural Allies: Women's Associations in American History*. Urbana: University of Illinois Press.

———, ed. 1984. *Making the Invisible Woman Visible*. Urbana: University of Illinois Press.

Scott, Mary Semple, ed. 1920. "History of Woman Suffrage in Missouri." *Missouri Historical Review* 14: 281–384.

Shaw, Barton C. 1984. *The Wool-Hat Boys: Georgia's Populist Party*. Baton Rouge: Louisiana State University Press.

Sinclair, Andrew. 1965. *The Emancipation of the American Woman*. New York: Harper and Row.

Skocpol, Theda. 1979. *States and Social Revolutions: A Comparative Analysis of France, Russia, and China*. Cambridge: Cambridge University Press.

———. 1992. *Protecting Soldiers and Mothers: The Political Origins of Social Policy in the United States*. Cambridge: Harvard University Press.

Smelser, Neil J. 1963. *Theories of Collective Behavior*. New York: Free Press of Glencoe.

Smith, A. K. 1969. "Socioeconomic Development and Political Democracy, A Causal Analysis." *Midwest Journal of Political Science* 13: 95–125.

Snow, David, and Robert Benford. 1988. "Ideology, Frame Resonance, and Participant Mobilization." *International Social Movement Research* 1: 197–217.

———. 1992. "Master Frames and Cycles of Protest," in *Frontiers in Social Movement Theory*, edited by Aldon D. Morris and Carol McClurg Mueller. New Haven: Yale University Press.

Snow, David, E. Burke Rochford, Jr., Steven K. Worden, and Robert Benford. 1986. "Frame Alignment Processes, Micromobilization, and Movement Participation." *American Sociological Review* 51: 464–81.

Snow, David, Louis Zurcher, and Sheldon Ekland-Olson. 1980. "Social Networks and Social Movements: A Microstructural Approach to Differential Recruitment." *American Sociological Review* 45: 787–801.

Snyder, David, and William Kelly. 1976. "Industrial Violence in Italy, 1878–1903." *American Journal of Sociology* 82: 131–62.

Die Staatsbürgerin. 1968. Number 10/11 (November). Special edition for the seventy-fifth anniversary of the woman suffrage organization in Zürich.

"Der STAKA Sektion Kanton Schwyz." 1969. *Schwyzer Zeitung*, September 16.

Stanton, Elizabeth, Susan B. Anthony, and Matilda Joslyn Gage, eds. 1881a. *The History of Woman Suffrage.* Vol. 1, *1848–1861*. Salem N.H.: Ayer.

———. 1881b. *The History of Woman Suffrage.* Vol. 2, *1861–1876*. Salem N.H.: Ayer.

———. 1886. *The History of Woman Suffrage.* Vol. 3, *1876–1885*. Salem N.H.: Ayer.

Stapler, Martha, ed. 1917. *The Woman Suffrage Year Book, 1917*. New York: National Woman Suffrage Publishing Company.

Statistische Bureau der Schweiz. 1910. *Eidgenössische Volkszählung 1910: 1. Band*. Bern: Statistische Bureau der Schweiz.

Steinberg, Jonathan. 1976. *Why Switzerland?* Cambridge: Cambridge University Press.

Steinberg, Ronnie. 1982. *Wages and Hours: Labor and Reform in Twentieth-Century America*. New Brunswick, N.J.: Rutgers University Press.

Steiner, Jürg. 1974. *Amicable Agreement versus Majority Rule: Conflict Resolution in Switzerland*. Chapel Hill: University of North Carolina Press.

Steiner Jürg, and Robert Dorff. 1980. *A Theory of Political Decision Modes: Intraparty Decision Making in Switzerland*. Chapel Hill: University of North Carolina Press.

Swidler, Ann. 1986. "Culture in Action: Symbols and Strategies." *American Sociological Review* 51: 273–86.

Tarrow, Sidney. 1989a. *Democracy and Disorder: Protest and Politics in Italy, 1965–1975*. Oxford: Clarendon Press.

———. 1989b. *Struggle, Politics, and Reform: Collective Action, Social Movements, and Cycles of Protest*. Western Societies Program, Occasional Paper no. 21. Ithaca, N.Y.: Cornell University.

———. 1992. "Mentalities, Political Cultures, and Collective Action Frames: Constructing Meanings through Action," in *Frontiers in Social Movement Theory*, edited by Aldon D. Morris and Carol McClurg Mueller. New Haven: Yale University Press.

———. 1994. *Power in Movement: Social Movements, Collective Action, and Politics*. Cambridge: Cambridge University Press.

Taylor, A. Elizabeth. 1944. "The Origin of the Woman Suffrage Movement in Georgia." *Georgia Historical Quarterly* 28: 63–79.

———. 1956. "The Woman Suffrage Movement in Arkansas." *Arkansas Historical Quarterly* 15: 17–52.

———. 1957a. "The Woman Suffrage Movement in Florida." *Florida Historical Quarterly* 36: 42–60.

———. 1957b. *The Woman Suffrage Movement in Tennessee*. New York: Bookman Associates.

———. 1958. "Revival and Development of the Woman Suffrage Movement in Georgia." *Georgia Historical Quarterly* 42: 339–54.

———. 1959. "The Last Phase of the Woman Suffrage Movement in Georgia." *Georgia Historical Quarterly* 43: 11–28.

———. 1961. "The Woman Suffrage Movement in North Carolina." *North Carolina Historical Review* 38: 173–89.

———. 1968. "The Woman Suffrage Movement in Mississippi, 1890–1920." *Journal of Mississippi History* 30: 1–34.

———. 1987. *Citizens at Last: The Woman Suffrage Movement in Texas*. Austin: Ellen C. Temple.

Tilly, Charles. 1978. *From Mobilization to Revolution*. Reading, Mass.: Addison-Wesley.

———. 1984. "Social Movements and National Politics," in *Statemaking and Social Movements*, edited by Charles Bright and Susan Harding. Ann Arbor: University of Michigan Press.

Timberlake, James. 1963. *Prohibition and the Progressive Movement, 1900–1920*. Cambridge: Harvard University Press.

Tocqueville, Alexis de. [1845] 1969. *Democracy in America*. Translated by George Lawrence and edited by J. P. Mayer. New York: Doubleday and Company.

Trout, Grace Wilbur. 1920. "Sidelights on Illinois Woman Suffrage History." *Illinois State Historical Society Journal* 13: 145–79.

Tschäni, Hans. 1987. *Wer regiert die Schweiz?* Munich: Piper.

United States. Bureau of the Census. 1900. Census. Reports. *Twelfth Census of the United States Taken in the Year 1900*. Vol. 2. Washington, D.C.: Bureau of the Census.

———. 1920. *Fourteenth Census of the United States Taken in the Year 1920*. Vol. 2, *Population: 1920*. Washington, D.C.: Bureau of the Census.

Venet, Wendy Hamand. 1991. *Neither Ballots nor Bullets: Women Abolitionists and the Civil War*. Charlottesville: University of Virginia Press.

Villard-Traber, Anneliese. 1984. *Der lange Weg zur Gleichberechtigung: Eine Chronik der Basler Frauenbewegung, 1916–1983*. Basel: Vereinigung für Frauenrechte Basel.

Van Voris, Jacqueline. 1987. *Carrie Chapman Catt: A Public Life*. New York: The Feminist Press at the City University of New York.

Vonwyl, Doris. 1988. *Einführung des Frauenstimmrechts im Kanton Luzern*. Unpublished Student Paper, Luzern.

Welch, Susan. 1975. "The Impact of Urban Riots on Urban Expenditures." *American Journal of Political Science* 19: 741–60.

Werder, Hans. 1978. *Die Bedeutung der Volksinitiative in der Nachkriegszeit*. Bern: Francke Verlag.

Wettstein, Susanna. 1990. "Der lange Weg des Frauenstimmrechts im Kanton Appenzell Ausserrhoden." Unpublished Student Paper.

———. 1991. "Frauenstimmrecht Nie!" Unpublished Student Paper.

Wheeler, Marjorie Spruill. 1993. *New Women of the New South: The Leaders of the Woman Suffrage Movement in the Southern States.* Oxford: Oxford University Press.

Wilhite, Ann L. W. 1968. "Sixty-five Years till Victory: A History of Woman Suffrage in Nebraska." *Nebraska History* 49: 149–63.

Women's Christian Temperance Union. Franchise Department. ca. 1900. *Franchise Department of the National Women's Christian Temperance Union.* n.p.

Woodtli, Susanna. 1983. *Gleichberechtigung: Der Kampf um die politischen Rechte der Frau in der Schweiz.* 2d ed. Frauenfeld: Verlag Huber.

Youmans, Theodora W. 1921. "How Wisconsin Women Won the Ballot." *Wisconsin Magazine of History* 5: 3–32.

Zald, Mayer N. and John McCarthy, eds. 1979. *The Dynamics of Social Movements.* Cambridge Mass.: Winthrop Publishers.

Zald, Mayer N. and John McCarthy, eds. 1987. *Social Movements in an Organizational Society.* New Brunswick, N.J.: Transaction Books.

INDEX

Aargau, 59, 60–61, 61t, 65, 147

Abbot, Andrew, 82

abolitionist movement: alliance with suffragists, southern view of, 111, 198; antislavery as first priority, 7; beliefs and values of as influence on suffragists, 67, 187, 188–91; blacks' rights as priority, 162, 190; compromises on women's rights, 189–91; as model for suffragists in techniques, 47, 67–68, 71, 188; suffrage movement ties to, 6, 7, 20, 66

access. *See* legislation introductions

action committees, Swiss: anti-suffrage, 124–25; local, role of in national organization, 166, 169–70, 171, 256n.4; national, role in national referendum (1971), 171; as public opinion-building, 118

Addams, Jane, 105

adoption of suffrage: and confrontational tactics, 178–179, 179t, 180; as final goal and measure of suffrage groups' success, 73, 74; and organization membership, 87t, 88t, 94–96; and organized lobbying tactics, 139–40, 142; timing of, regional variations in U.S. and Switzerland, 95–96, 253n.19; and use of initiative, 182–184, 183t, 184t, 184–85; values of western states of U.S., 196–97. *See also* cantonal suffrage; full suffrage; partial suffrage

Agrarian party (SVP), in Vaud, 123

Alabama, 111

Alaska Territory, 11

alcoholism, and women's vote, 191, 192, 257n.2

alliances: absence of in Swiss suffrage movement, 69–70, 112, 124, 130, 200, 219; anti-suffrage backlash in U.S., 98, 100, 107–12, 129–30; building of, in Swiss referenda campaigns, 251n.3; constraints and opportunities of, 28–29, 215, 220; effect on success of suffrage movements, 42, 43; impact on pro-suffrage coalitions in U.S., 129–30; with Swiss political parties, 70; tactics, influences on, 188, 212, 213; with temperance movement, 100–

101; and timing of suffrage adoption, 130–31; of U.S. and Swiss movements compared, 20, 40, 212; values derived from, 39–40, 212, 213, 218–19, 222. *See also* coalitions, anti-suffrage; coalitions, pro-suffrage

American Anti-Slavery Society, 66, 190

American Equal Rights Association (AERA), 6, 7, 162

American Woman Suffrage Association (AWSA), 7, 9

Anthony, Susan B., 10, 56, 57, 247n.3; in abolitionist movement, 7, 66; attempt to vote, 164; on black rights, 198; compromising on demands, 163; finances of organization, 47, 80; legislative lobbying campaign in New York, 136; at Philadelphia centennial (1876), 164; reaction to Fourteenth Amendment, 7, 190; as temperance activist, 68, 100, 191, 254n.1; on women in public life, 191

anti-abortion groups, 250n.23, 250n.27

anti-nuclear power groups, 53

Anti-Saloon League, 109

anti-slavery movement, 5, 6, 7, 189. *See also* abolitionist movement

anti-suffrage coalitions: in Switzerland, 98, 124–29; U.S., 98, 100, 107–12, 129–30

anti-suffrage movement, 124–26; arguments of, 125–26, 257n.1

Appenzell Ausserrhoden; anti-suffrage stance, 146, 209, 210–12; local autonomy values, 209, 210–12, 213; woman suffrage in, 4, 19, 152

Appenzell Innerrhoden: anti-suffrage stance, 209, 210–12; initiative laws in, 181; local autonomy values, 209, 210–12, 213; woman suffrage in, 4, 19

Arbeitsgemeinschaft fur die politischen Rechte der Frau, 17; creation of by BSF (1957 or so), 113; national organization coordinated but didn't direct locals, 166; role as clearinghouse, 113; translation of, 255n.8

Argersinger, Peter, 102

Arizona: initiative petition introduced, 180; suffrage amendments, 11, 106

About the Author

Lee Ann Banaszak is Associate Professor of Political Science
at the Pennsylvania State University